DATE			
MAR 1990			

RUSSIAN VIEWS

OF PUSHKIN'S

EUGENE ONEGIN

RUSSIAN VIEWS
OF PUSHKIN'S
EUGENE ONEGIN

TRANSLATED, WITH AN INTRODUCTION AND NOTES BY

Sona Stephan Hoisington

VERSE PASSAGES TRANSLATED BY

Walter Arndt

INDIANA UNIVERSITY PRESS

Bloomington & Indianapolis

Manufactured in the United States of America

Library of Congress Cataloging-in-Publication Data

Russian views of Pushkin's Eugene Onegin.

  "Bibliography: criticism on Eugene Onegin in English": p.
  Includes index.
  1. Pushkin, Aleksandr Sergeevich, 1799–1837.
Evgeniĭ Onegin. I. Pushkin, Aleksandr Sergeevich,
1799–1837. Evgeniĭ Onegin. English. II. Hoisington,
Sona Stephan, 1941–
PG3343.E83R87 1988   891.71′3   87-45980
ISBN 0-253-35067-0

1   2   3   4   5   93   92   91   90   89

To my family:
Thomas, Rena, and Haik

CONTENTS

Foreword

The problems faced by the non-Russian reader of Pushkin's *Eugene Onegin* are legion, but they might be reduced to a single fact: so much in it does not translate. On the plane of language there is the miraculous tension of a novel in verse, a multiplicity of voices embedded in the flawless "Onegin stanza," whose subtle rhythms and rhyme scheme can be accommodated only partially and—despite the heroic efforts of gifted translators—with considerable strain in our weakly inflected English. On the plane of plot, *Onegin* is a banal society tale whose charm and profundity is most often in the telling, in the narrator's ambivalent play with the tale. On both planes, paraphrase fails. Yet Russians see this text as the masterpiece of their master poet and take for granted an intimacy with its form, flavor, and most intricate details. How can Western students of Russian culture hope to approximate this knowledge?

The present volume offers one approach to the problem. It attempts to "translate" *Onegin* critically, not so much to advance an appreciation of the text itself as to argue for an appreciation of the *status* of the text. *Eugene Onegin* is so central an element of Russian culture that almost every important critical movement or literary theory has been tried out on it. Thus, in retrospect, *Onegin* can be used as a lens through which to view the Russian critical imagination.

Such an access point is valuable for two reasons. First, Russian literary critics (like Russian authors) have traditionally been allocated a monumental role in defining their own culture. The line between fiction, political journalism, philosophy, and theology has been very flexibly drawn, and by some writers—notably Gogol, Dostoevsky, Tolstoy, and Solzhenitsyn—deliberately blurred. Pushkin himself, writing the cantos of *Eugene Onegin* during the very decade that professional journal criticism was establishing itself in Russian society, incorporated into his novel a "struggle with his critics," part ironic and part deadly serious. Until its appearance in book form in 1833, *Onegin* was, in the words of J. Douglas Clayton, a "contemporary literary phenomenon surrounded by the critical birds of passage."[1] The text's calculated stance of openness to unreliable and shifting addressees has teased readers ever since. As the present selection of essays ably demonstrates, commentators soon began to respond as much to earlier critical readings as to Pushkin's text. A secondary dialogue developed among these critics, one that was at times more focused and insightful than any illumination these writers could offer about *Onegin*.

Second, many of the most celebrated Russian critics of *Eugene Onegin* have responded to the text in a way quite incomprehensible to any currently accepted tradition of Western literary scholarship. This gap is most apparent when one considers the work of nineteenth-century social critics. Vissarion Belinsky, the "father" of Russian literary criticism, speaks of Onegin and Tatyana as if they were living people and real-life social types, burdening their relationship with the suffering and sociopolitical impotence expected of educated subjects of the Russian Empire. Dmitry Pisarev resents equally and on the same plane the author Pushkin, his hero Eugene Onegin, and the critic Belinsky—the first two for their aristocratic enthusiasms and ennui, and Belinsky for being taken in, for blaming the moral weakness of the Pushkins and the Onegins on society and not on the men themselves. Pisarev does not touch upon questions of irony, narrative voice, or fictionality.

Fyodor Dostoevsky presents a peculiar and even more extreme case. His "Pushkin Speech," one could argue, mistakes the tonality of *Onegin* at almost every crucial point. He invests Tatyana's decision not to leave her elderly husband for Onegin with the moral and millenarian pathos of Ivan Karamazov's challenge ("Can anyone possibly build his happiness on the unhappiness of another?"). And in his reading of Pushkin's earlier work *The Gypsies,* Dostoevsky even adjusts the poet's very words, transforming the old gypsy's sorrowful graveside sermon to Aleko, "Leave us, proud man!" *(Ostav' nas, gordyi chelovek),* into quite different, and essentially Dostoevskian, advice: "Humble yourself, proud man" *(Smiris', gordyi chelovek).* Dostoevsky thus transmutes social ostracism—so clear in Pushkin's original—into a call for inner spiritual rebirth through fusion with the folk and withdrawal from radical political action. Pushkin, that enlightened conservative with profound sympathy for his own beleaguered class, has been successfully reinvented as a left-wing radical in one decade and a right-wing nationalist in another.

The Russians developed a healthy countertradition to their own social critics, first among the Formalists of the 1920s and then, in the 1960s and 70s, among Structuralists, cultural semioticians, and Bakhtin school scholars. These Russian schools of criticism have their Western analogues in the New Criticism, Structuralism, and various post-Structuralisms. The very popularity—and perhaps cult—of Yury Lotman and even more of Mikhail Bakhtin in the West suggests a degree of translatability among cultures that would delight both theorists. It is a strength of the present volume, not to be taken for granted in anthologies of literary criticism, that these twentieth-century essays succeed so well in transmitting technical points about formal structure *in translation.*

The Tynyanov essay and the first Lotman entry constitute what might be called a socially informed Structuralist approach. Here the word is not pressed into the service of extraliterary events (as in the work of social critics), but neither are outside events exiled; they are organized, rather, to elucidate the changing status of the word. Tynyanov explores the prose/poetry boundary in *Onegin* through variously weighted mechanisms of deformation—of sound, meaning, and protagonist—and through the dynamic function of marked omissions in the text. Always sensitive to questions of literary reception, Tynyanov's work somewhat resembles that of Jauss and Iser; in the pantheon of Western critical thought, Tynyanov could be called a patron saint of such journals as *New Literary History and Poetics Today.*

Tynyanov's essay on *Onegin* was written in the early 1920s, but was not published in full in the Soviet Union until 1975. Western readers must always keep this peculiar non-continuum in mind. Russian literary criticism in the Soviet period has not developed organically, accumulating a placid network of cross-references and freely competing schools. From 1930 to the early 1950s, when New Criticism was flourishing in American universities, Soviet literary studies were cast back into a neo-Belinskian naive realism. Post-Stalinist theorists have had to exercise considerable care as they reintroduce—and occasionally code—fifty-year-old concepts back into sanctioned critical vocabulary.[2] We see just such judicious care in Lotman's first essay, which uses Formalist categories to reconsider *Eugene Onegin* but clearly has a second and larger agenda: to use a canonized text like *Onegin* as the ground for reintroducing Formalist categories.

Lotman's 1966 essay continues Tynyanov's task by analyzing the contradictions in *Onegin* as deliberate structural elements that define various relations between system and subject. Similar to many Western Structuralists, Lotman in this essay believes in system and in binary opposition; his text is supplemented by several double-column charts, and he makes subtle points about Pushkin's "multiple recoding of systems" from one semantic plane to another. Never, however, does Lotman's brand of Structuralism generate the autonomous, grammatically pure fantasies of an analysis by Genette or the early Barthes. Soviet Structuralism bears permanent traces of its nineteenth-century heritage. As Douglas Clayton correctly observes, Lotman strives to "synthesize the formalist approach with the traditional Soviet emphasis on realism."[3] Indeed, the second essay by Lotman, a chapter from his 1975 book on *Onegin,* invokes a much richer concept of the cultural boundary—and even celebrates those moments when the unstructured immediacy of life appears to break through the surface of the text, thus confirming it as a novel.[4]

Enter here Mikhail Bakhtin. For the past two decades his legacy has been claimed by rival groups in the Soviet Union, and it is likely that Lotman's move from Structuralism to cultural semiotics was inspired in part by the powerful ideological field generated by Bakhtin's work. The piece here entitled "Discourse in *Eugene Onegin*" was originally part of a lecture delivered by Bakhtin in Moscow in October 1940. That text appeared in print only in 1965, however, and whether Lotman was responding to Bakhtin in his own essay published one year later is difficult to determine. But we do have a record of Bakhtin's response to Lotman's 1966 essay. Those comments might serve as a good starting point for the Lotman/Bakhtin (and later Bocharov) debate. As Bakhtin writes in a passage from his notebooks of 1970–71:

> An understanding of the multistyled nature of *Eugene Onegin* (see Lotman) as a recoding (romanticism into realism and so forth) leads to a falling away of that most important *dialogic* aspect and to the transformation of a dialogue of styles into a simple coexistence of various versions of one and the same style. Behind styles lies the integral viewpoint of the integral individual personality. A code presupposes content to be somehow ready-made and presupposes the realization of a choice among various *given* codes.[5]

Bakhtin's response to Lotman is a comment on Structuralism not only as a literary method but also as a view of the world. What Bakhtin finds inadequate in Lotman's 1966 essay is the whole idea of codes, even those as flexibly open to unfinishedness as Lotman's codes often were. When one reads Bakhtin's above comment, made at the end of his life, back into the 1940 lecture and into the even earlier essay "Discourse in the Novel" (to which the comments on *Onegin* are closely linked), these forty-year-old pieces sound uncannily, anachronistically post-Structuralist.[6] In place of codes and binary oppositions, Bakhtin suggests a potentially infinite world of consciousness centers and voice zones.

In his sophisticated reading of *Eugene Onegin* (1974), Bakhtin's disciple and literary executor Sergey Bocharov makes creative use of Bakhtin's essays on the novel. But he draws as well on Bakhtin's early, and still untranslated, archival manuscripts (1919–23?), which contain—among much astonishing material—a lengthy analysis of a lyric poem by Pushkin.[7] Since Bakhtin's treatment of poetry in the early manuscripts differs so markedly from the harsh "monologic" role later assigned to poetic form in "Discourse in the Novel," we might briefly discuss that early text here, as a bridge back to the Formalists and forward to Bocharov's essay.

In discussing Pushkin's lyric, Bakhtin does indeed employ formal categories—but of a very different sort than Shklovsky's and Tynyanov's models make possible.[8] In those Formalist models, artistic material is organized by a "dominant" and creatively deformed by device or by reader expectation. Bakhtin posits another sort of dominance and a very different concept of "deformation." Throughout the early manuscripts, Bakhtin stresses two prerequisites for artistic creation.[9] First, at the center of the aesthetic project there must always be a human being, a second consciousness in addition to the author. And second, what makes a work "aesthetic" is the degree to which this other consciousness can follow its *own* laws—in the presence of a second force that would surmount it. In this project, form belongs to the author, content to the hero. The work of art is the product of their struggle.

Bakhtin chooses Pushkin's lyric "Dlia beregov otchiznoi dal'noi" [For the Shores of Your Distant Country] to illustrate this aesthetic struggle. He begins with the assertion that every poem—and in fact every aesthetic event—is "the reaction to a reaction." In highly structured metric poetry this dialogic situation can result in wonderfully rich tensions, especially between *intonation* and *rhythm*. Intonation, as Bakhtin uses the word, refers to the more or less "realistic" reaction of a created character (the hero) to isolated events from within the whole. Rhythm, on the other hand, is the "formal" reaction of the author to the event of the poem *as* a whole—and from a perspective outside the whole. The hero, with his own consciousness and autonomous point of view on events, possesses a whole slate of realistic reactions, realistic intonations, realistic rhythms of his own. The author counters them with a formal reaction, formal intonation, formal rhythm. Since all these variables must of necessity be expressed externally on the same verbal plane, they will struggle for dominance. The subtler and better-crafted this struggle, Bakhtin suggests, the more satisfying the poem.[10]

Within this early Bakhtinian framework, and in dialogue with both Tynyanov and Lotman, Bocharov discusses the prose/poetry boundary in *Eugene Onegin*. Where the earlier critics saw the "novelness" of *Onegin* in its multiple, and multiplying, systems, Bocharov concentrates on a much more open-ended realm of possibility, on the subjunctive mode so often used at crucial moments in the plot. Following Bakhtin's lead in his essay "Epic and Novel," Bocharov suggests that it is only the unrealized potential of a character that keeps him out of the epic world of actualized reality. The story that does *not* occur is the real story. And thus a novel will imitate real life to the extent that it imitates not the palpably real (however prosaic, unplanned, and idiosyncratic that might be), but the *un*realized potential of every moment. Not since Tolstoy has Russian Realism had so canny a defense.

The essays in this volume cover a wide spectrum of approaches to literature. The critics engage in complex polemics, enrich and misrepresent one another, and call each other out on various issues—often over Pushkin's almost silenced text. And yet these essays might well strike the Western reader as unusually integrated. This integration is no accident, and in closing we should consider the parameters and constraints on Russian critical readings of *Onegin*. What, from our contemporary Western perspective, is missing from this anthology?

First, there is no deconstructionist impulse, no suspicion or subversion of the author's intent or of the capacity of words to mean. Formalist critics did question the autonomy of the author, to be sure, but even the most doctrinaire of them generally conceded that properly chosen devices would have their calculated verbal effect, however temporary. Russian literary critics tend not only to be solicitous of the author, however; they are enormously protective of the canon as well. As any participant in Soviet-American literary symposia will attest, an unorthodox or potentially disrespectful attitude toward Pushkin—or toward any of Pushkin's characters—causes an instant uneasiness. At the 1985 Soviet-American Conference on "Pushkin's Shorter Prose" at the Kennan Institute in Washington, D.C., several American Pushkinists discussing possible feminist approaches to *Eugene Onegin* were cut short in the corridor with the curt retort of one Soviet delegate: "Leave Tatyana alone."

This leads to a second and related absent area in Russian Pushkin studies: gender consciousness. The work being done in the United States and Canada by, among others, Barbara Heldt, J. Douglas Clayton, and Stephanie Sandler on feminist issues and the erotic in Pushkin appears to have no real Soviet counterpart.[11] There is also little interpretive work attempted, beyond neutral documentation, on race and ethnic difference. This is surprising, in light of Pushkin's pride in his genealogy (one-eighth Ethiopian) and frequent reference to his non-European origin (in *Onegin,* for example, the narrator—a stylization of Pushkin himself—dreams of escape to the "noonday heat of my Africa," I, 50). In sum, critical movements in the West that are pledged to making the marginalized central, giving silenced groups a voice, and thus altering radically the way we read our literary canon appear to have no official academic equivalent in Russian or Soviet scholarship.

This state of affairs imparts to the essays in this volume a certain comfortable respectability. The fallacies they commit have all been long familiar, while what works remains robust. Opinions and methods may differ, but even at its most antagonistic the dialogue among these critics takes place within a coherent, even a reverent, tradition where everyone acknowledges the seriousness of what is at stake. Perhaps the greatest paradox of Russian literary criticism is that a tradition so centrally concerned with revolution should nevertheless constitute so organic a whole and so unbroken a continuum.

CARYL EMERSON
PRINCETON UNIVERSITY

NOTES

1. J. Douglas Clayton, *Ice and Flame: Aleksandr Pushkin's* Eugene Onegin (Toronto: University of Toronto Press, 1985), p. 19. The first chapter, "The Repainted Icon: Criticism of *Eugene Onegin,*" provides detailed background for the essays in the present volume.

2. For an account of attempts to recuperate aspects of the Formalist tradition in the Soviet Union in the 1960s–80s, see Peter Seyffert, *Soviet Literary Structuralism* (Columbus, OH: Slavica, 1983).

3. Clayton, p. 63.

4. Mention should be made of the most creative application to date of Lotman's cultural semiotics in the field of Pushkin studies: William Mills Todd III, *Fiction and*

Society in the Age of Pushkin: Ideology, Institutions, Narrative (Cambridge: Harvard University Press, 1986), especially chapters I–III. Todd considers the problem of *Onegin* as one of "the relationship between art and life, the limits imposed upon social action and artistic expression by a culture's grammar of conventions." It is his thesis that *Onegin* offers its characters almost none of the nature/culture options of conventional Romantic literature: *all* is culture. Tatyana triumphs because she can creatively master and combine convention; Eugene has only the hollow options of a London dandy or a Byronic hero, and neither can satisfy him (or the reader) for long.

5. M. M. Bakhtin, *Speech Genres and Other Late Essays,* trans. Vern W. McGee, ed. Caryl Emerson and Michael Holquist (Austin: University of Texas Press, 1986), p. 135.

6. One contemporary literary scholar has suggested that Bakhtin had precisely that in mind at the end of the 1920s: to forestall the development of Structuralism out of Formalism. See Wlad Godzich's Foreword to M. M. Bakhtin/P. M. Medvedev, *The Formal Method in Literary Scholarship,* trans. Albert J. Wehrle (Cambridge: Harvard University Press, 1985), p. x.

7. These manuscripts have since been published as M. M. Bakhtin, "K filosofii postupka" [Toward a Philosophy of the Act], in a 1984–85 yearbook for the Soviet Academy of Sciences, *Filosofiia i sotsiologiia nauki i tekhniki* (Moscow: Nauka, 1986), pp. 80–160. The reading of the Pushkin lyric, "Dlia beregov otchiznoi dal'noi," appears on pp. 131–137 and 141–151.

8. In the first chapter of her *Distant Pleasures: Reading Pushkin in Exile* (Stanford: Stanford University Press, forthcoming), Stephanie Sandler suggests that Bakhtin's analysis of this poem might be a response to the quasi-Formalist poetician V. M. Zhirmunsky, who, in his influential essay "Zadachi poetiki" [The Tasks of Poetics, 1921–23] had selected just this Pushkin lyric to illustrate quite different, more conservative techniques of poetic analysis.

9. M. M. Bakhtin, "Avtor i geroi v esteticheskoi deiatel'nosti" [Author and Hero in Aesthetic Activity], in *Estetika slovesnogo tvorchestva* (Moscow: Iskusstvo, 1979), pp. 170–175. The exact chronology and textual relationship between this segment and the recently published "Toward a Philosophy of the Act" is undetermined.

10. Bakhtin does not directly apply these categories of intonation and rhythm to *Onegin,* but one could profitably view the "Onegin stanza" as a distancing, teasing, formal sheath for the warring intonational variations within. Such a reading lends support to the idea that Pushkin—like Chekhov—had no interest in theater (or art in general) that pretended to complete realism or verisimilitude, that ignored the "absence of the fourth wall." Rhythm (in Bakhtin's sense) *is* a temporal expression of that absent wall, which serves formally to separate art from life. The tension between rhythm and intonation would then constitute the art-generating moment.

11. See Barbara Heldt, *Terrible Perfection: Women and Russian Literature* (Bloomington: Indiana University Press, 1987); J. Douglas Clayton (*Ice and Flame,* as well as his essay "Towards a Feminist Reading of *Evgenii Onegin,*" *Canadian Slavonic Papers* XXIX/2, 3 [June–September 1987]); Stephanie Sandler, *Distant Pleasures,* especially Part IV.

Preface

Eugene Onegin occupies a unique place in the history of Russian culture. Yet outside the Soviet Union this work, which has long been regarded as Russia's national epic, is little known, despite the fact that three English translations of it have appeared since 1963. Most Americans, if they know *Onegin* at all, associate it with the operatic version by Pyotr Tchaikovsky. The purpose of this anthology is to help English-speaking readers to appreciate the hold *Eugene Onegin* has on the Russian imagination. The criticism selected for this volume will enable readers to understand the cultural significance of Pushkin's novel in verse and at the same time shed light on its meaning for world literature.

The eight essays translated here are regarded as the most influential pieces in the vast body of Russian criticism devoted to *Onegin*. They are of special interest because they illuminate not only a great work of Russian literature but also Russian criticism and its history. Although the Russians have produced a very important body of criticism and have been the secret legislator of much criticism in the West (they invented both social criticism and Structuralism), outside the Soviet Union their contributions are little known. Russia's greatest critic, Vissarion Belinsky, called *Eugene Onegin* "an encyclopedia of Russian life." In the same spirit this anthology is intended as "an encyclopedia of Russian criticism."

A word should be said about the arrangement of the essays. The nineteenth-century texts are ordered chronologically, opening with a famous essay by Belinsky, the father of social criticism, from the 1840s. It is followed by a vituperative essay by the radical critic Dmitry Pisarev, written in the 1860s, and Dostoevsky's celebrated "Pushkin Speech," composed for the dedication of the Pushkin monument in Moscow in 1880. The twentieth-century pieces of criticism are arranged according to a different principle—to demonstrate linkages rather than adhere rigidly to chronology. Thus Yury Lotman's essay on the structure of *Onegin* follows that of Yury Tynyanov on its composition, since Soviet Structuralism is in a sense an outgrowth of Russian Formalism. Then comes a short but highly significant essay by Mikhail Bakhtin, the fountainhead of a second seminal twentieth-century tradition—one that is anti-formalistic and stresses the importance of semantics. It is followed by a meditation on the stylistic world of *Onegin* by Sergey Bocharov, whose understanding of style is strongly influenced by Bakhtin. Another essay by Lotman closes the collection because it points forward, dealing with the impact of *Onegin* on the subsequent development of the Russian novel.

All the translations in this collection are my own, with the exception of the Bakhtin article, which was translated by Caryl Emerson and Michael Holquist and is reprinted from *The Dialogic Imagination* with the permission of the University of Texas Press. While the essays have been edited for an English-speaking audience, only one of them— that of Pisarev—has been abridged. All the verse translations quoted are by Walter Arndt. His rendition of *Eugene Onegin* deftly captures the stylistic nuances and ever-shifting tonal registers of Pushkin's verse. In some instances, particularly in the Tynyanov and Bocharov essays, I have modified Arndt's translation to illustrate a critic's point. Occasionally I have given a literal translation of an individual word or cited the Russian in brackets.

To assist the reader, authors and works which are frequently cited in the articles are identified in the glossary. Authors and works which are cited only once are identified in notes marked "—Tr." to distinguish them from those of the critics whose essays are translated. Russian names in the text reflect the most common English spelling. Russian names in the notes are given according to the Library of Congress system of transliteration, as are all Russian titles. In many instances the authors of the essays have quoted Pushkin's comments on his own works or other poems by him. When a translation of such a passage already exists, I have cited it in brackets in the text. When no translation exists, reference is made to the seventeen-volume Academy of Sciences edition: *Polnoe sobranie sochinenii* (Moscow/Leningrad, 1937–1959), with volume and page given in arabic numerals. Passages from *Eugene Onegin* are identified by a roman numeral for the chapter and an arabic one for the stanza (for example, V, 5); lines from "Onegin's Journey" are indicated by the letter J and the number of the stanza.

The following abbreviations are used for these frequently cited works:

Arndt

Eugene Onegin, trans. Walter Arndt, 2d rev. ed. (New York: E. P. Dutton, 1981).

Arndt, *PuCP*

Alexander Pushkin: Collected Narrative and Lyrical Poetry, trans. Walter Arndt (Ann Arbor: Ardis, 1984). Quotations from "Onegin's Journey" are taken from this edition, pp. 451–459.

Nabokov

Eugene Onegin, trans. Vladimir Nabokov, rev. ed., 4 vols. (Princeton: Princeton University Press, 1975). Translations of Pushkin's Notes are quoted from this edition.

Proffer

The Critical Prose of Alexander Pushkin, trans. Carl R. Proffer (Bloomington: Indiana University Press, 1969).

PSS

A. S. Pushkin, *Polnoe sobranie sochinenii,* 17 vols. (Moscow/Leningrad, 1937–1959).

Shaw

The Letters of Alexander Pushkin, trans. J. Thomas Shaw, 3 vols. in one (Madison: University of Wisconsin Press, 1967).

A bibliography of criticism on *Onegin* in English is provided at the back of this volume.

Acknowledgments

Work on this collection was begun thanks to a Summer Fellowship from the Research Board of the Graduate College of the University of Illinois at Chicago. A generous grant from the Translations Program, then headed by Susan Mango, of the National Endowment for the Humanities permitted me to go on leave for a year and translate the bulk of these essays and write a draft of the Introduction.

This collection has been long in the making and at each stage there have been friends and colleagues who have been most helpful. To each of them I owe a special debt of gratitude: to my sister Paula Stephan, who judiciously guided me in formulating my grant proposal to the NEH; to Paulina Lewin of the Ukrainian Research Center of Harvard University, who painstakingly checked my translations for accuracy and patiently explained passages in the Russian texts which I found difficult to decipher; to Robert Maguire of Columbia University, who taught me how to recast my translations into good English and who very generously went over all of these translations, helping me push and pull difficult phrases into acceptable English; to Walter Arndt of Dartmouth College, who not only allowed me to quote from his translation of *Eugene Onegin* but also generously provided verse translations of other poetry quoted by the critics I translated; to Michael Holquist of Yale University, who inspired me to rewrite the introduction and helped me to see the articles I had translated not as discrete pieces but as part of a larger tradition; to Janet Rabinowitch, Senior Sponsoring Editor of Indiana University Press, whose wise counsel helped make this collection a much better book than it would have been otherwise; to Curtisteen Steward, who retyped the bulk of these articles efficiently and cheerfully and who sacrificed weekends to do it. My deepest debt of gratitude is owed to my family, who have endured this project for much longer than they would care to remember—and especially to my husband, Thomas, for his sound judgment, encouragement, sense of perspective, and help at all stages in producing this book.

RUSSIAN VIEWS
OF PUSHKIN'S
EUGENE ONEGIN

Introduction

1

When we in the West think of nineteenth-century Russian literature, we think of the Russian novel, and we associate it with Dostoevsky and Tolstoy. Russians, however, are quick to point out that Alexander Pushkin created the Russian novel and that Dostoevsky's and Tolstoy's works are an extension of his genius. They regard Pushkin as their greatest writer, their Shakespeare. Why is this so? In order to understand Pushkin's unique role in the history of Russian culture, we must remember that Russian literature was late to mature. Only in the eighteenth century, in the wake of the reforms of Peter the Great, did a secular literature begin to emerge, and only in the nineteenth century did Russian literature truly come into its own. Pushkin was Russia's first great writer in the modern tradition. After self-consciously practicing European literary genres for almost one hundred years and groping for a national literary language, Russia suddenly produced a dazzling and sophisticated poet who wrote with complete assurance. It was as if he had simultaneously created and perfected the Russian literary language. He seemed both the creator and the supreme embodiment of Russian literature.

Pushkin, however, is more than the creator of modern Russian literature. He is the "beginning of all beginnings," to quote Gorky. He has such a powerful hold on the Russian imagination because literature means much more to Russians than it does to us in the West. To Russians literature is both an affirmation and an expression of national identity, *narodnost'*. Moreover, literature is regarded as an embodiment of social and moral truths. Therefore, the writer is viewed as a sacred voice, a prophet, and is revered in a way we in the West find difficult to imagine. The Russians regard Pushkin not only as the first but also as the fullest expression of Russianness in literature. The work of Pushkin's which best articulates this national quality is *Eugene Onegin*.

Begun in 1823 and completed in 1831, *Eugene Onegin* is the most original of all of Pushkin's writings and the most difficult to characterize. On the one hand, it is a dazzling poetic masterpiece. No other poem of Pushkin's contains such an abundance of perfect poetry, all the more astonishing because the work is executed in intricate fourteen-line stanzas. On the other hand, *Onegin* is a novel—the story of love twice rejected set against a broad picture of contemporary Russian life. Its hero and heroine—Onegin, the disillusioned sophisticate, and Tatyana, the appealing, sincere young woman—became the prototypes for many characters in nineteenth-century Russian fiction.

Onegin is an intriguing hybrid. In some ways it resembles the nineteenth-century realistic novel which was to follow it; in other ways it is very different. Pushkin deliberately called attention to the hybrid nature of his work by giving it the subtitle "novel in verse." In his very first mention of *Onegin* he emphasized its elusive quality: "As for what I am doing," he confessed in a letter to a friend, "I am writing, not a novel but a novel in verse—a devil of a difference."[1]

This "devil of a difference" disturbed Pushkin's contemporaries. They were quick to find fault with *Onegin* because it did not fit their preconceptions. Since it was full of sparkling play and amusing chatter, they did not regard it as serious poetry nor could they accept it as a novel. They complained about its digressive quality, "improvisatory" nature, and weak plot. Moreover, they saw nothing "Russian" about *Onegin*. Living in an age dominated by Byron, they were quick to conclude that Pushkin's work was marred by the influence of the English poet. Their views were summed up by Pushkin's fellow poet Evgeny Baratynsky:

> The form belongs to Byron, the tone also. Many poetic details are borrowed . . . the characters are pale. Onegin is not well developed, Tatyana lacks distinctive qualities, Lensky is insignificant. The descriptions of locale are beautiful but are only an exercise in purely plastic art. There is nothing here which definitively characterizes our Russian way of life.[2]

Like many Russians of the period, Baratynsky believed that genuine literature did express national character—that it embodied the inner, as well as the external, life of a people. This view, propounded by the German Romantics, had great appeal to Russians in the 1830s because they, like the Germans before them, relied on literature to aid them in self-definition. Russians, however, believed in the crucial role of literature more intensely than did the Germans because there were few other signs of cultural life in their country. Russia had a repressive censorship. She had no secular philosophical tradition and no tradition of political or social thought. She had not yet made important contributions in the fields of secular art or music. She could look to literature and little else, although Russians suspected that their own literature did not express the national character. They were afraid that the Russian character did not exist, that they lacked an identity of their own, that they had received everything from without and given nothing to the world. They feared that theirs was a country without a history in the Western European sense, and they had a great feeling of inferiority.

In an attempt to resolve this cultural dilemma Russian intellectuals of the 1840s put forward two opposing sets of views. Some—labeled Slavophiles—insisted that the true national identity had been preserved among the peasants, whose way of life had not been violated by the reforms of Peter the Great, and that Russians could regain a sense of wholeness by returning to the ideals and traditions of the people. Others—called Westernizers—argued that the reforms of Peter the Great had awakened Russia from her lethargy and that in order to come fully into her own Russia must continue to learn from the West and follow the European pattern of development.[3]

The chief spokesman for the Westernizers was Vissarion Belinsky, who played a more important role in Russia's cultural history than has any other critic and who has no real counterpart in Western criticism.[4] Belinsky was an ardent polemicist, and in a sense his 1844 essay in the present collection is a polemic against the Slavophiles. At the same time it reveals his ability to transcend the controversies of his day and to perceive what was actually happening in and to Russia.

Belinsky had an acute sense of history. He realized that profound changes had occurred in Russia during his own lifetime. (He was born in 1811, on the eve of the Great Patriotic War of 1812.) Belinsky possessed, as it were, a double vision. He was able simultaneously to see what had happened and to relive it, to outline the broad contours of Russia's cultural development and to bring events alive and give them a sense of immediacy. His excellence as a critic stemmed from his finely tuned historical sense, his remarkable judgment, and his forceful and impassioned manner of writing. Belinsky realized that in his own time modern Russian society had come into being and modern Russian literature had been born. Aware that he had been present at the genesis of modern Russian culture, he simultaneously traced this process, recreated it, and celebrated it.

Belinsky recognized that Pushkin's novel in verse, which he termed an "encyclopedia of Russian life," had played a crucial role in the development of national self-awareness, that it both affirmed the existence of Russian culture and the Russian character and embodied them. *Onegin* was testimony to the fact that the Russian consciousness had awakened; at the same time, the work was an act of consciousness itself. Belinsky saw *Onegin* as the center which made everything cohere. Thanks to *Onegin,* Russia had a past and was moving, organically, toward the future. *Onegin* was an affirmation that Russia had entered universal history and, simultaneously, had her own unique history. It was also evidence of the rapidity with which Russia was changing, proof that the pace of her cultural development was radically different from that of the West. Time, Belinsky observed, was compressed in Russia: "Five years for her is almost a century."[5]

Belinsky grasped, as no one else had, the unique cultural significance of *Eugene Onegin.* He dramatized its meaning more compellingly than has any other critic. At one stroke, he elevated Pushkin's work to the status of a national epic and forged a link between *Onegin* and Russia's identity. Thus the centrality of Pushkin's novel in verse for the national life was quickly established. What would probably have been a gradual process in other European countries happened overnight in Russia.

Belinsky devoted considerable attention to the major characters, discussing them as if they were real people.[6] Ardently defending Pushkin's hero, he blamed the age in which Onegin lived for his egotism and inactivity. He treated Onegin's dilemma as if it mirrored the dilemma of Belinsky's own generation, many of whom felt their talents stifled by the repressive regime of Nicholas I. Moreover, Belinsky interpreted the similarity between Pushkin's hero and Pechorin, the hero of Mikhail Lermontov's novel, *Hero of Our Time,* as evidence that this dilemma was an ongoing problem in Russian society. Indeed, the degree to which Russians would read their own social and spiritual history in the lives of their literary heroes became one of the most striking features of nineteenth-century Russian criticism. The Onegin-type hero was labeled the "superfluous man," and both his progeny and his genealogy were traced by later critics. The first to emphasize the social significance of literary heroes like Onegin, Belinsky defined the malady of the superfluous man and introduced the notion of a recurring social type.

Today, Belinsky is regarded as the father of social criticism, which became the dominant approach to literature in Russia in the nineteenth century and was enshrined as the official creed in the Soviet Union in the 1930s. However, Belinsky was strongly influenced by German Romanticism and never abandoned its basic doctrines, even though he modified his views toward the end of his life. Like the German Romantics, Belinsky conceived of society as a spiritual entity, the embodiment of consciousness, and he believed that genuine literature—i.e., literature that is truly national—was an expression of that consciousness. Increasingly, however, Belinsky also came to identify society with empirical reality, to regard literature as society's mirror, and to assume that literature evolved along with society.[7] The tension between these two impulses is evident again and again in the articles on *Onegin.* It helps to explain inconsistencies: why, for example, Belinsky in one breath referred to *Onegin* as a poem and in the next as a novel, why he insisted that the characters were typical and then argued that they were extraordinary beings. Belinsky was neither troubled nor impeded by the contradictions inherent in his views. Those who followed him, however, were much more rigid. In the next generation a conflict arose between critics of the Left and of the Right, each claiming to be Belinsky's true heirs. Actually, Belinsky fathered two traditions yet remained distinct from both of them.

Dmitry Pisarev's 1865 essay on *Eugene Onegin* demonstrates how different from Belinsky's were the attitudes and sensibility of the radical sons. Pisarev, the most talented and outspoken of the "new men,"[8] was a passionate utilitarian and had little respect or sympathy for culture. (In a heated moment he once said that a pair of boots was of more value than all the plays of Shakespeare.) Pisarev tolerated literature that was critical of existing social conditions and educated the reader to fight against the existing order, but he had little feeling for art as such and did not hold its great practitioners in high esteem.

Unlike Belinsky, Pisarev had nothing but contempt for Pushkin and *Eugene Onegin*. He accused Pushkin of turning his back on social issues, of failing to portray Russian reality as it really was, of sweeping the "dirt of real life" under the rug and chattering away about inconsequential matters like restaurants, balls, and the little feet of ladies. (In an effort to demonstrate the inanity of *Eugene Onegin,* Pisarev twisted quotations, deliberately destroying Pushkin's rhythm and rhyme.) Pisarev strongly disapproved of the exuberance of Pushkin's novel in verse. He insisted that the tone of *Onegin* was misleading, that Pushkin duped his reader into believing he lived in Arcadia, that far from being an encyclopedia of Russian life, *Eugene Onegin* was nothing more than an apotheosis of the status quo.

Pisarev hungered for a new kind of hero—a man of action who would shape the future and serve as a model for others to follow. He insisted that Onegin, like Pushkin himself, was shallow and spineless. Whereas Belinsky blamed Onegin's inactivity on the age in which he lived, Pisarev argued that the times were the inevitable cumulative result of such men as Onegin.

Pisarev considered Pushkin's novel in verse to be the epitome of a superfluous culture deserving of repudiation. Yet we should not completely dismiss his interpretation of *Onegin*. Pisarev raised important questions about the nature of Pushkin's hero. Although he was blind to the ironic distance created by Pushkin and persisted in identifying the poet with his flawed protagonist, he surely was right to question the authenticity of Onegin's ennui. Moreover, he pointed to a significant peculiarity in the language of *Eugene Onegin:* Pushkin's use of "elastic"—i.e., ambiguous—words, which the reader should be wary of accepting at face value.

Pisarev's radical views were opposed by a group of conservative critics who called themselves *pochvenniki,* "men of the soil."[9] The *pochvenniki* were intensely nationalistic, and their understanding of nationhood was tinged with mysticism. They believed in the powers of intuition rather than reason, religiosity rather than science. They valued organic growth, man's connections with history and tradition. They revered things Russian and felt an antipathy to Europe, Catholicism, and socialism. They sought a renewed sense of wholeness, a reaffirmation of national principles, a return to the soil. The mentor of the *pochvenniki* was Apollon Grigoriev, a gifted critic who considered himself a follower of Belinsky.[10] The most outspoken member of the group was Grigoriev's disciple Fyodor Dostoevsky. It was Dostoevsky who led the counterattack against the radicals, polemicizing heatedly with them both in his journalistic writings and in such works of fiction as *Notes from Underground* and *The Possessed.*

The conservative critics regarded art as the highest of human achievements. They held that the artist possessed prophetic powers as well as a special intuitive, synthetic understanding of life and of truth. They stressed the artist's organic connection to his native soil, which permitted him to grasp and represent different facets of the national psyche and to delineate truly national types. In their eyes the consummate artist was Pushkin.

The *pochvenniki* made a cult of Pushkin, but their adoring voices were drowned out by the tumult of the 1860s. By 1880, however, the mood of the country had changed. There was a resurgence of nationalism in the wake of the Russo-Turkish War. At last the conservative critics saw their position vindicated and Pushkin enshrined. The occasion was the erection of a monument to the poet in Moscow (it still occupies a central place in the nation's capital); the most celebrated speech at the dedication ceremony was delivered by Dostoevsky.

Dostoevsky's "Pushkin Speech" is actually a speech about Russia—her spiritual identity and her destiny. It is important for two reasons: it reveals with striking clarity Dostoevsky's view of his native land and his vision of her future, and it demonstrates that for Dostoevsky these matters were inextricably bound up with Pushkin and *Eugene Onegin*. To talk about them was to talk about Russia; to make extraordinary claims for Pushkin the poet was to make extraordinary claims for Russia. Dostoevsky insisted that Pushkin was an unprecedented phenomenon in world literature and that his greatness was a sign of Russia's future greatness; his unique ability to reincarnate himself in the spirit of other nations was a foretoken of Russia's messianic mission.

Dostoevsky invoked Pushkin to vindicate Russia and the Russian spirit, and he invoked *Eugene Onegin* to explain the Russian psyche. As a *pochvennik*, Dostoevsky believed that the Russian character had been split in two as a result of the reforms of Peter the Great and that Russia, Janus-like, had one face turned outward toward the West and the other turned inward toward the people. (The former he viewed as a sign of disease, the latter as an indication of health.) Dostoevsky insisted that Pushkin's hero and heroine incarnated the two sides of the Russian character. He portrayed Onegin as the negative type, the Westernized intellectual who had lost contact with the people and wandered about aimlessly, seeking salvation in Europe and in socialism. Tatyana became the positive type, close to the people, their traditions, and their religious beliefs. Dostoevsky stressed the opposition between the two characters—that Onegin was an abstract reasoner, while Tatyana instinctively knew the truth and was faithful to it; that Onegin came from Petersburg, the cosmopolitan city built by Peter the Great, while Tatyana came from the country; that Onegin was uprooted, like a blade of grass carried hither and yon by the wind, while Tatyana was firmly rooted in her native soil. Dostoevsky argued that Tatyana's rejection of Onegin and her pledge of conjugal fidelity proved that she was morally superior to Onegin in the same way that Russia was morally superior to the West.

The "Pushkin Speech" deified the poet, treated *Eugene Onegin* as scripture, and strangely transformed Pushkin's characters. Tatyana was elevated to sainthood, Onegin was recast as a restless intellectual (much like the heroes in

Dostoevsky's own novels), and Tatyana's husband was brought to life, portrayed as an honest old man who dearly loved his wife (thereby acquiring a psychological presence never granted him by Pushkin, who deliberately left him undeveloped).[11]

2

In the 1920s the Russian Formalists radically reinterpreted Pushkin by shifting attention from content to form. A seminal critical movement, Russian Formalism left an impressive legacy whose impact on criticism—both in the Soviet Union and in the West—is still felt today.[12] Among its founders was the linguist Roman Jakobson, who later became one of the main creators of Structuralism.

Formalism was part of the broader modernist trend which emerged in Russia, as in other parts of Europe, just before World War I. It was closely allied with the Russian avant-garde movements in literature and art—Futurism and Constructivism—and shared their enthusiasm for technology and innovation, their desire to break with tradition, and their taste for nonobjective, stylized art. Formalism was a reaction against social criticism, on the one hand, and philosophical criticism on the other. The Formalists insisted that art does not reproduce reality. Art, they argued, is not a reflection of society or a battleground for ideas. Rather it is both artful and artificial—invented and shaped through the deliberate manipulation of materials.

The Formalists disregarded extraliterary factors and turned their attention solely to the work of literature itself.[13] What interested them was *literaturnost'* [literariness], i.e., that which distinguishes literary works from other uses of the word. In an attempt to discover the specific properties of literary art, they focused on technique, on the "devices" employed.[14] They sought to discover how literary works are constructed or put together.[15] Their overriding concern was with language as the medium of literature. They assumed that literary speech is different from practical speech, autonomous rather than subordinate to objective reality, sign-oriented rather than referential. They were particularly interested in poetic language, since poetry enables one to experience speech in its totality.

The Formalists sought to redefine the study of literature radically and make it a science. They were not interested in traditional critical concerns: plot, characters, and ideas; nor were they committed to the traditional task of the critic: making value judgments. They regarded literature as a construct, analogous to a clock, and they wanted to take it apart and determine what makes it tick. At the same time they sought to challenge readers' perceptions, to make them see literary works in a new light by restoring the orientation toward form.

As a school of thought, Russian Formalism was far from unified, and there were marked differences among its members. This state of affairs is illustrated by the two Formalist essays on *Eugene Onegin*. The first, Viktor Shklovsky's "Pushkin and Sterne: *Eugene Onegin*," has been available in translation since 1975[16] and is not included in this collection; the second, Yury Tynyanov's "On the Composition of *Eugene Onegin*," is translated here for the first time.

The *enfant terrible* of the Formalist movement, Viktor Shklovsky was an initiator, a gadfly, the creator of slogans, and the brash promoter of Formalism.[17] In his article he boldly challenged traditional views of *Onegin*. He dismissed the characters and the plot, disavowed the work's social significance, and focused on the playfulness of Pushkin's novel in verse, the ways in which Pushkin deliberately flaunted his craft. Shklovsky insisted that *Eugene Onegin* bore a close resemblance to *Tristram Shandy*, that, like Sterne's work, it was highly form-conscious and parodied the techniques and conventions of the novel.[18] He pointed out that Pushkin mocks conventional narrative schemes by playing with his story: digressing, omitting stanzas, rearranging the time sequence and calling attention to it, deliberately breaking off the narrative at the end; and he argued that this playing with the "story" is in fact the true "plot" of *Eugene Onegin*.

By focusing on Pushkin's form-consciousness, Shklovsky rendered *Eugene Onegin* "perceptible" again—to use another favorite term of the Formalists. Yet he overstated the case, ignoring the fundamental differences between *Onegin* and *Tristram Shandy* (*Tristram Shandy* was Shklovsky's favorite novel and the one he deemed "most typical"). Moreover, he assumed that the work of literature is the sum total of devices employed in it, and he mechanically juxtaposed the parodistic devices used in Pushkin's novel in verse to similar devices found in Sterne.

Yury Tynyanov was a very different kind of critic: a systematic thinker, brilliant theoretician, and astute literary historian. From the very beginning of his career he had a dynamic conception of literature and the literary process. He conceived of the literary work as a hierarchical system in which one group of elements "dominates" and "deforms"—i.e., alters the nature of—all other elements. Thus, when Tynyanov used the term "composition," he had in mind the dynamic integration of elements and not their static and symmetrical arrangement. His notion of the aesthetic structure as a dynamic system anticipated the Czech Structuralists.[19]

In his article on *Onegin*, Tynyanov addressed one of the fundamental questions of literary theory: What is it that distinguishes poetry from prose? He took an approach to this problem that was characteristic of mature Formalism. He did not assume an inherent difference between the two, as many critics have done. Rather he argued that the difference hinges on function—that in poetry rhythm (in the broad sense encompassing all perceptible phonic phenomena) is dominant, while in prose the semantic aspect is dominant. Tynyanov recognized that poetry and prose are closed categories or systems, yet he did not insist that they are mutually exclusive. He realized that the systems overlap, that they enrich and cross-fertilize each other, and he substantiated this argument with the example of *Eugene Onegin*. Pushkin's work provided rich material because it is a borderline case, poised between poetry and prose, where there is maximum tension between the two systems.

Tynyanov stressed the differences between the novel in verse and the novel in prose, pointing out that in *Eugene Onegin,* meaning—the characters, the story, even the digressions—is deformed by the verse. (As if rebutting Shklovsky's argument, Tynyanov observed that *Tristram Shandy* and *Onegin* are very different kinds of works precisely because of their systemic differences.) At the same time Tynyanov demonstrated how verse itself is exploited in *Eugene Onegin* to make the "novel" more perceptible. By "novel" Tynyanov meant: (1) novel as a literary genre with a defined tradition and (2) novel as an embodiment of the colloquial intonations of everyday speech. The latter concept particularly interested him, and he subjected it to rigorous analysis.

At the end of the 1920s Russian Formalism was suppressed in the Soviet Union. The official criticism that dominated the next three decades was not really Marxist (the Marxist school too came under attack at the end of the 1920s) but a more "neutral" form of sociological criticism. It evaded the issue of class origin and was actually reminiscent of nineteenth-century social criticism. Therefore, it is not represented in the present collection.[20]

The 1950s brought a change in intellectual climate in the Soviet Union. As has often been the case in Russian history, one cause of the change was political—the death of Stalin; another was technological—the advent of cybernetics. The "thaw" that followed Stalin's demise prompted renewed interest in the culture of the 1920s—in the contributions of writers and artists and in the critical studies of the Russian Formalists and, by extension, the Czech Structuralists, since the two schools overlapped. The coming of the computer age, by contrast, sparked an interest in machine translation, in semiotics, and in structural linguistics. Out of this complex interplay of factors emerged Soviet Structuralism, which flourished in the 1960s and early 1970s.

Yury Lotman, a professor at Tartu University in Estonia, quickly became one of the leaders of the movement, although he was not involved in the group's activities before 1964. Because of his abundant energy and productivity, Tartu became a major locus of Structuralist activities in the mid-1960s, achieving international prominence. Lotman is well known in the West. Many of his articles and three of his books have been translated into English.[21] A specialist in Russian literature, Lotman has written widely on eighteenth- and nineteenth-century Russian culture. By examining his two articles on *Eugene Onegin* in the present collection, we can trace his development from a Structuralist stage into a new phase, perhaps best termed the "semiotics of culture."

Lotman's 1966 article, "The Structure of *Eugene Onegin*," was one of his early Structuralist pieces. In it Lotman called attention to the fact that he had ceased to practice sociological criticism and stressed his links with the Russian Formalists—Shklovsky, Tynyanov, Boris Eikhenbaum, and Grigory Vinokur—and with Mikhail Bakhtin. Criticizing the work of his teacher, Grigory Gukovsky, and his own earlier work on *Eugene Onegin*, Lotman emphasized that the purpose of this article was to determine what makes *Onegin* cohere as a structural whole. In an attempt to answer this question, Lotman set out to analyze the internal structure of Pushkin's novel in verse on three levels: point of view, intonation, and character. The article represented a search for an appropriate methodological model. Lotman experimented—testing out different ideas on Pushkin's novel in verse and diagramming the results. Analyzing point of view, Lotman applied Bakhtin's notion that the text is a series of overlaid utterances.[22] Discussing intonation, he drew on the theories of the Russian Formalists. Investigating character, he adopted a Jakobsonian approach, looking at the novel as synchronic sections and reducing the characters to a series of binary oppositions.

Lotman's "The Structure of *Eugene Onegin*" was a pioneering piece. It signaled a change in the critical climate and was itself instrumental in bringing about that change. Lotman resurrected Formalist techniques in order to apply a Structuralist approach to one of the sacred texts in Russian literature. At the same time he challenged the authority of official criticism by pointing out the limitations of extrinsic approaches to literature. Here, too, Lotman emphasized the semantic energy of art, thereby opening the door for new and diverse readings of *Onegin*.

At the end of the 1960s Lotman's critical orientation began to change. He ceased to view literature as a closed system and came to regard it as an integral part of the larger field of culture. He recognized that literature influences other cultural systems and is in turn influenced by them.

This recognition of the interrelatedness of cultural series informs Lotman's 1975 article on *Eugene Onegin* and the Russian novel. Here, Lotman, examining the tradition generated by *Onegin*, approached the problem of *Onegin*'s impact on that tradition, not in terms of mechanistic reproduction, as critics have traditionally done, but as a process of continual transformation caused by the interaction between systems. Lotman stressed that for subsequent writers *Onegin* was not so much a literary as a cultural fact. He showed the way in which writers like Lermontov and Turgenev, far from duplicating *Onegin*, adapted elements from it to meet their own needs and how in turn their interpretations of Pushkin's novel in verse began to influence perceptions of the work itself. *Onegin*, for example, came to be perceived through the prism of

Turgenev's novels, which are characterized by a strong heroine and a weak hero. (Undoubtedly this had an impact on both Dostoevsky and Tchaikovsky.)

In his 1975 article Lotman radically redefined the notion of the "superfluous man," whose roots he traced back to the Romantic hero, demonstrating that the phenomenon was the result of a complex interaction between "literature" and "life." He argued that the notion of the superfluous man was later projected onto Pushkin's hero rather than being characteristic of him and stressed that *Eugene Onegin* stands outside the novelistic tradition generated by it.

Lotman's evolution may be said to parallel that of the mature Formalists, such as Yury Tynyanov, who became increasingly aware that literature is not a closed field of inquiry but a social construct. Lotman and his fellow semioticians of culture have once again taken up the question of literature's social role, but their assumptions and methodology are quite different from those of the nineteenth-century social critics.[23]

The 1960s witnessed not only the flourishing of Structuralism in the Soviet Union but also the rediscovery of Mikhail Bakhtin, whose seminal study, *Problems of Dostoevsky's Poetics,* was reissued in 1963 by two of his young disciples, Vadim Kozhinov and Sergey Bocharov.[24] Following the publication of a major work on Rabelais in 1965,[25] Bakhtin came to the attention of Western critics, and soon he was influential in the West as well. His influence has continued to grow as more of his work has become available, and he has come to be regarded as one of the major thinkers of the twentieth century.[26]

Bakhtin began his career in the 1920s during the prime of Russian Formalism. But in many ways his approach was antithetical to that of the Formalists. They concentrated on what might be termed the technical aspects of literature, while he focused on semantics, insisting that language cannot be divorced from meaning but that meaning is itself open-ended since it depends on a variety of contexts. Bakhtin was given to speculation and broad synthesis, the Formalists to systemization and close analysis. Bakhtin conceived of the work of literature as animate, living, and therefore unfinished—hence his preference for organic metaphors; while the early Formalists viewed the literary work as a construct, a finished object—hence their preference for technical metaphors.

Bakhtin regarded the novel as a genre unlike all other genres. What made the novel radically different in his view was the fact that it presumes its own highly peculiar relationship to language. According to Bakhtin, the language of other genres is fixed, homogeneous, direct, while the language of the novel is heterogeneous—a living mix of varied and opposing voices. Bakhtin argued that this heterogeneity must be taken into consideration if the novel's stylistics is to be understood, that it is erroneous to identify one particular style in the novel with its author, for he speaks through all of its languages, simultaneously representing in them and distancing himself from them—criticizing them, arguing with them, ridiculing them. In Bakhtin's view, the novel is a complex dialogical system of languages with the author serving as the unifying aesthetic center.

Bakhtin presented his theory about the way discourse functions in the novel in remarkably concise form in remarks here entitled "Discourse in *Eugene Onegin*."[27] For Bakhtin, *Onegin* proved the uniqueness of novelistic discourse, since it is not characterized by a single uniform style, as one finds in Pushkin's poetry, but by a variety of languages or styles connected to one another through dialogical relationships. Bakhtin pointed out that different parts of *Onegin* are constructed in different "speech zones" and that each of these major voice zones is associated with one of the novel's central characters: the Sentimental Romantic poetic style with Lensky, the Byronic style with Onegin, the complex combination of dreamy sentimental Richardsonian language and folk language with Tatyana. Thus, each of these stylistic systems is inseparable from a living being, a character who is its agent, and from his world view. Bakhtin stressed that none of these speech zones can be directly identified with the author Pushkin. He is closer to some languages than to others, yet not one of them, not even that of the lyrical digressions, is completely free of parodically stylized or parodically polemicizing elements. Bakhtin called attention to the fact that Pushkin participates in the novel with almost no direct language of his own. He is present, however, as the organizing center where all these images of language intersect.

In "Discourse in *Eugene Onegin*" Bakhtin succeeded in demonstrating, as no other critic has done, the novel-ness of *Eugene Onegin*. He did this by radically shifting ground, focusing attention on discourse. Incisively characterizing the major speech zones found in Pushkin's work and revealing their links to the novel's central characters, he showed that discourse functions in *Eugene Onegin* as a dialogized system composed of images of languages and consciousnesses that are concrete and inseparable from language.

Bakhtin's disciple Sergey Bocharov, a research fellow at the Gorky Institute of World Literature in Moscow, is one of the finest Pushkin scholars in the Soviet Union today. Bocharov was not associated with the Structuralist movement in the Soviet Union; neither can he be called a cultural semiotician. Rather, he is akin to the Phenomenologists—critics like Georges Poulet, Gaston Bachelard, and the early J. Hillis Miller. To some degree he has been influenced by the writings of Maurice Merleau-Ponty. (Bocharov reads French and has been in France.) At the same time his understanding of the novel and in particular of the way discourse functions in the novel has been shaped by Bakhtin, to whom he was close in the 1960s and early 1970s and whose works he has been instrumental in bringing into print.

Bocharov has written on Cervantes; he had produced a study of Tolstoy's *War and Peace,* which Edward Wasiolek has called remarkable and praised for its originality and perceptiveness;[28] and he has written articles on Gogol and on the philosophical poet Evgeny Baratynsky, who was Pushkin's contemporary. His substantial essay in the present collection is taken from his book on Pushkin's poetics.[29]

In order to understand Bocharov's interpretation of *Eugene Onegin,* it is crucial to understand his view of discourse. Like the Phenomenologists, Bocharov believes that language is open to the lived world of experience rather than being an autonomous and closed system of signs, as the Structuralists conceived it to be. For Bocharov, as for the Phenomenologists, style is of overriding importance because it can capture and constitute the fullness of reality, since it is the incarnation of intentional consciousness, the writer's experience of the world given verbal form.

In "The Stylistic World of the Novel" Bocharov attempts to show how the fullness of life is constituted, *stylistically* speaking, in *Eugene Onegin.* Here the crucial notion for him is "translation," not in the sense of a literal copy or a deflation (although these meanings enter in as well—particularly with reference to Onegin). Rather, by "translation" Bocharov means the continual switching from one *stylistic* language to another which pervades Pushkin's novel in verse. However, since Bocharov assumes that language is a living phenomenon and not a closed system, he does not regard this switching as an automatic mechanism but as a dynamic process in which varied and opposing voices animatedly interact. To characterize this interaction Bocharov uses the musical analogy of counterpoint.[30] Broadly speaking, he sees the stylistic interaction in *Eugene Onegin* as that of two independent voices which sound simultaneously and yet remain distinct, which coalesce and yet retain their active differences. For Bocharov this interaction forms a kind of tension between "poetry," on the one hand, and "prose," on the other. With "poetry" is associated the verse tradition, the periphrastic style, the lofty, the ideal, the subjective; with "prose" the bare word, simple language, the plain, the real, the objective. "Poetry" is identified with the young poet Lensky, "prose" with the cynical Onegin. In Bocharov's view the stylistic world of Pushkin's work is a dynamic synthesis of these polar opposites. One does not negate the other; rather the two collide, yet come together in the unity of authorial speech.

Bocharov is remarkably attuned to the stylistic richness and vitality of *Onegin* and able to convey that, to make his reader experience what he terms the "heterostylism" of authorial speech.[31] Because he is so sensitive to context, he is able to bring the verse culture of the period to life and demonstrate the living links between it and Pushkin's text, both in a broad sense and in a narrow one—that of Pushkin's own poetry. Bocharov succeeds in showing how *Onegin* grew out of the verse culture of the period and simultaneously how it transcended that culture, how Pushkin moved from the closed world of poetry into the open, consciously heterostylistic world of the novel by joining verse with prose, its polar opposite.

Nineteenth-Century
Views

Eugene Onegin

An Encyclopedia of Russian Life

VISSARION BELINSKY
(1844)

We must confess that we are somewhat hesitant to undertake a critical exam-
ination of a poem like *Eugene Onegin*.[1] There are many reasons for this. *Onegin*
is Pushkin's most sincere work, the most beloved child of his imagination.
There are very few works of literature in which the personality of the poet is
reflected as fully, as clearly and distinctly, as it is in *Onegin*. Here everything
mirrors him; the work embodies his feelings, his concepts, his ideals. To
evaluate this work is to evaluate the poet himself in the full range of his literary
endeavors. Furthermore, apart from its aesthetic merit, *Eugene Ongein* has for
Russians enormous historical and social significance. From this point of view
even that which now could justifiably be called weak or outdated in *Onegin* is
full of deep significance and great interest. We find ourselves in a difficult
position. We fear that we are not up to the task of evaluating this work, and yet
we feel called upon to note both the shortcomings and the merits of *Onegin*.
The majority of the public has not yet risen above abstract and one-sided
criticism—criticism which acknowledges only absolute shortcomings or abso-
lute merits in works of literature and does not understand that the conditional
and the relative also constitute a form of the absolute. And this explains why
some critics sincerely believed that we do not respect the eighteenth-century
poet Derzhavin, because, while we recognize that he was a great talent, we
cannot say that even one of his works is fully artistic or fully capable of
satisfying the aesthetic needs of our age. With regard to *Onegin,* our views may
seem to many even more contradictory, for it seems to us that in terms of form
Onegin is supremely artistic, while in terms of content its very shortcomings
constitute its greatest merit. Our entire article on *Onegin* will be devoted to
developing this idea—however strange it may seem at first glance.

First of all, *Onegin* is a poetically rendered picture of Russian society
captured at one of the most interesting stages in its development. From this
standpoint *Eugene Onegin* is a *historical* poem in the full sense of the word,
although there is not a single historical personage among its heroes. The
historical merit of this poem is all the greater, because it was the first attempt of
its kind—and what is more a brilliant one—to be undertaken in Russia. Here

Pushkin is not simply a poet but the representative of a newly awakened social consciousness. This is an enormous achievement!

Until Pushkin, Russian poetry, no matter how facile, was nothing more than the slavish pupil of the European muse, and, therefore, all the works of Russian poetry produced before Pushkin were more like sketches and copies than original creations, freely inspired. It took Ivan Krylov[2]—that mighty talent, so national, so Russian—a long time to summon up the courage to decline the unenviable honor of being translator and imitator of La Fontaine. In Derzhavin's poetry there are flashes of Russian speech, Russian intellect, but they quickly vanish—drowned in a flood of artificial foreign forms and concepts. The dramatist Ozerov[3] wrote a Russian tragedy, even a historical one— *Dimitry of the Don*—but in it only the names are "Russian" and "historical." All the rest is no more Russian and historical than it is French or Tartar. The poet Zhukovsky wrote two "Russian" ballads, *Lyudmila* and *Svetlana*. But the first is actually an adaptation of a German ballad (what is more, a rather ordinary one), and the second, though noteworthy for its truly poetic depictions of Russian Christmas customs and Russian winter landscapes, is completely permeated with German sentimentality and German phantasma. Batyushkov's muse wandered eternally under foreign skies and did not pluck a single flower on Russian soil. People soon concluded that there was no poetry in Russian life and that Russian poets had to seek inspiration in foreign lands, galloping off on Pegasus not only to the West but to the East.

With Pushkin, however, Russian poetry ceased to be a timid pupil and became a talented and experienced master. To be sure, this did not happen overnight, because nothing happens overnight. In his narrative poems, *Ruslan and Lyudmila* and *The Bandit Brothers,* Pushkin, like his predecessors, was nothing more than a pupil—not only in his attempt to create poetry, but also in his attempt to create a poetic representation of Russian reality. It is because of this that there is so little of Russia and so much of Italy in *Ruslan and Lyudmila;* this also explains why *The Bandits* is so much like a noisy melodrama. Like Zhukovsky, Pushkin produced a Russian ballad, *The Bridegroom,*[4] which he wrote in 1825, the same year Chapter I of *Eugene Onegin* was published.[5] But Pushkin's ballad is permeated to the core with the Russian spirit, both in terms of form and of content. One can say of it a thousand times more than of *Ruslan and Lyudmila*

There's Russia's spirit . . . Russian scent![6]

All the Russian folk songs taken together do not give expression to the Russian national character [*narodnost'*] any better than does this one ballad. However, it would be wrong to think that works of this sort are exemplary, and consequently the public paid little attention to this lovely ballad. The world which it portrays so faithfully and clearly is too accessible to any poet, if only because its salient characteristics are so obvious. Moreover, this world is so limited, shallow, and uncomplicated, that a truly gifted poet would not portray it repeatedly, fearing that his works would become one-sided, monotonous, boring, and, ultimately, banal—no matter what their merits. That is why a talented poet will usually make, at most, two attempts in this genre. For him, undertaking to write a ballad is more a test of strength than an indication of special esteem for the form.

Rich soil for the flowers of poetry is found where there is diversity of passions, infinitely subtle gradations of feeling, innumerably complex relations between people. Only a strongly developing or developed civilization can prepare this soil. Only in France, for example, are works like George Sand's *Jeanne* possible, because France is blessed with a very rich civilization which has created conditions whereby social estates [*sosloviia*] interact in a close and electrifying manner. By contrast, our poets must seek their materials almost exclusively in that one class which shows development and intellectual activity. The expression of national spirit [*natsional'nost'*] constitutes one of the highest merits of poetic works. In Russia only works that draw their content from the life of the estate which came into being as a result of the reforms of Peter the Great can be deemed truly national, since it was that estate which adopted the forms of civilized life. But even now the majority of the public views this matter differently.

Say that *Ruslan and Lyudmila* is imbued with *narodnost'* or *natsional'nost'*, and everyone will agree with you. You will gain even more support if you hail as a national work any play in which *muzhiks* and *babas* [i.e., peasants], bearded merchants, and townsfolk parade on the stage, or where characters intersperse their "artless" conversation with Russian proverbs and crudely slip in rhetorical statements about *narodnost'* and the like. Those who are more intelligent and educated recognize (quite justifiably) a national Russian quality in Krylov's fables and are even prepared to see it (less justifiably) not only in Pushkin's fairy tales, *Tsar Saltan* and *The Dead Tsarevna and the Seven Heroes,* but also (quite unjustifiably) in Zhukovsky's fairy tales, *Tsar Berendey* and *Sleeping Beauty.* However, you will find little support—in fact, many will think it strange—if you say that the first truly national Russian poem in verse was and remains Pushkin's *Eugene Onegin* and that more *narodnost'* finds expression in it than in any other "national" Russian work. But this is as true as two times two is four. If the national character of the poem is not recognized by everyone, it is because we have been brought up with the strange notion that a Russian man in a frock coat or a Russian woman in a corset is no longer a Russian, and that the Russian spirit manifests itself only where there are *zipuns,*[7] bast sandals, crude vodka, and sour cabbage. In this respect even many so-called educated people unintentionally imitate the common folk, who call every foreigner from Europe a *nemets.*[8] And this explains the unfounded fear some Russians have that we will be Germanized! In their naiveté, our self-styled patriots do not realize that, by constantly fearing for the Russian national character, they do it a great injustice. After all, when did the Russian army become ever-victorious, if not when Peter the Great outfitted it in European dress and inculcated the military discipline that went with this dress?

Some of our ardent Slavophiles say, 'Just look at the German. No matter where he goes, he is a German—whether he is in Russia, or in France, or in India. The Frenchman too is always a Frenchman, no matter where fate may take him. But the Russian in England is an Englishman, in France a Frenchman, in Germany a German.' To be sure, there is an element of truth in this which cannot be denied, but it does credit, not discredit, to the Russians. And this knack for successfully adapting to any people, to any country, is by no means the exclusive property of the educated estates in Russia; it is characteristic of the entire Russian tribe, the whole of northern Russia. However, just because a Russian can pass for an Englishman in England and a Frenchman in France, it does not mean that he has ceased even for a moment to be a Russian or even could for a moment become in earnest an Englishman or a Frenchman. Adopting foreign ways is hardly tantamount to renouncing one's own nature.

We had to digress in order to refute the unfounded opinion that only those works whose content is drawn from the life of the lower and uneducated classes can express the Russian character. Because our public holds this strange view, everything that is best and most civilized in Russia is proclaimed "un-Russian"; on account of it any crude farce with *muzhiks* and *babas* is hailed as a national work, but Griboedov's great comedy *Woe from Wit,* though admittedly Russian, is not considered to be one. Any vulgar novel, no matter how bad, is hailed as a national work, but Lermontov's novel, *A Hero of Our Time,* though a superb work, though Russian, is not regarded as one. This is absolutely wrong! It is high time we struck out against this opinion with all the power of common sense, with all the strength of inexorable logic! That "blessed" pseudoclassical age, where only people from high society and the educated estates were portrayed in literature (common people could be used only if they were washed, combed, and decked out and spoke in a language that was not their own) is a thing of the past. But now we are "blessed" with pseudoroman-ticism. The proponents of this school are so excited at the word *narodnost'* and so overjoyed that they can portray not only honest people of a lower rank but even thieves and scoundrels in poetry and drama that they fall prey to a misconception. They assume that true *natsional'nost'* lies hidden under a *zipun* or in a smoke-filled hut, that the nose of a drunken lackey broken in a fist fight is a truly Shakespearian feature, and, most importantly, that no signs of *narodnost'* are to be found among educated people.

It is high time we realized that a Russian poet can only prove himself to be a truly national poet by portraying in his works the life of the educated estates. For in order to discover the national elements in a life half-enveloped in forms that were originally alien to it, a poet must possess enormous talent and be national to the core. As Gogol pointed out, "True *natsional'nost'* rests not in the description of a peasant *sarafan*[9] but in the expression of the very spirit of the people. A poet can be a national poet even when he is describing a totally alien world, provided he looks at it through native eyes, through the eyes of his people, and provided that he feels and talks in such a way that his compatriots can identify with him."[10] To unriddle the mystery of the national psyche, a poet must have the ability to be faithful to reality, whether he is portraying the lower, the middle, or the upper estates. A poet who can only grasp the bold shades of the common people's crude life and is unable to grasp the subtler and more complex shades of civilized life will never be a great poet and still less will have the right to claim the celebrated title of national poet. A great national poet is able to make both the master and the peasant speak, each in his own language. And if a work whose content is drawn from the life of the educated estates does not deserve to be called a "national work," then it is worthless in an artistic sense too, because it is not faithful to the spirit of the reality it purports to portray. Therefore, Griboedov's *Woe from Wit*, Gogol's *Dead Souls,* and Lermontov's *A Hero of Our Time* are all every bit as national as they are superb poetic works.

And the first such national masterpiece was Pushkin's *Eugene Onegin*. The young poet's resolve to represent the moral physiognomy of the most Europeanized estate in Russia is proof that he was a national poet and, what is more, that he was deeply conscious of being one. He understood that the time for epic poems had long passed and that in order to portray contemporary society, in which the prose of life had so deeply penetrated the poetry of life, a novel was needed and not an epic poem. He took life as it really is and did not merely abstract the poetic moments from it. He took life with all its coldness, with all its prose and banality. Such boldness would have been less surprising had Pushkin written his novel in prose, but the audacity of writing such a novel in verse—and at a time when no Russian writer had even produced a single decent novel in prose! This was indisputable evidence of his genius, and his daring met with tremendous success. True, Russian poetry had produced something on the order of a story in verse which was good (for its time). We have in mind Dmitriev's *Modish Wife,*[11] but this work has nothing in common with *Eugene Onegin*. It could just as easily be taken for a free translation or an adaptation from the French as for an original Russian work. If any of Pushkin's works have something in common with Dmitriev's witty tale, then it is *Count Nulin*. But again this does not mean that the two works are of equal merit.

The form used in novels like *Onegin* was created by Byron. He was responsible for its features: the manner in which the story is told, the mixture of prose and poetry in the portrayal of reality, the digressions, the poet's addresses to himself, and particularly the all too perceptible presence of the poet in his own work. Of course, adopting the form created by another poet for one's own content is not the same as inventing it oneself. Nevertheless, if we compare Pushkin's *Onegin* with Byron's *Don Juan, Childe Harold,* and

Beppo, we find that they have nothing in common—aside from the form and manner. Not only the content but the spirit of Byron's poems preclude the possibility of any significant resemblance between them and Pushkin's *Onegin.* Byron wrote about Europe for Europe. This subjective spirit, so mighty and profound, this being, so colossal, proud, and unbending, did not so much aspire to portray contemporary mankind as to pronounce judgment upon its past and present history. We repeat: it is futile to look for even the slightest trace of a resemblance. Pushkin wrote about Russia for Russia. And it is indicative of his originality and genius that Pushkin remained true to his own nature (which was exactly the opposite of Byron's), true to his own artistic instincts, and did not permit himself to be tempted to create something "Byronic," in writing a Russian novel. Had he done so, he would have been praised to the skies. For this false tour de force he would have been covered with great glory, however transitory. But Pushkin was too extraordinary a poet to be tempted by such foolishness, which would have been so alluring to mediocre talents. His concern was not to be like Byron but to be himself and to be true to that untried and untouched reality which cried out for his pen. And that is why his *Onegin* is a supremely original and supremely national work.

Pushkin's novel in verse, together with Griboedov's brilliant comedy *Woe from Wit* (which was written at about the same time), laid the foundation for modern Russian poetry, for modern Russian literature. Before these two works, Russian poets knew how to be poets when they sang of subjects alien to Russian reality but hardly knew how to be poets when they undertook to portray the world of Russian life. The only exceptions were Derzhavin, whose poetry contains flashes of Russian life, Krylov, and lastly Fonvizin.[12] However, Fonvizin's comedies were more like skillful copies of Russian reality than creative renderings. For all the shortcomings of Griboedov's play (and there are major ones), it was the first Russian comedy to be free of imitation, false motifs, and unnatural colors. In it the whole and the parts, the plot and the characters, the passions and the actions, the opinions and the language are permeated with the profound truth of Russian reality. Many of the lines from Griboedov's play have become proverbs. No matter what the situation, his comedy comes to mind; it is a veritable gold mine of witty sayings!

Although there is no way to prove that Krylov's fables directly influenced Griboedov's comedy (from the standpoint of language and of verse), there is no way to deny it either. Where literature develops organically and historically, everything is interconnected and linked together! Khemnitser's[13] and Dmitriev's fables relate to the fables of Krylov as talent to genius; yet Krylov owes a great deal to Khemnitser and to Dmitriev. The same can be said of Griboedov. He was not a pupil of Krylov; he did not imitate him. He simply availed himself of Krylov's achievements in order to proceed further along his own path. Had there been no Krylov in Russian literature, Griboedov's verse would not have been so free, so spontaneous, so original. In short, Griboedov would not have made such tremendous advances. But his achievement was greater than this. His *Woe from Wit* and Pushkin's *Onegin* were the first exemplary poetic representations of Russian reality in the broad sense of the word. In this respect both works laid the foundation for the literature that followed and formed the school from which Lermontov and Gogol emerged. Without *Onegin,* there would have been no *Hero of Our Time,* just as without *Onegin* and *Woe from Wit,* Gogol would not have felt prepared to portray Russian reality with such profundity and truth.

Everyone knows the plot of *Onegin* so well that there is no need to describe it in detail. But, in order to get at the underlying idea, we will summarize it briefly. A young dreamy girl, brought up in the backwoods, falls in love with a young Petersburg lion (to use an expression now in vogue) who, bored with life in high society, has come to the country to be bored on his estate. She writes him a letter permeated with naive passion. He answers her in person, telling her that he cannot love her and that he does not consider himself created for the "bliss of family life" [IV, 14, line 1]. Then for some trivial reason Onegin is challenged to a duel by Lensky, the fiancé of our heroine's sister, and he kills the young poet. Because of Lensky's death, Tatyana and Onegin are separated for a long time. The poor girl, disappointed in her youthful dreams, bows to her old mother's tears and entreaties and marries a general, since it no longer makes any difference to her whom she weds, if wed she must. Onegin meets Tatyana in Petersburg and hardly recognizes her. She has changed so much. The simple country girl he remembers bears little resemblance to this grand Petersburg lady. Onegin is smitten by passion. He writes Tatyana a letter, and this time she answers him in person, telling him that although she loves him, she cannot be his because of pride of virtue. That exhausts the whole plot.

Many maintained and still maintain that the novel has no plot because there is no denouement. As a matter of fact, there is no death (either from consumption or a dagger wound) or wedding—that privileged ending of all novels, stories, and dramas, particularly Russian ones. Moreover, there are so many incongruities! When Tatyana was a girl, Onegin met her passionate confession with coldness; but, when she became a woman, he fell madly in love with her without even knowing for sure that she loved him. This is unnatural, extremely unnatural! And what an immoral character the man has. He coldly preaches to the girl who is in love with him instead of falling head over heels in love with her. Had he done so, then acted properly and obtained her dear, sweet parents' blessing forever and ever, and been joined with her in the bonds of holy matrimony, he would have become the happiest man in the world. Worse, Onegin kills poor Lensky, that young poet with high hopes and radiant dreams, for no reason whatsoever. If he had just once shed a tear of remorse or at least uttered a pathetic speech, made mention of the bloody specter, and so on. Many "respected readers" voiced opinions like this about *Onegin* and even now still voice them. At least we have had occasion to hear such opinions expressed. At one time they infuriated us, but now we are simply amused by them.

One great critic even said in print that *Onegin* lacks wholeness, that it is simply poetic chatter about everything and nothing.[14] The great critic based his judgment on the fact that the poem does not end with either a wedding or a funeral and on the following testimony of the poet himself:

> Ah, many, many days have hied
> Since first Tatyana's image hovered,
> *A cloudy vision,* in my mind,
> With her Onegin's form outlined,
> And when as yet there was discovered
> This rambling novel's trend and sense
> *But darkly* in my magic lens.

> (VIII, 50) [All italics in the verse, except
> those signifying foreign words, are
> Belinsky's.]

The great critic did not realize that the poet, by virtue of his creative instinct, could write a complete and finished work without planning it in advance and that he could stop precisely at the point where the novel on its own ends and reaches a denouement—namely, with the picture of Onegin, nonplussed, after his final meeting with Tatyana. But we will have more to say about this when the time comes, just as we will have more to say about the fact that nothing could be more natural than Onegin's treatment of Tatyana throughout the novel. Onegin certainly is not a monster, not a debauchee, although at the same time he is not a hero of virtue. It is one of Pushkin's great achievements that he made monsters of vice and heroes of virtue seem passé, and depicted instead ordinary people.

We began this article with the statement that *Onegin* is a poetic representation of Russian society in a certain period, one which is faithful to reality. This picture appeared at just the right time, that is, precisely when that which could serve as its model appeared—i.e., society. As a result of the reforms instituted by Peter the Great, a new society was supposed to take shape in Russia—a society whose way of life would be completely divorced from that of the masses. But one exceptional set of circumstances is not enough to create a society. Special underpinnings were required to ensure its existence, and education was required to give it internal, as well as external, unity. In her Charter of 1785,[15] Catherine the Great defined the rights and duties of the nobility. This completely changed the character of the great nobles, the only estate under Catherine the Great to attain full development and to be enlightened and educated. However, in the wake of the Charter of 1785, a class of lesser nobility began to emerge as well. By "emerge" [*voznikat'*] we mean "take shape," "come into being [*obrazovyvat'sia*]. During the reign of Alexander I the significance of this estate grew greater and greater, and it grew because education penetrated ever more deeply into the provinces where the landowners lived. Thus a society was taking shape which increasingly regarded the noble pleasures of existence as a necessity, signaling an emerging spiritual life. This society was not content any longer simply to hunt and live sumptuously, to dance and play cards. It spoke and read French; it demanded that music and drawing be part of its children's education. It became familiar with the works of Derzhavin, Fonvizin, and Bogdanovich[16]—poets who in their own day were known only at court. Most important, this new society developed its own literature, which tended to be light, lively, and sophisticated rather than ponderous, dull, and pedantic.

Novikov,[17] through his publishing activities, fostered an interest in reading and the book trade and thereby created a large number of readers. Karamzin, through his reform of the literary language and through the tenor, spirit, and form of his own works, molded literary taste and created a reading public. And at this point poetry became part of the life of the new society. Fair maidens and young men by the score rushed to Liza's pond[18] to shed a "tear of sentimentality" in homage to the memory of the piteous victim of passion and seduction. The lyric poetry of Dmitriev, which was marked by intellect, taste, wit, and grace, enjoyed the same success and influence as did Karamzin's prose. The sentimentality and dreaminess they fostered, although somewhat ludicrous, marked a great step forward for the young society. Ozerov's tragedies imparted even more vigor and brilliance to this literary school. Krylov's fables had long been read by grown-ups and children alike. Soon a young poet[19] appeared who injected into this sentimental literature romantic elements of deep feeling, fantastic dreaminess, and a strange longing for the realm of the miraculous and the mysterious. It was he who introduced and wedded the Russian muse to the muse of Germany and England. Literature's influence on society was much more important than we are inclined to think. By drawing together people of different estates and linking them through the bonds of taste and a desire for the noble pleasures of life, literature transformed *estate* into *society*. But, despite this, there is no doubt that by and large the class of the nobility was synonymous with society and the direct source of education for all of society. The increase in appropriations for public education, the establishment of universities, gymnasia, and schools made society grow not by the day but by the hour.

The period from 1812 to 1815 was a splendid one for Russia. We have in mind here not only Russia's great victory in the War of 1812 but also the inner growth Russia experienced, in terms of societal development and education, during this period. It can be said without exaggeration that Russia lived through more and advanced further from 1812 to the present, than from the reign of Peter the Great to 1812. On the one hand, the War of 1812 shook the whole of Russia, awakened her slumbering powers, and revealed new, hitherto unknown, sources of strength within her. By appealing to a sense of common danger, the War of 1812 fused the inert, disconnected individual wills into one enormous mass, awakened national consciousness and national pride, and in this way helped to bring into being a sense of public-spiritedness and the beginnings of public opinion. Moreover, the War of 1812 inflicted a powerful blow on atrophied traditions. In its wake the nonserving nobles disappeared— those who had come peacefully into the world and died in their own villages, without ever venturing beyond the sacred boundaries of their estates. The backwoods and wilds quickly disappeared, together with the scattered remnants of time-honored traditions. On the other hand, all of Russia, in the person of its victorious army, came face to face with Europe, through which it advanced amidst victories and triumphs. All this greatly furthered the growth of and strengthened the emerging society.

In the 1820s Russian literature aspired to achieve originality. Pushkin appeared. He loved that social estate [*soslovie*] which was almost the sole expression of Russian society's progress, the one to which he himself belonged, and in *Onegin* he resolved to present to us the inner life of this estate and with it society as it was in that period, that is, in the 1820s. And here we cannot help marveling at the speed with which Russian society moves forward. We view *Onegin* as a novel about an age from which we are already far removed. The ideals and the aspirations of that age are already so alien to us, so remote from the ideals and aspirations of our own age. Lermontov's novel, *A Hero of Our Time,* was a new *Onegin*. Hardly four years have passed since it was published, and its hero, Pechorin, is no longer the contemporary ideal. And this is what we meant when we said at the beginning of our article that *Onegin*'s very shortcomings constitute its greatest merit. These shortcomings can be summed up in one word: "obsolete." But is it really Pushkin's fault that everything moves forward so quickly in Russia? Is it not rather an indication of his great talent that Pushkin was able to grasp with such fidelity the reality of a certain stage in the life of our society? If nothing in *Onegin* now seemed antiquated or outdated, it would be a clear indication that the poem lacks truth, that it represented an imaginary society and not society as it really was in the 1820s. If such were the case, what sort of poem would it be, and would it be worth discussing?

We have already touched on the plot of *Onegin*. Let us turn to an analysis of the characters. Despite the fact that the novel bears the name of its hero, it contains not one but two heroes, Onegin and Tatyana. They should be regarded as the representatives of both sexes of Russian society in that period. Let us turn to Onegin. The poet did well to choose a hero from the upper stratum of society. This does not mean that Onegin is a great noble (great nobles flourished in the age of Catherine the Great). Onegin is a man of the world.

Most of the public flatly denied that Onegin possessed a heart and soul and viewed him as a cold, unfeeling person and an egoist by nature. Nothing could be further from the truth! But what is more, many sincerely believed and still believe today that the poet himself wanted to portray Onegin as a cold egoist. This is like having eyes but seeing nothing. The life of high society did not destroy feeling in Onegin but only dampened it, so far as empty passions and trivial pastimes were concerned. Recall the stanzas in which the poet describes his own acquaintance with Onegin:

> Of worldly bustle and unreason
> I'd shed the burden, as had he,
> And we became good friends that season.
> His features fascinated me,
> *His bent for dreamy meditation,*
> His strangeness, free of affectation,
> *His frigidly dissecting mind.*
> He was embittered, I maligned;
> We both had drunk from Passion's chalice:
> In either, life had numbed all zest;
> Extinct the glow in either breast;
> For both, too, lay in wait the malice
> Of reckless fortune and of man,
> When first our lease of life began.
>
> He who has lived and thought can never
> Look on mankind without disdain;
> He who has felt is haunted ever
> By days that will not come again;
> No more for him enchantment's semblance,
> On him the serpent of remembrance
> Feeds, and remorse corrodes his heart.
> All this is likely to impart
> An added charm to conversation.
> At first, indeed, Onegin's tongue
> Used to abash me; but ere long
> I liked his acid derogation,
> His humor, half shot-through with gall,
> Grim epigrams' malicious drawl.
>
> How often summer's radiant shimmer
> Glowed over the Nevá at night,
> Her cheerful mirror not aglimmer
> With Dian's image—and the sight
> Would hold us there in rapt reflection,
> *Aware again in recollection*
> *Of love gone by, romance of yore;*
> *Carefree and sentient once more,*

> We savored then, intoxicated,
> The night's sweet balm in mute delight!
> As some fair dream from prison night
> The sleeping convict may deliver
> To verdant forests—fancy-lorn
> We reveled there at life's young morn.

(I, 45–47)

These verses clearly demonstrate that Onegin was neither cold, nor unfeeling, nor callous, that poetry lived in his soul, and that in general he was not of the ordinary run of men. A bent for dreamy meditation, sensitivity, an ability to savor the beauties of nature and to recollect love gone by, romance of yore—all this attests more to feeling and poetry than to coldness and callousness. It is simply that Onegin did not like to "wallow" in dreams, that he was more sensitive than he let on, and that he did not open up to everyone. An embittered mind is also the sign of a higher nature, because a man with an embittered mind is dissatisfied not only with other people but with himself as well. The run of the mill are always satisfied with themselves, and, if fortune smiles on them, then with everyone else as well. Life does not disappoint fools, since they ask so little of it: plain food, a roof over their heads, and a few playthings to gratify their banal and petty self-love. Disillusionment with life, with other people, and with one's self (if only it is genuine and natural, devoid of high-flown phrases and the affectation of fashionable sorrow) is only characteristic of men who desire "much" and are not content with a mere "pittance." Readers will recall the description of Onegin's study in Chapter VII. All of Onegin is embodied in that description. Particularly striking is the fact that Onegin had lost interest in books, except for two or three novels

> . . . with a power
> To focus and reflect the age,
> Where shown upon the current stage,
> Man moves with truth and animation:
> Unprincipled, perversely bent
> Upon himself, his talents spent
> In reverie and speculation,
> With his exacerbated mind
> In idle seething self-confined.

(VII, 22)

People will say that this is a portrait of Onegin. Perhaps, but this attests even more to his moral superiority. It shows that he recognized himself in this portrait, which is the perfect likeness of so many but in which so few are willing to see the resemblance. Most say, 'That looks like Peter, not me.'[20] Onegin did not self-complacently admire this portrait, but mutely suffered from the striking likeness of this portrait to the children of the present age. It

was not nature, or passions, or personal delusions that made Onegin resemble
this portrait, but the age.

The strongest argument of all against Onegin's alleged callousness is the
fact that he formed a friendship with Lensky, the young dreamer who so
captivated our public. Onegin felt contempt for people,

> . . . but did exempt
> A few (no rule without exception):
> *Their feelings,* as beyond reproof,
> *He honored*—though himself aloof.

> The poet's [Lensky's] fiery effusions
> Eugene met with a smiling glance,
> The judgments riddled with delusions,
> And the habitual look of trance—
> All this to him seemed strange and novel;
> But he was careful not to cavil,
> Or check the flow with caustic curb,
> And mused: Who am I to disturb
> This state of blissful, brief infection?
> Its spell will pass without my help;
> Meanwhile, allow the dear young whelp
> To glory in the world's perfection;
> We must forgive youth's fever blaze
> Both youthful heat and youthful craze.

> All subjects led to disputations
> Between them and engendered thought;
> The covenants of ancient nations,
> The useful works by science wrought;
> And Good and Evil, time-worn errors,
> The great Beyond's mysterious terrors,
> And Destiny and Life in turn
> Engaged their serious concern.

(II, 14-16)

The matter speaks for itself. Proud coldness and callousness, arrogance and
heartlessness were attributed to Onegin simply because many readers were
unable to comprehend his character, which Pushkin created so faithfully. But
we will not stop here. We will go right to the heart of the matter:

> A strangely bleak and reckless creature,
> Issue of Heaven or of Hell,
> Proud demon, angel—who can tell?
> Perhaps he is all imitation,
> An idle phantom or, poor joke,
> A Muscovite in Harold's cloak,

An alien whim's interpretation,
Compound of every faddish prose. . . ?
A parody, perhaps . . . who knows?

(VII, 24)

"And is he mellowed by migration,
Or still the crank he was before?
Tell us, what new impersonation,
What pose is held for us in store?
Well? Cosmopolitan, Melmotic,
Childe Haroldesque or patriotic,
Tartuffe or Quaker, may one ask,
Or yet another faddish mask?
Or will he be like everybody,
Like you and me, just a good egg?
At all events, one thing I beg:
Discard the style that's worn and shoddy,
One tires of the stale old show . . ."
"Why, do you know him?"—"*Yes and no.*"

Why then attempt to be so clever,
So merciless at his expense?
Because we sit in judgment ever
And pry with ceaseless vigilance?
Because the rash missteps of heroes
Invoke from self-complacent zeros
Resentment or a gloating grin?
Because broad minds hem small ones in?
Or since too often we are willing
To take reported talk for deeds,
And idle spite on dullness feeds,
And pompous men find rubbish thrilling?
Do we feel snugly "in our own"
With mediocrity alone?

Blest he who, green in adolescence,
Matured at the appointed stage,
Who tasted of life's acrid essence
And learnt to stomach it with age;
Who for strange transports never lusted,
Through worldly slime strode undisgusted,
At twenty was a fop or blade,
At thirty a good marriage made,
At fifty shed by liquidation
All debts, both private and the rest,
And issued painlessly possessed
Of money, rank, and reputation,

And whom you hear throughout his span
Referred to as "an excellent man!"

But sad to feel, when youth has left us,
That it was given us in vain,
That its unnoticed flight bereft us
And brought no harvest in its train:
That our most fondly nursed ambitions,
Our fancy's freshest apparitions,
Have swiftly wilted one by one,
Like leaves by autumn blasts undone;
To see no prospect but an endless
Array of meals in solemn row,
To watch life like a puppet show,
Do as the Romans do, yet friendless,
And sharing with that titled crew
No single passion, taste, or view.

(VIII, 8–11)

These verses contain the key to the mystery of Onegin's character. Onegin is not Melmoth, not Childe Harold, not a demon, not a parody, not a faddish whim, not a genius, not a great man, but simply "*like everybody,*/ Like you and me, just a good egg." The poet is absolutely right when he calls it "worn and shoddy" to be always on the lookout for men of genius, for extraordinary men. We will say it again: Onegin is simply a nice fellow; at the same time, however, he is not of the ordinary run of men. He is not cut out to be a genius, he does not aspire to be a great man, but the inertia and banality of life oppress him. He does not even know what he needs or wants, but he knows, and only too well, that he does not need or want that which so easily satisfies and pleases smug mediocrity. And for this, smug mediocrity not only declared him "immoral" but robbed him of his ardor, his warmheartedness, and his receptivity to all that is good and beautiful. Remember how Onegin was brought up, and you will have to agree that his nature was extremely fine, not to have been ruined by such an upbringing. As a young man, he was carried away by the glitter of society, like many. But he soon tired of it and abandoned it, as too few are willing to do. He still had a glimmer of hope that he would be revived, refreshed in the tranquility of solitude, in the lap of nature. But he soon realized that a change of scene cannot alter matters which do not lie within our power to control:

Two days the solitary meadows
Retained for him their novel look,
The leafy groves with cooling shadows
And the sedately murmuring brook;

Next day he did not take the trouble
To glance at coppice, hill, and stubble,
Then they brought on a sleepy mood,
And he was ready to conclude:
Spleen does not spare the landed gentry,
It needs no palaces or streets,
No cards or balls or rhymed conceits.
Spleen hovered near him like a sentry
And haunted all his waking life
Like a shadow, or a faithful wife.

(I, 54)

We have demonstrated that Onegin is not cold, not unfeeling, not heartless, but so far we have avoided using the word *egoist*. Since a profusion of feeling and a craving for the beautiful do not exclude egoism, then we will admit that Onegin is an egoist—but a *suffering egoist*. Egoists come in two kinds. The first are men without any arrogant or dreamy pretensions. They do not understand how a person can love anyone except himself, and therefore they make no effort to conceal the ardent love they feel for themselves. If things go badly for them, they turn pale; grow thin; become malicious, contemptible and mean; turn into traitors and slanderers. If things go well for them, they become fat, fleshy, rosy-cheeked, cheerful, and kind. They will not share their profits with anyone, but they willingly entertain not only people who are useful to them but even people who are utterly useless. They are egoists by nature or because of bad upbringing. The second kind of egoists are almost never fat and rosy-cheeked. For the most part they are sickly men, always bored. Casting about in search of happiness and diversion, they fail to find either from the moment the blandishments of youth leave them. These men often develop a passion for good deeds, a desire to sacrifice themselves for dear ones. But the problem is that they seek happiness and diversion in doing good, when they should only seek good in doing good. If such men live in a society which fully affords each of its members the opportunity to strive for the attainment of truth and happiness, then it can be said without a moment's hesitation that vanity and petty self-love have stifled the good in them and made them egoists. But Onegin is not like either of these kinds of egoists. He is an *egoist against his own will*. In his egoism we see what the ancients called *fatum* [fate]. Why didn't Onegin pursue a good, beneficial, useful occupation? Why didn't he seek satisfaction in it? Why? Why? Because, dear sirs, it is easier for empty-headed men to ask questions than for sensible men to provide answers.

Bored in his lordly isolation,
Just to relieve the daily norm,
Eugene at first found occupation
In bold agrarian reform.

The backwood wiseacre commuted
The harsh *corvée* and instituted
A quitrent system in its stead;
The serf called blessings on his head.
Whereat his thrifty neighbor, highly
Incensed, swelled in his nook and fought
The wicked and expensive thought;
Another only snickered slyly,
And one and all they set him down
As a subversive kind of clown.

At first the neighbors started calling;
But when he kept by the back stoop,
Their visits artfully forestalling,
A Cossack cob (to fly the coop
When rumbles of a homely coach
First warned him of a guest's approach),
Such conduct struck them as ill bred,
And all the County cut him dead.
"Our neighbor is uncouth; he's crazy;
A freemason; he only drinks
Red wine in tumblers; never thinks
To kiss a lady's hand—too lazy;
It's 'yes' and 'no,' no 'ma'am' or 'sir.' "
In this indictment all concur.

(II, 4–5)

Only in society, only on the basis of real social needs (and not in accordance with some theory) is it possible to accomplish something. But what could Onegin have accomplished in the company of such lovely neighbors, such fine folks? To alleviate the lot of the peasant meant a great deal, of course, to the peasant, but Onegin did not accomplish much in this regard. There are men who, if they succeed in accomplishing anything at all, complacently tell the whole world about it and thus agreeably occupy themselves for the rest of their lives. Onegin was not like these men; what seemed important and noteworthy to many was absolutely unimportant to him.

By chance Onegin and Lensky met. Through Lensky, Onegin made the acquaintance of the Larin family. Returning home from his first visit to the Larins, Onegin yawns [III, 4]. From his conversation with Lensky we learn that he mistook Tatyana for his friend's fiancée. When he realizes his mistake, he expresses his surprise at Lensky's choice saying that, if he were a poet, he would choose the elder sister, Tatyana [III, 5]. It took this indifferent, jaded man only one or two inattentive glances to understand the difference between the two sisters, whereas it never even occurred to the ardent, impassioned Lensky that his beloved Olga was not an ideal, poetic creature but just a good-looking, simple girl for whose sake it was not worth risking his friend's life or his own. While Onegin yawned from *habit,* to use his own expression [III, 4], and did not give any further thought to the Larin family, within this family his visit created quite a stir.

The majority of the public was extremely surprised that Onegin, upon receiving Tatyana's letter, was able to refrain from falling in love with her and, still more, that this very same Onegin, who so coldly spurned the pure, naive love of the noble girl, later fell passionately in love with the sophisticated lady. Indeed, there is reason to be surprised, but the heart has its own laws. Therefore, Onegin had a perfect right, without fearing the stern judgment of critics, not to fall in love with the girl Tatyana and to fall in love with the woman. In neither case did he act morally or immorally. We have said quite enough to vindicate him, but we will add something else. Onegin was so intelligent, so perceptive and experienced, he understood human nature so well, that he could not help but realize from Tatyana's letter that this poor girl was endowed with a passionate nature, that she yearned for celestial food, that her soul was pure as a babe's, her passion as naive as a child's, and that she did not bear the slightest resemblance to those coquettes who had so wearied him with their frivolous and forced feelings. In fact, he was profoundly moved by Tatyana's letter. Yet how could he, who was burned-out, disillusioned with life and mankind, yet still seething with vague aspirations, be carried away by the childish love of a starry-eyed girl, who viewed life as he could no longer view it? And what would this love portend for the future? What would he discover later in Tatyana? Either a capricious child, who would cry because he could not share her naive view of life and naively play at love—that you will agree would be very boring—or a creature so overcome by his superiority that she would fall completely under his sway and lose all feeling and all sense of self. This would make things more peaceful but, in return, even more boring. And this is what men call the poetry and bliss of love!

Separated from Tatyana by Lensky's death, Onegin was deprived of every-thing that linked him to other people:

> When he had killed his friend and neighbor—
> Now twenty-six, still vague of aim,
> Void of employment—he became
> A martyr to his leisure's labor:
> No service, business, or wife
> To occupy his empty life.
>
> The travel-fever took possession
> Of him, the up-and-going fit
> (A most unfortunate obsession,
> Though some do volunteer for it).

(VIII, 12–13)

Among other places, Onegin visits the Caucasus and gazes on the pallid patients swarming around the healing streams of Mount Mashuk:

> Engrossed in bitter meditations
> Amidst this melancholy crew,
> Onegin looks with wry impatience
> Upon the waters dim with dew
> And thinks: why could not I be blessed
> With such a bullet in my chest?
> Why am I not a senile coot
> Like that poor sack of landed loot?
> Why, like the alderman from Tula,
> May I not lie there stiff with gout?
> Could not at least my shoulder sprout
> Rheumatic pains? O Lord and Ruler,
> I'm young, and life is strong in me,
> And what's ahead? Ennui, ennui!

(J, 14)[21]

What a life! Suffering is the subject of so much poetry and prose, so many complain about it—as though they had really experienced it themselves. Here is real suffering—without melodrama, without high-sounding words, without embellishment, without pompous phrases. Here is true suffering which, although it does not rob you of sleep, or appetite, or health, is all the more terrible for it. To sleep at night, to yawn during the day, to see all around you people bustling about, occupied with one thing or another: one with making money, another with getting married, a third with illness, a fourth with want and the bloody sweat of toil. To see around you joy and sadness, laughter and tears. To see all this and yet feel alienated from it all, like the Wandering Jew, who amidst the bustle of life realizes that he is a stranger and dreams of death, regarding it as the greatest blessing. Suffering like this is not comprehensible to everyone, but it is no less terrible. Youth, health, wealth combined with intellect and sensitivity. What more does it take to live and be happy? This is the way the masses think, and they dismiss such suffering as a modish whim. The more natural and unaffected was Onegin's suffering, the more removed it was from theatricality, the less could the majority of the public understand and appreciate it. To have experienced so much at age twenty-six without having tasted life, to be so exhausted and weary without having accomplished anything, to have reached such absolute negation without having held any convictions—this is death!

Onegin, however, was not fated to die without having tasted the cup of life. A strong and profound passion soon roused his soul from its ennui. Onegin could hardly recognize Tatyana when he met her at a Petersburg ball. She had changed so!

> She was not cold, nor too vivacious,
> Not taciturn, nor yet loquacious;
> No forward glance or bold address,
> No conscious straining for success,
> Without affected mannerism
> Or specious second-hand conceit—
> All calm, all simple, all discreet,
> She seemed a living catechism
> *Du comme il faut.* . . .
>
> .   .   .   .
>
> One hardly found in her what passes
> For beauty, but no more could find
> A single blemish of the kind
> That London's fashionable classes
> In their fastidious slang decry
> As *vulgar.* . . .

(VIII, 14–15)

Tatyana's husband is so marvelously captured in the following characterization:

> . . . and none more proudly
> Raised nose and shoulders in the air
> Then he who was her escort there.

(VIII, 15)

It is the husband who introduces Onegin to Tatyana as an old and dear friend [VIII, 18]. Many readers, when they read this chapter for the first time, expected Tatyana to cry out and faint dead away, and then, when she had regained consciousness, to cling to Onegin. But what a disappointment they were in for!

> She met him with a level gaze . . .
> If she was poignantly affected,
> If she was shaken or unnerved—
> Her calm eyes never flinched or swerved.
> Cool, imperturbable, collected,
> Her voice in no wise changed in key,
> Her bow was easy, gracious, free.
>
> .   .   .   .
>
> . . . What strange trance
> Has seized him, what absurd romance
> Upset his torpid self-possession?
> Hurt pride? Frivolity? Or, bane
> And bliss of youngsters, love again?
>
> .   .   .   .

Tanya was changed—past recognition!
How she had grown into her role,
The weary pomp of her position
Fused in the substance of her soul!
Who dared to seek the lovelorn maiden
In this assured, decorum-laden
High Priestess of the polished floor?
Yet he had stirred her heart before!
Of him, ere Morpheus' pinions wafted
Down veils of night and slumber brought,
She had with girlish grieving thought,
And, moonbeams in her eyes, had drafted
Some longed-for future, dreamy-dim,
Of walking down life's path with him.

(VIII, 18, 21, 28)

We are not ultra-idealists. We readily admit that there is a touch of pettiness in even the loftiest of passions, and therefore we think that *hurt pride* and *frivolity* did play a part in arousing Onegin's passion. But we emphatically disagree with the following opinion of the poet, which he pronounced so solemnly and which met with such a response, since the masses found it so easy to grasp:

Ah, men! The curse of Eve, our far
Progenetrix is still enduring:
The proffered palls, but half-concealed,
The tree, the serpent ever wield
Their immemorial mystic luring.
Forbidden fruit we still implore,
Or Eden Eden is no more.

(VIII, 27)

We think better of human nature and are convinced that man is born not for evil but for good, not for crime, but for the rational and rightful enjoyment of life's blessings, that his aspirations are just, his instincts noble. Evil lurks not in man but in society.

Now Onegin had to see Tatyana in a completely new light. No longer was she the starry-eyed girl who confided her most intimate thoughts to the moon and used Martin Zadeka's book[22] to interpret dreams. She was a woman, she knew the value of everything she received, she could demand much but give much as well. The aura of sophistication surrounding her could not help but enhance her in Onegin's eyes. In high society, just as everywhere else, there are two kinds of people. There are those who are attracted to form and see in adherence to it life's purpose; these are the crowd of vulgar men. And there are

those who acquire from society a knowledge of people and life, sound judg-
ment, and the ability to utilize completely all that nature has given them.
Tatyana was one of the latter, and the fact that she was a sophisticated lady only
enhanced her significance as a woman. Moreover, in Onegin's eyes love with-
out a struggle did not hold any fascination, and Tatyana did not promise to be
an easy conquest. So he threw himself into the struggle without any hope of
victory, without calculation, with all the recklessness of true passion. Every
word of his letter breathes with this passion:

> I know now: always to behold you,
> Devoutly follow all your steps,
> With loving scrutiny enfold you
> When you look up or move your lips;
> Be drinking in your voice, be bathing
> My soul in all your loveliness,
> Writhe in your sight with torment scathing,
> Wane, be extinguished—there is bliss!
>
> . . . .
>
> But if you knew my mortal anguish—
> To be with love's wild fever cursed,
> Grope for detachment while I languish,
> Sense, while my flesh is parched with thirst;
> To long to clutch your knees and, sobbing,
> In supplication bent, confess
> With pleas, avowals, prayers throbbing,
> All, everything I might express;
> Instead, with lying self-possession
> To armor daily speech and gaze,
> Hold converse in well-tempered phrase,
> And meet you with a gay expression! . . .
>
> ("Onegin's Letter," ll. 23–30, 45–56)

But Onegin's ardent passion had no effect on Tatyana. When he met her,
after sending her several messages, he saw no signs of anxiety, no suffering, no
tearstains on her face. Cold wrath alone showed on it [VIII, 33]. Onegin then
locked himself up in his apartment for the whole winter and took to reading:

> To what end? While the letters tumbled
> Across his sight beyond control,
> Desires, dreams, regrets were jumbled
> In dense profusion in his soul.
> *Between the lines of printing hidden,*
> *To his mind's eye there rise unbidden*
> *Quite other lines,* and it is these
> That in his trance alone he sees.
> They were dear tales and droll convictions

Alive among us as of old,
Weird, disconnected dreams untold,
And threats and axioms and predictions,
A spun-out fable's whimsy purl,
Or letters from a fresh young girl.

And while a drowsy stupor muffles
All thought and feeling unawares,
Imagination deals and shuffles
Its rapid motley solitaires:
He sees on melting snow-sheet dozing
A lad, quite still, as if reposing
Asleep upon a hostel bed,
And someone says: "That's that—he's dead . . ."
He sees old enemies forgotten,
Detractors two-faced and afraid,
A swarm of beauties who betrayed,
A circle of companions rotten,
A rustic house—and who would be
Framed in the window? . . . Who but She!

(VIII, 36–37)

We will not stop now to discuss the scene where Onegin confronts Tatyana and hears her explanation, because the principal role in that scene belongs to Tatyana. The novel ends with Tatyana's rebuke, and the reader parts forever with Onegin at the most painful moment in his life. But wait a minute. What is this? What happened to the love story? What does it all mean? And what kind of novel can this be without an ending? We think that there are novels whose idea consists in the very fact that they have no ending, because in reality there are events that have no denouement, lives with no goal, individuals who are ill-defined, comprehensible to no one, not even to themselves—in short, what the French call *les êtres manqués* [individuals frustrated in the fulfillment of their aspirations or talents], *les existences avortées* [aborted lives]. And these individuals are often endowed with great moral advantages, with great spiritual powers. They promise much; they fulfill little or nothing at all. The matter does not depend on them. It is *fatum* [fate] which is present in the reality surrounding them like air, from which man does not have the strength or power to free himself.[23] Another poet [Lermontov] gave us another Onegin under the name of Pechorin [in his novel, *A Hero of Our Time*]. Pushkin's Onegin with a kind of self-abnegation resigns himself to yawning. Lermontov's Pechorin is engaged in mortal combat with life and wants to wrest his share from it by force. Their paths are different, but the result is the same. Both novels have no ending, like the lives and careers of both poets.[24]

What happened to Onegin? Was his passion rekindled? Did he suffer anew, this time for something more commensurate with human dignity? Or were all his spiritual powers spent, and did his joyless ennui turn into lifeless apathy? We do not know, and what need have we to know, knowing as we do that the powers of this rich nature remained unutilized, that here is a life without meaning and a novel without an ending. Knowing this is enough to make us not want to know any more.

There is nothing dreamy or fantastic about Onegin. He could be happy or unhappy only in reality and through reality. In Lensky, Pushkin portrayed a character who is the complete opposite, a character who is completely abstract, completely alien to reality. At that time [in the 1820s] this was a completely new phenomenon, and men of this sort actually began to appear in Russian society:

> . . . impregnated to the core
> With Göttingen and Kantian lore.
> From German mists the poet-errant
> Brought Teuton wisdom's clouded brew,
> Dreams of a libertarian hue,
> A spirit fiery, though aberrant,
> Relentlessly impassioned speech,
> And raven locks of shoulder reach.
>
> .   .   .   .
>
> Of love he sang, love's service choosing,
> And limpid was his simple tune
> As ever artless maiden's musing,
> As babes aslumber, as the Moon
> In heaven's tranquil regions shining,
> Goddess of secrets and sweet pining;
> He sang of *partings, mists* afar,
> Of *sorrow,* of *je ne sais quoi:*
> *Romantic roses,* distant islands
> He used to sing of, where for years
> He poured a generous toll of tears
> Into the soothing lap of silence;
> *He mourned the wilt of life's young green*
> *When he had almost turned eighteen.*

(II, 6, 10)

Lensky was a romantic both by nature and in accordance with the spirit of the times. Needless to say, he was a pure and noble creature, receptive to all that is beautiful and sublime. But at the same time he was a "dear ignoramus in the science of life" [II, 7]; he talked endlessly about life but never knew it. Reality had no effect on him; his joys and sorrows were the creation of his own imagination. He fell in love with Olga. Little did it matter to him that she did not understand him, that once married she would have become a carbon copy of her Mama, that it was all the same to her whether she married him, the poet and friend of her childhood games, or the uhlan so satisfied with himself and his horse. Lensky adorned her with virtues and perfections, ascribed to her feelings and thoughts which she did not possess and to which she was indifferent. Good, sweet, and cheerful, Olga was charming—as are all "young ladies" until they become "wives." But Lensky regarded her as a fairy, a sylphid, a romantic dream and had not the slightest suspicion what she would be like, once she was a wife. He even managed to discover a poetic side to old man Larin. Witness the sincere, serious "graveside dirge" dedicated to him [II, 37]. Lensky regarded Onegin's simple desire to tease him as treachery, seduction, a mortal insult. All this resulted in his own death, which he celebrated beforehand in foggy romantic verses [VI, 21–22]. Of course, we do not excuse Onegin, who, as the poet says:

> Ought to have proved himself in truth
> No helpless play-ball of convention,
> No gamecock bristling with offense,
> But man of honor and good sense.

(VI, 10)

But society's prejudices have such a tyrannical hold over men that heroes are required to do battle with them. The description of Onegin's duel with Lensky is the height of perfection in an artistic sense. The poet loved the ideal he had realized in Lensky and lamented his passing in beautiful verses:

> My friends, you will lament the poet
> Who, flowering with a happy gift,
> Must wilt before he could bestow it
> Upon the world, yet scarce adrift
> From boyhood's shore. Now he will never
> Seethe with that generous endeavor,
> Those storms of mind and heart again,
> Audacious, tender, or humane!
> Stilled now are love's unruly urges,
> The thirst for knowledge and for deeds,
> Contempt for vice and what it breeds,
> And stilled you too, ethereal surges,
> Breath of a transcendental clime,
> Dreams from the sacred realm of rhyme!
>
> Perchance the world would have saluted
> In him a savior or a sage;
> That lyre of his, forever muted,
> Might have resounded down the age
> In ceaseless thunder, and have fated
> Its bearer to be elevated
> To high rank on the worldly grade;

Or haply with his martyred shade
Some holy insight will they bury,
A gem, who knows, of wisdom choice,
Now perished with his living voice.
The hymn of ages will not carry
Deep into his sepulchral den
The benedictions of all men.

Or we might guess with equal reason
A fate of far more common cast
For our poet, once the season
Of effervescent youth had passed.
The flame within him would have faltered;
Deep in the country, greatly altered,
He'd live in wedded bliss and horned,
In quilted robe, the Muses scorned.
There he would learn life's essence truly,
By forty would contract the gout,
Would eat and drink, be dull, grow stout,
Sicken, and on his own couch, duly
Wreathed in his offspring, would have died,
While doctors fussed and women cried.

                                        (VI, 36–39)

We are convinced that the latter fate undoubtedly would have befallen Lensky. There was a lot of good in him, but what was best about him was the fact that he was young and died at just the right time. He would not have developed and moved forward. He, we repeat, was a *romantic* and nothing more. Had he lived, Pushkin would have had no other choice than to spread out over an entire chapter what he expressed so succinctly in a single stanza. Men like Lensky, for all their undeniable merits, either degenerate into complete philistines or, if they remain romantics, become old-fashioned mystics and dreamers and are even greater enemies of progress than ordinary, vulgar men. Forever wrapped up in themselves, they think that they are the center of the universe. Calmly they look at everything that is going on in the world and assert over and over that happiness lies within us, that we ought to aspire to the starry heights of dreams and not think about the problems of this world, where there is hunger and want. Even now the Lenskys have not died out; they have only degenerated. They no longer possess any of the charm and nobility which were characteristic of Lensky. They lack the virginal purity of his heart and have only pretensions to greatness and a passion for scribbling. They are poets, and it is they who are responsible for the verse "ballast" in journals. In short, they are now the most unbearable, the most vapid, the most ordinary of men.

Pushkin and Belinsky:
Eugene Onegin

DMITRY PISAREV
(1865)

According to Belinsky, "*Eugene Onegin* is Pushkin's most sincere work, the most beloved child of his imagination. Here everything mirrors the poet; the work embodies his feelings, his concepts, his ideals."[1] Let us see whether Pushkin's novel really merits the high acclaim accorded it by our great critic. First of all, we must decide just what sort of person Pushkin's hero is. Belinsky insists that Onegin is not of the ordinary run of men: "He is not cut out to be a genius, he does not aspire to be a great man, but the inertia and banality of life oppress him." Pushkin himself treats his hero with respect and love:

> His features fascinated me,
> His bent for dreamy meditation,
> His strangeness, free of affectation,
> His frigidly dissecting mind.
> He was embittered, I maligned;
> We both had drunk from Passion's chalice:
> In either, life had numbed all zest;
> Extinct the glow in either breast;
> For both, too, lay in wait the malice
> Of reckless fortune and of man,
> When first our lease of life began.

> He who has lived and thought can never
> Look on mankind without disdain;
> He who has felt is haunted ever
> By days that will not come again;
> No more for him enchantment's semblance,
> On him the serpent of remembrance
> Feeds, and remorse corrodes his heart.
> All this is likely to impart
> An added charm to conversation.
> At first, indeed, Onegin's tongue
> Used to abash me; but ere long
> I liked his acid derogation,
> His humor, half shot-through with gall,
> Grim epigrams' malicious drawl.

How often summer's radiant shimmer
Glowed over the Nevá at night,
Her cheerful mirror not aglimmer
With Dian's image—and the sight
Would hold us there in rapt reflection,
Aware again in recollection
Of love gone by, romance of yore;
Carefree and sentient once more,
We savored then, intoxicated,
The night's sweet balm in mute delight!
As some fair dream from prison night
The sleeping convict may deliver
To verdant forests—fancy-lorn
We reveled there at life's young morn.

(I, 45–47)

In these stanzas, however, Pushkin keeps using elastic words which in and of themselves have no defined meaning and which consequently can be interpreted in a variety of ways. A man possesses a frigidly dissecting mind, he has drunk from passion's chalice, he has lived and thought and felt, the glow within his breast is extinct, in him life has numbed all zest, the malice of men and reckless fortune lies in wait for him. All these words could be applied to a man of importance, to an outstanding intellect, even to a historical figure who tried to bring people to their senses but was misunderstood, mocked, or cursed by his narrow-minded contemporaries. Belinsky was deceived by these fine elastic words—by the very words which he himself as a thinker and a doer was accustomed to using to denote a real, live human being, and he regarded Onegin favorably. He boldly assumed that Onegin was not one of the crowd, that he was not an ordinary person. But Belinsky was wrong. He believed Pushkin's *words* and overlooked the fact that all too often people utter fine words without clearly understanding what they mean, or they attribute to such words some narrow, paltry meaning. Let us ask ourselves: *What* had made Onegin's mind frigid? *What* had made him drink from passion's chalice? *On what* had he spent his ardor? *What* did he mean by the word *life,* when he said to himself and to others that life had numbed all zest? *What* does it really mean, in Pushkin and Onegin's language, to *live,* to *think,* and to *feel*?

The answers to these questions must be sought in the description of those diversions which Onegin indulged in from early youth, diversions which finally gave him a case of the blues. In Chapter I, beginning with stanza 15 and extending all the way to stanza 37, Pushkin describes a day in the life of Onegin, from the moment he wakes up in the morning to the moment he lies down to sleep, which is also in the morning. While still abed, Onegin receives three invitations to parties. He gets dressed and in his morning attire goes out to parade on the boulevard

Till the repeater's watchful peal
Recalls him to the midday meal.

(I, 15)

He then goes to dine at the restaurant Talon, and, since it is winter, his beaver collar conveniently glistens with a hoarfrost dusting [I, 16]. This memorable incident prompted Belinsky to note that Pushkin possessed an amazing ability "to make the most prosaic objects seem poetic."[2] If Belinsky had lived longer he would have renounced these aesthetic ideas and realized that the ability to celebrate beaver collars is hardly a great achievement.

Having celebrated Onegin's beaver collar, Pushkin goes on to celebrate all the foods which await Onegin at Talon. The dinner is not bad. There is bloody roast beef, a truffle which Pushkin for some reason calls "youth's delight," deathless pie Strasbourg, bold Limburger cheese, luscious gold pineapple, and cutlets which are sizzling and so greasy that a lot of champagne has to be downed [I, 16–17]. Regrettably, Pushkin does not explain in what order these poetic objects are served, and thus it is the duty of antiquarians and bibliophiles to fill in this important gap through painstaking research.

Dinner is not yet finished, the sizzling grease of the cutlets is not yet doused in waves of champagne (what brand you may well ask; this is also a very interesting problem for assiduous commentators), when the repeater's peal informs Onegin that a new ballet has begun [I, 17]. As the exacting arbiter of the stage, as the fickle worshiper of charming actresses, and as established freeman of the wings [I, 17], Onegin rushes off to the theater. (Here I suddenly realize to my horror that we have absolutely no idea what color Onegin's horse was and that very likely no commentator, no matter how hard he tries, will be able to solve this great mystery for us.) Entering the theater, Onegin begins to display the frigidity of his mind. Having scrutinized all the tiers, he seems bored by the gowns and faces. In Pushkin's words, he had "seen it all" [I, 21]. Absentmindedly he glances at the stage, then turns away with a yawn, and says:

. . . "In all things change is needed;
On me ballets have lost their hold;
Didelot himself now leaves me cold."

(I, 21)[3]

Here Pushkin seemed to sense that he had put his hero in a rather ludicrous position. After all, people who really have frigidly dissecting minds do not waste their irony pooh-poohing the balletmaster Didelot and the gowns of society women. So Pushkin appended the following humorous note to stanza 21: "A trait of chilled sentiment worthy of Childe Harold. The ballets of Mr. Didelot are full of liveliness of fancy and extraordinary charm. One of our romantic writers found in them much more poetry than in the whole of French literature" [Nabokov, 1, 323n5]. Obviously, through this note Pushkin wanted to show that he himself did not take Onegin's sally seriously and that he did not consider it a sign of real disenchantment. But the note has little effect on the discerning and distrustful reader. He realizes that apart from amusing sallies Onegin's frigidly dissecting mind does not produce anything at all. In I, 21, Onegin negates the ballets of Didelot; in III, 4–5, Onegin negates bilberry elixir, Olga's beauty, the moon, and the sky. And these infrequent, harmless sallies totally exhaust the malice of Onegin's grim epigrams, with which Pushkin tried to frighten us in I, 46. Nothing more malicious or grimmer ever emerges from Onegin's lips. If all of Onegin's epigrams were really this malicious and grim, no wonder Pushkin grew accustomed to them so quickly.

Onegin continues to exude disenchantment as he leaves the theater, while cupids, devils, and monkeys prance and swoop behind the footlights [I, 22]. Since he is not interested in their prancing and swooping, he goes home to dress for a ball and then off to dance until the wee hours of the morning. While Onegin is preening before the mirror, Pushkin transforms the combs, files, scissors, and brushes which adorn the boudoir of the "philosopher at age eighteen" [I, 23] into poetic objects. Very likely Onegin appeared to be a philosopher because he had so many combs, files, scissors, and brushes. But Pushkin does not want to be outdistanced by Onegin in philosophical matters, and so he categorically states that philosophical truth which was so much to Pavel Kirsanov's liking,[4] that one can be moral and capable and still have manicure on one's mind [I, 25]. This great truth Pushkin supports with another, even greater truth. "Why," he asks, "vainly chide one's age?" (Obviously, if one is indifferent to manicured nails it means that one is a reactionary and an obscurantist.) "Custom," continues Pushkin the philosopher, "is lord of all mankind" [I, 25]. It goes without saying that custom will always be lord to *such* philosophers as Onegin and Pushkin. Regrettably, the number of such philosophical gems begins to diminish. Pushkin would like to go on uttering philosophical truths, but Onegin is already dressed and has driven off to the ball *in a headlong flurry* [I, 27; the italics are Pisarev's]—very likely, a consequence of the frigidity of his mind. Of course, Pushkin hurries after him, and so the stream of philosophical truths dries up for a while.

At the ball we completely lose sight of Onegin and have absolutely no idea how his indisputable superiority over the crowd of vulgar men manifested itself. Escorting his hero into the ballroom, Pushkin falls to reminiscing about feet and passionately recounts how he once enviously watched "the waves repeat / Their onrush of tumultuous motion / To stretch in love about her feet" [I, 33]. The skeptical reader will perhaps doubt that waves could actually stretch *in love* about her feet, but I assure such an uncultured reader that here prosaic waves are transformed into a poetic object and therefore it is very laudable of the poet to ascribe to them—for poetic effect, of course—love for woman in general or her feet in particular. After Pushkin has explained to readers that he adores little feet much more than lips, cheeks, or breasts, he remembers his hero and takes him home from the ball and tucks him into bed while working-class Petersburg is already beginning its day. When Onegin wakes up, the same thing begins all over again. He goes out to walk on the boulevard, then off to dine at Talon, then to the theater, then home to dress for a ball, then off to the ball, and finally home to sleep.

And so Onegin eats, drinks, criticizes ballets, dances whole nights away—in a word, leads the good life. His consuming interest is the "science of tender passion" [I, 8], which he pursues assiduously and with great success. But was Onegin "content with his condition?" asks Pushkin [I, 36]. It turns out that Onegin was not content, and this leads Pushkin to conclude that Eugene is on a higher level than the contemptible, self-complacent crowd of vulgar men. As we have seen, Belinsky agrees with this conclusion, but I, to my great regret, must disagree with both our greatest poet and our greatest critic. Onegin's boredom bears no resemblance to real dissatisfaction with life. Here there is not even the slightest trace of an instinctive protest against those unbearable rituals and attitudes which the silent majority accepts—out of habit, out of sheer inertia. Onegin's boredom is nothing more than the physiological consequence of a very disorderly life. This boredom is simply a variant of what the Germans call *Katzenjammer,* a condition which usually visits every rake the next day after a good bout of drinking. Man is so constituted that he cannot continually gormandize, get drunk, and study the "science of tender passion." Even the strongest organism breaks down or at least grows weary when it enjoys the gifts of nature to excess.

Imagine to yourself that you really like some kind of nutritious and wholesome food—for example, rice pudding. One fine day your favorite food is prepared especially well. You eat too much of it and upset your stomach. After this you develop an aversion to rice pudding which you cannot overcome, no matter what you think of rice pudding in theory. You know perfectly well all the ingredients that go into rice pudding; you know that nothing poisonous is put in it. You see other people eating it with pleasure in your presence, and yet you simply cannot bring yourself to eat it, even though you used to love rice pudding. Onegin's attitude toward the pleasures of life is exactly like your attitude toward rice pudding. Onegin has eaten too much of everything and is revolted by it all.

Now let us see what means Onegin adopted to overcome his *Katzenjammer* and reconcile himself once more to life. When a man has become sick and tired of life's pleasures and senses that he is young and strong, he inevitably begins to look for something challenging. A time of serious reflection sets in. He examines himself; he examines society. He carefully weighs his own abilities. He sizes up the obstacles which he will have to struggle to overcome and the needs of society which beg to be answered. Finally after long reflection he reaches a decision and begins to act. Life shatters his plans. It tries to deprive him of his individuality, to water down his convictions and make them like everyone else's. But he stubbornly fights for his intellectual and moral independence, and in the unavoidable struggle that ensues the magnitude of his own powers is revealed. When a man has graduated from this school of reflection and hard knocks, we have the right to ask if he stands head and shoulders above the conforming, idle masses or not. But so long as a man has not undergone this reeducation, he is like an infant—in an intellectual and moral sense. If a man who is weary of life's pleasures does not even know how to find this school of reflection and hard knocks, then we can definitely say that this embryo will never become a thinking person and consequently will never have a legitimate reason to look with contempt on the idle masses. Onegin is one of these eternal and hopeless embryos:

> Apostate from the whirl of pleasure,
> He did withdraw into his den
> And, yawning, reached for ink and pen.
> He tried to write—from such tenacious
> Endeavor, though, his mind recoiled;
> And so the paper stayed unsoiled.

(I, 43)

Onegin does not suffer from boredom because he cannot find some kind of intellectual activity to occupy himself or because he is a higher nature, but simply because he has extra money lying in his pocket which allows him to eat a lot, to drink a lot, to pursue the "science of tender passion" and assume all sorts of expressions—depending on the effect he wants to create. Nothing has made his mind frigid. It is simply untouched and totally undeveloped. He has drunk from *passion's chalice* to the extent that this is part of the "science of tender passion," but he has absolutely no understanding of other, stronger passions—like the consuming passion for an idea. He has wasted the *glow within his breast* on boudoir scenes and masquerade balls. If Onegin thinks that *life has numbed him,* he is thinking utter nonsense. A person who has really been numbed by life does not gallop off in pursuit of an inheritance from a dying uncle. To *live,* in Onegin's language, means to parade on the boulevard, to dine at Talon's, to frequent the theater and go to balls. To *think* means to criticize Didelot's ballets and to call the moon insipid because it is too round. To *feel* means to envy the waves which stretch out at the feet of a good-looking woman.

Onegin goes off to the country, only to discover that he is bored there as well. His young neighbor Lensky becomes his friend and companion. If we analyze the conversations they have, we are forced to conclude that they do not talk about any lofty subjects at all and that Pushkin has absolutely no idea what it means to carry on a serious discussion, one leading to true reflection, that he has no notion what it means to have real and deeply felt convictions. In Onegin's relationship with Lensky, Pushkin wanted his hero to reveal grace and gentleness of character. Pushkin, who was well versed in grace and gentleness and completely ignorant of convictions, did not stop to think that in endowing his hero with these refined traits he was condemning him to pathetic insipidity so that he could only chatter on about the weather, the merits of champagne, and—oh, yes—Oleg's treaties with the Greeks. If Onegin had really had any convictions, then, out of affection for Lensky, he would have tried to share openly with the youth his own views on life and to dispel those youthful delusions which sooner or later are so ruthlessly destroyed by the contemptible prose of everyday life. But because Onegin was undeveloped and totally lacking in convictions, he practiced the celebrated policy of concealment and pedagogical deceit, which all parents and teachers who possess warm feelings and narrow minds practice with their charges.

Lensky challenges Onegin to a duel because he becomes infuriated by the attentions Onegin showers on Olga, his intended, at Tatyana's name-day party. After Onegin has received Lensky's "urbane, high-minded, and polite" challenge [VI, 9] from the latter's second, Zaretsky, he, like the model dandy he is, does not demand any further explanations but answers in an urbane, high-minded, and polite manner that he is "at Lensky's command" [VI, 9]. Zaretsky departs, and Onegin, "left alone with his soul" [VI, 9], begins to think that he has committed a lot of blunders. Onegin is dissatisfied with himself. Pushkin observes:

> And rightly so: for self-indicted
> In secret court, he could defend
> But little, and was sternly cited
> For many wrongs: First, that a friend,
> Who loved so tenderly and gently,
> Last night was duped so nonchalantly.
> And second: if that friend had been
> A silly ass, well, at eighteen
> He could be pardoned. Not to mention
> That he, who dearly loved the youth,
> Ought to have proved himself in truth
> No helpless play-ball of convention,
> No gamecock bristling with offense,
> But man of honor and good sense.
>
> He could have curbed his angry feeling,
> Instead of snarling; have appeased
> That hot young spirit by appealing
> To reason, friendship—had he pleased.
> "But it's too late; that chance was squandered . . .

And now, to make things worse," he pondered,
"We're saddled with this dueling hawk,
Sharp, fond of gossip, quick to talk . . .
The best, of course, is to ignore him;
But still, one will not be exempt
From snickers, whispers, fools' contempt . . ."
Our god, Good Repute, rose before him,
To which we feel our honor bound:
This is what makes the world go round!

(VI, 10–11)

You see, Eugene dearly loves the youth. Moreover, the stern indictment handed down by the secret court of his conscience tells him that a man of honor and good sense would not bristle with offense and would not permit himself to shoot at an eighteen-year old who had made a fool of himself. On one scale Onegin places the life of the youth he dearly loves and the sensible demands of honor and good sense—those demands that were sternly formulated by the secret court. On the other Onegin places the whispers and snickers of fools which the dueling hawk and gossip Zaretsky would be only too happy to provoke—the dueling hawk who in Onegin's own opinion would be best ignored. The second scale is heavier and immediately tips the balance. The observant reader quickly sizes up the situation and surmises just how capable Onegin is of love and how highly he values his own self-esteem. 'I must kill my friend,' Onegin reasons. 'I must show the secret court of my conscience that I am a man without honor and good sense. I absolutely have to do this because, otherwise, fools whom I despise will whisper and snicker.'

From the way Onegin reasons, it is obvious that the words "friend," "conscience," "honor," "good sense," "fools," "contempt" do not have any real meaning for him. Oppressed by intellectual emptiness and the prejudices of society, Onegin has irreparably lost his ability to feel, to think, and to act without seeking the approbation of that crowd of vulgar men he so utterly despises. Onegin's own ideas, feelings, and desires are so weak and amorphous that they cannot possibly have any appreciable effect on his actions. In any case he acts just the way the crowd demands that he act. In fact, he does not even wait for the crowd to state its demand; he guesses it in advance. With the abject servility of a slave, raised in slavery from the cradle, he anticipates all the desires of this crowd, which, like a pampered master, does not even take notice of the sacrifices its faithful slave Onegin makes in order to buy the right to stay in its good graces.

The question arises: How should Pushkin have regarded Onegin's servility? I think he should have sensed the profound humor implicit in this trait, that he should have used the whole arsenal of his talent to expose the ludicrous aspects of this servility. He should have derided it, trivialized it, vilified it—without showing the slightest bit of sympathy for that vile cowardice which makes a sensible man play the role of a harmful idiot, just so he will not be subjected to the timid ridicule of real idiots who are worthy of utter contempt. If the poet had acted this way, he would have rendered a great service to social consciousness. He would have compelled the masses to make fun of those forms of ignorance and conformity which they are all too accustomed to regard with indifference—and sometimes even favorably.

But did Pushkin act this way? No, he acted just the opposite. In his assessment of Onegin's situation he revealed himself to be one of the crowd. He used the whole arsenal of his talent to turn a petty, cowardly, spineless, idle dandy into a tragic figure, exhausted from battling the inordinate demands of people and the age. Instead of telling the reader that Onegin is spineless, ludicrous, and contemptible because he kills his friend to please fools and scoundrels, Pushkin says: "This is what makes the world go round"—as if to refuse an utterly absurd challenge is to break a universal law.

Thus, Pushkin elevates those types and those traits which in and of themselves are base, banal, and contemptible and uses the whole arsenal of his talent to put to sleep social consciousness. A true poet would awaken and educate social consciousness through his works. Pushkin stifles personal initiative, disarms personal protest, and reinforces the prejudices of society—those very prejudices which every thinking person is called upon to eradicate. *"This is what makes the world go round,"* Pushkin naively confesses. You see, for him the whole world is concentrated in those exclusive circles of fashionable society where people worship "Good Repute" and out of reverence for it go against their own convictions and exchange shots with their friends.

After Lensky's death, Onegin sets out to travel across Russia. Everywhere he goes, he frowns and groans; everywhere he goes, he gazes with ridiculous contempt on the pursuits of the idle public. Finally he reaches such absurd extremes that he begins to envy the sick and wounded he sees taking mineral baths in the Caucasus:

> Engrossed in bitter meditations
> Amidst this melancholy crew,
> Onegin looks with wry impatience
> Upon the waters dim with dew
> And thinks: why could not I be blessed
> With such a bullet in my chest?
> Why am I not a senile coot
> Like that poor sack of landed loot?
> Why, like the alderman from Tula,
> May I not lie there stiff with gout?
> Could not at least my shoulder sprout
> Rheumatic pains? O Lord and Ruler,

> I'm young, and life is strong in me,
> And what's ahead? Ennui, ennui!

                                                                              (J, 14)

Belinsky's comments apropos of these ridiculous complaints are extremely curious. They clearly reveal the profound sincerity of our great critic, his extraordinary truthfulness, and his remarkable credulity—his willingness to take for gospel truth every word a man says, even those which are the crudest, most obvious lies, the most impudent form of charlatanism. Obviously Belinsky mistook Onegin for someone else—for example, for Beltov, the civil servant who did not serve out his fourteen years and six months.[5] But, see here, Beltov did not waste his youth seducing inveterate coquettes. He was incapable of vile cowardice; he could not have killed a friend. He never lamented the fact that he did not have a bullet in his chest. He never envied an alderman from Tula or a senile coot. In short, Beltov is as far from Onegin as Beltov's creator, Herzen, is from Pushkin.

I simply cannot understand how Belinsky could have confused these two totally different types. Onegin is nothing more than a Mitrofan Prostakov decked out in the fashion of the 1820s. Even their ways are almost the same. Mitrofan says: "I don't want to study, I want to marry."[6] And Onegin studies the "science of tender passion" and draws mourning crepe around all the thinkers of the eighteenth century [a reference to I, 44]. Beltov is quite the opposite. He, together with Chatsky and Rudin,[7] represent the agonizing awakening of the Russian consciousness. These are thinking people, people who are capable of loving passionately. If they are bored, it is not because their minds are idle but because the questions long ago resolved in their own minds cannot even be raised in real life.

The day of the Beltovs, the Chatskys, and the Rudins was over the moment the Bazarovs, the Lopukhovs, and the Rakhmetovs came on the scene.[8] But we, modern realists, sense our kinship with this type, which has had its day. We recognize that the Chatskys, the Beltovs, and the Rudins are our forerunners. We respect and love them as our teachers, and we understand that, without *them, we* would not be here. Absolutely nothing, however, binds us to the Onegin type. We are not obligated to it in any way. It is a completely sterile type, capable of neither development nor rebirth. Onegin's boredom cannot give rise to anything except absurd and vile acts. Onegin is bored like a fat merchant's wife who has drunk three samovars of tea and complains about the fact that she cannot drink thirty-three. If a man's belly did not have its limits, then Onegin would not be bored. Belinsky loves Onegin because he mistakes him for someone else, but the same cannot be said of Pushkin.

We have analyzed the hero of Pushkin's novel. Now we must decide whether Belinsky was right when he extolled *Onegin* as an "encyclopedia of Russian life," as "an act of consciousness for Russian society."

If consciousness means that society is fully aware of its needs, sufferings, prejudices, and flaws, then on no account can *Eugene Onegin* be called an "act of consciousness." Pushkin's attitude toward the phenomena of life he portrays is so biased, his ideas about the needs and moral obligations of men and citizens are so vague and misleading that the "beloved child" of Pushkin's muse acts on the reader like a soporific drink, which is so delightful that a man forgets everything he should constantly be mindful of and is reconciled to everything he should tirelessly oppose. *Eugene Onegin* is nothing more than a vivid and glittering apotheosis of the dreary and senseless *status quo*. All the pictures in this novel are drawn in such bright colors, all the dirt of real life is so carefully pushed to the side, the profound foolishness of our morals and manners is made to look so grand, the tiny mistakes are laughed at so good-naturedly, the poet himself leads such a gay life and breathes so easily, that inevitably the impressionable reader imagines that he is the happy inhabitant of some Arcadia at the dawning of the Golden Age.

Suppose you would like to find out how educated people in the 1820s spent their time, the encyclopedia of Russian life will answer that they ate, drank, danced, frequented theaters, fell in love and suffered—now from boredom, now from the pangs of love. 'Is that all?' you will ask. 'That's all,' the encyclopedia will answer. 'That's very jolly,' you will think, 'but not entirely believable.' You will learn almost nothing that would tell you about the physiology or the pathology of society in that period. You will definitely not find out what ideas or illusions informed that society. You will definitely not find out what gave it meaning and direction or what fostered apathy and absurd behavior. You will not get a historical picture. You will only discover a collection of outdated costumes and hairdos, outdated menus and playbills, outdated furniture, and outdated grimaces. Everything may be described in an extremely lively and playful manner—but so what? In order to create a historical picture one must be not only an attentive observer but also a real intellect. One must be able to select from the variety of persons, ideas, words, joys, sorrows, stupidities, and base deeds that which epitomizes the character of a given period, that which leaves its mark on all the secondary phenomena, that which influences and shapes all the remaining spheres of private and public life.

It was Griboedov who accomplished this enormous task for Russia in the 1820s. So far as Pushkin is concerned, I have to say it: he did not come anywhere close to accomplishing this task. He did not even have any real notion what this task was. First of all, his choice of a hero is very unfortunate. In a novel which purports to depict the life of an entire society at a particular stage in its development, the hero must either be the kind of person who typifies the *status quo* or the kind of person who bears within himself the seeds of the future and who clearly understands the real needs of society. In other words the hero must be either a knight of the past or a knight of the future, but in any event a person who is active, who has some goal in life. Only the life of an active person can clearly reveal the merits and shortcomings of society's machinery and morals.

If the critics and the public had understood Pushkin's novel the way he himself understood it, if they had regarded it as an innocent and frivolous piece like *Count Nulin* or *Little House in Kolomna,* if they had not put Pushkin on a pedestal, which he did not in the least deserve, if they had not thrust on him great tasks, which he did not know how to undertake, did not want to undertake, and never even thought of undertaking, then I would not have taken it upon myself to upset the sensitive souls of the Russian aesthetes with my irreverent articles on the works of our so-called great poet. But unfortunately in Pushkin's day the public was so undeveloped that it mistook polished verses and vivid descriptions for great events in its intellectual life.

Twenty years passed, and a first-rate critic undertook to resolve the question of Pushkin, a critic who was an honest citizen and a real intellect. I am speaking of Vissarion Belinsky. It would seem that he should have been able to resolve this question and assign Pushkin the modest place in the history of our intellectual life which he rightfully deserves. However, just the reverse happened. Belinsky wrote eleven excellent articles on Pushkin, pouring into them lots and lots of good ideas concerning the rights and duties of man, relations between men and women, love and jealousy, private and public life, but the question of Pushkin's place in the history of our intellectual life was completely fogged. To readers and perhaps even to Belinsky himself it seemed that Pushkin had generated all these remarkable ideas. In fact, however, they were entirely Belinsky's, and most likely they would not have pleased the poet at all. Belinsky exaggerated the significance of all of Pushkin's major works and ascribed to each of them some serious and profound meaning which the author himself never intended and was incapable of articulating.

As essays, Belinsky's articles on Pushkin were extremely useful and promoted the intellectual development of our society. But these articles also did their share of harm, because they extolled an old idol and entreated people to enter an old temple which harbored food for the imagination but no food for the intellect. Belinsky loved the Pushkin he himself created, but many of Belinsky's fervent followers have fallen in love with the real Pushkin in his natural and unadorned dress. They have begun to extoll the weak aspects of the poet's works, those very aspects which Belinsky either ignored or interpreted in his own way. As a result, Pushkin's name has become the banner of incorrigible romantics and literary philistines. All of Apollon Grigoriev's criticism and that of his followers is based on the notion of universal love, which allegedly permeates Pushkin's works.

At the same time these romantics take refuge in Belinsky's great name, hoping that it will act as a lightning rod and save them from being suspected of having philistine tastes and tendencies. 'We are one with Belinsky,' the romantics say, 'and you, nihilists or realists, are simply egotistical brats, trying to get the public's attention by flaunting your irreverence for esteemed authorities.'

We hope to prove to the public that old literary idols crumble as soon as a serious critic turns his attention on them. As for Belinsky's estimable name, it will ring out against our literary enemies. Although we part company with Belinsky in small matters, although we find that he is excessively trusting and too impressionable, we come much closer than our opponents to sharing his fundamental convictions.

Pushkin

FYODOR DOSTOEVSKY
(1880)

"Pushkin is an extraordinary phenomenon and perhaps the most singular manifestation of the Russian spirit," observed Gogol.[1] And I would add: he is a prophetic phenomenon. Indeed, in his coming there is unquestionably something prophetic for all us Russians. Pushkin appears exactly at the dawning of our true consciousness, for it was a whole century after the reforms of Peter the Great before that consciousness awakened within us. Pushkin's coming, like a guiding light, greatly helped to illuminate the dark road in front of us. And in this sense Pushkin is prophetic, pointing toward the future.

I divide the works of our great poet into three periods. I do this, speaking not as a literary critic but in order to explain my idea about Pushkin's prophetic significance for us Russians and what I mean by the word "prophecy." In passing, however, I would note that Pushkin's works do not fall neatly into periods. For example, the beginning of *Eugene Onegin* in my opinion belongs to the poet's first period, but that work was completed in the second period. By that time Pushkin had found the ideals he longed for in his native land, had taken them to heart, and had come to love them with all his being. It is often said that in his first period Pushkin imitated European poets like Parny, Chenier, and, above all, Byron. Undoubtedly, European poets did greatly influence the development of Pushkin's genius and continued to do so throughout his life. Nevertheless, even Pushkin's first poems were more than mere imitations; already the extraordinary originality of his genius shone brightly in them. Poems that are imitations would never give expression to the intense suffering and profound self-awareness found, for example, in *The Gypsies,* a work which in my opinion falls wholly within the first period of Pushkin's literary development. If this work were merely an imitation, it would not be suffused with such dramatic power, such impetuosity.

A powerful, profound, purely Russian idea clearly manifests itself in Aleko, the hero of *The Gypsies*. The idea finds even fuller expression in *Eugene Onegin,* in which Aleko appears again, no longer wearing a fantastic guise but assuming a completely comprehensible form. In Aleko Pushkin's genius grasped and masterfully delineated a specifically Russian type: the unhappy wanderer, uprooted, cut off from his own people, a stranger in his native land. Pushkin did not simply borrow this type from Byron. This is a real Russian type, and Pushkin's genius grasped it. The type has been with us a long time. It settled among us, on Russian soil, and even now homeless Russian wanderers of this sort continue their peregrinations, and they are not likely to vanish for a long time. Today they no longer go off to gypsy camps, hoping to find their ideals realized in the primitive gypsy way of life and seeking a refuge from the hurly-burly of civilization in the bosom of nature. Now they get caught up in socialism, which did not exist in Aleko's day, and go out armed with a new faith into a different vineyard, where they work zealously, believing, just like Aleko, that through such a fantastic enterprise they will attain their goal of bringing about happiness not only for themselves but for all mankind. This is essential: the Russian wanderer must attain happiness for all mankind in order to find peace. He will not settle for less. Of course, at the present all this remains in the realm of theory. But this is the very same Russian type; it is just that the times have changed. The type, I repeat, was born exactly a century after the reforms of Peter the Great, reforms which uprooted and cut off the educated part of our society from the people, from their strength.

In Pushkin's time the vast majority of educated Russians were content to serve as civil servants and work in the treasury or for the railroads or in banks. Or they simply found various ways to make money or occupied themselves with science, delivered lectures; and it is still like that today. These people draw their salaries, play cards, and have absolutely no desire to run off to gypsy camps or anywhere else more in keeping with the times. Many of them play the liberal "with a touch of European socialism," a stance which has acquired a certain benign Russian character, but it is simply a matter of time. What difference does it make that some have yet to become restless, while others have already succeeded in reaching the locked door and have beat their heads against it? They can all expect to end the same way, unless they find the road to salvation and humbly commune with the people. Maybe this will not happen to all of them. Maybe it will only be the fate of the "chosen." But even if it is the fate of only one-tenth of those who become infected with socialism, it will be enough to prevent all the rest from finding peace.

Of course, Aleko does not know how to express his anguish except in a rather abstract way: he longs for nature, he complains about society, he has universal aspirations, he laments the truth, which has somehow vanished, which, try as he may, he cannot find. In all of this there is a touch of Rousseau. Just what this truth is, where and in what form it will appear, and when exactly it vanished, he of course cannot say; but he suffers deeply. This fantastic and impatient man thirsts for salvation and believes that he will find it in external phenomena, and that is the way it must be. 'The truth,' he says, 'lies outside me, perhaps abroad, for example, in Europe, where political systems are firmly entrenched and society has long, established traditions.' He will never understand that truth is found within. And how can he? In his own country he is a stranger. He has forgotten how to work, he has no culture, he was raised like a cloistered schoolgirl, he has performed strange and inexplicable duties defined by his particular civil service rank.[2]

The Aleko type is uprooted, cut off, like a blade of grass tossed about in the wind. And he feels this and suffers because of it—often terribly! What difference does it make that he, a hereditary nobleman (chances are he owned serfs), finds the idea of people living in a state of nature attractive, and that he chooses to live for a time in a gypsy camp and lead a gypsy bear on a chain? It is understandable that a "primitive woman" should give him hope of escaping his anguish, and so, foolishly but passionately believing that Zemphira offers salvation, he throws himself at her feet. 'This,' he says, 'may be the way out. Perhaps I will find happiness here in the bosom of nature, far away from society, among people who possess neither civilization nor laws!' And what happens? The first time he collides with the primitive nature in these people, he cannot control himself and stains his hands with blood.[3] This unhappy dreamer is unfit not only for universal harmony but even for gypsies, and so they cast him out—but without any desire for revenge, without any malice. Simply and majestically the old gypsy says:

> "Depart from us, oh man of pride!
> We are but wild, a lawless nation,
> We keep no rack or hempen knot."

(Arndt, *PuCP,* p. 287)

Naturally, all of this is fantastic, but the "man of pride" is real. And Pushkin first grasped and delineated this type. We should not forget this. Should anything happen which is not to his liking, the "man of pride" is prepared to torment and punish cruelly for the wrong done him. Better still, remembering that he belongs to one of the fourteen ranks, he will invoke (for this indeed has happened) the law of torture and punishment to avenge a personal wrong. No, this extraordinary poem is no imitation! Already in it the Russian answer to the "cursed question" is suggested. 'Humble yourself, oh man of pride, and above all crush your pride. Humble yourself and above all devote yourself to honest labor on your native soil.' This answer is in accord with the people's sense of truth and their wisdom. 'Truth lies not outside you but within. You must look within to find yourself, you must subdue and control yourself, and then you will behold the truth. This truth is not to be found in material things; it is not outside you, not somewhere abroad, but rather in your own honest efforts to gain control of yourself. Conquer yourself, subdue yourself, and you will become free, freer than you ever dreamed, and you will begin a great work and you will make others free and you will see happiness, for your life will be made full and at last you will understand your people and their sacred truth. You will not find universal harmony among the gypsies; you will not find it anywhere if you are unworthy of it. You must not be spiteful, proud, and demanding; you must realize that life costs something.' This answer is suggested in Pushkin's poem *The Gypsies*. It is expressed even more clearly in *Eugene Onegin,* a poem which is not fantastic but quite real, a poem in which genuine Russian life is embodied with a power and a completeness unknown before Pushkin and not equalled since.

Onegin is from Petersburg—without question from Petersburg. This is absolutely essential to the poem, and Pushkin could not have omitted such an important, realistic detail from his hero's biography. I will say it again: Onegin is just like Aleko, especially when he cries out in anguish:

> Why, like the alderman from Tula,
> May I not lie there stiff with gout?

(J, 14)

But at the beginning of the poem he is still something of a fop and man of the world. He has lived too little to have become completely disillusioned with life. Nevertheless he is visited and tormented by "the noble demon of secret boredom."[4]

Naturally, in the country, in the heart of his native land, Onegin feels out of his element. He does not know what he should do; he feels like a guest in his own home. Later, when he wanders despondently across his native land and abroad, he, a man indisputably intelligent, indisputably sincere, feels even more estranged from himself in strange surroundings. It is true that he loves Russia, his native land, but he does not trust her. Naturally he has heard about native Russian ideals, but he does not believe in them. He believes only that it is utterly impossible to labor at any task on his native soil, and he looks upon those few who believe in this possibility with a sad but mocking smile. He kills Lensky simply because he is suffering from spleen; perhaps he longs for a universal ideal. This is so Russian that it is very possible.

Tatyana is quite different. She is a resolute type, firmly rooted in her native soil. She is more profound than Onegin and, of course, wiser. Thanks to her noble instincts, she senses what truth is and where it lies, as is clear from the final scene in the poem. Perhaps it would have been better had Pushkin named his poem for Tatyana rather than for Onegin, because unquestionably she is the real hero. She is a positive type, not a negative one. She embodies positive beauty; she is the apotheosis of the Russian woman. The poet chose her to express the true idea of the poem in the famous scene in which she meets Onegin for the last time. One could even say that there is no other woman in Russian literature who is such a positive type and possesses such beauty, except perhaps Turgenev's heroine Liza in *A Nest of Gentle Folk*.[5] Because Onegin is used to looking down his nose at people, he does not appreciate Tatyana when he meets her for the first time in the country. She is so modest, so innocent, so shy in his company. He is unable to discern her completeness, her perfection; perhaps he really does take her for a "moral embryo."[6] She an embryo—after her letter to Onegin!

If there is a moral embryo in the poem, then without a doubt it is Onegin himself. He is totally incapable of appreciating Tatyana. Can someone like him possibly understand the human soul? He is an abstract person, a restless dreamer. Nor does he appreciate Tatyana later in Petersburg when she has become a *grande dame*. Although he tells her that he longs to bathe his soul in all her loveliness [Onegin's letter], these are mere words. Tatyana passes through Onegin's life unrecognized and unappreciated by him. Herein lies the tragedy of their love. If only Childe Harold or somehow even Lord Byron himself could have been present when he met her for the first time in the country. If one of them had noticed Tatyana's shy, modest charm and had pointed her out to Onegin, he would have been smitten immediately, for at times world sufferers like Onegin are such lackeys. But this is not what happened. Instead, the seeker after universal harmony reads her a sermon (yet acts very honorably) and sets out with his *Weltschmerz* and his bloodstained hands (in a foolish fit of anger he has killed Lensky) to wander across Russia without really observing his native land. Bursting with health and strength, he cries out:

> I'm young, and life is strong in me,
> And what's ahead? Ennui, ennui!

(J, 14)

Tatyana understands this. In immortal stanzas the poet describes her visit to Onegin's home, to the home of the man who continues to hold such fascination for her. What beauty and profundity these verses possess! Now she is in Onegin's study, examining his books, his objects, trying to divine his soul, to solve the riddle. And at last the "moral embryo" stops, and deep in thought, with a strange smile on her lips and a presentiment that the riddle has been solved, she whispers quietly:

> A parody, perhaps . . . who knows?

(VII, 24)

Indeed, Tatyana must whisper this; she has solved the riddle. Much later when she and Onegin meet again in Petersburg, she knows him through and through. By the way, who claimed that Tatyana's soul was tainted by her life in high society, that her exalted social standing and worldly notions in part explain why she refuses Onegin? This is not the case at all. No, Tatyana remains the very same person; she remains just the way she was earlier in the country. Life in high society has not corrupted her. On the contrary, she is depressed by the glamor of Petersburg life, suffocated by it. She suffers deeply.

She hates being a *grande dame,* and anyone who judges her differently does not understand what Pushkin wanted to say. Remember what she says to Onegin, when they meet for the last time:

> "But I was pledged another's wife
> And will be faithful all my life."

(VIII, 47)

Tatyana utters these words as a Russian woman, and that is why she is the apotheosis of womanhood. She articulates the truth of the poem. Oh, I will not say a single word about her religious convictions, about her views on the sanctity of marriage. No, I will not go into this at all. Why does she refuse to go away with Onegin, despite the fact that she says to him: "I love you" [VIII, 47]? Is it because as a Russian woman (as opposed to a Mediterranean or a French woman) she is not capable of taking such a bold step, of casting off her chains, of sacrificing her wealth, status, and virtue? No, the Russian woman is bold. The Russian woman will boldly pursue that which she believes in, and Tatyana demonstrates this. But she "was pledged another's wife and will be faithful all her life." Faithful to whom and to what? To what obligations? Faithful to some old general, whom she cannot possibly love because she loves Onegin, whom she married simply because her mother tearfully entreated her to do so [VIII, 47], because her insulted and wounded heart harbored only despair and no hope for a bright future? Yes, faithful to this general, her husband, an honest man who loves her, respects her, and is proud of her. While it is true that her mother did entreat her, she and she alone gave her consent. She vowed to be his faithful wife. It is true that she married him out of despair, but now he is her husband, and, were she to betray him, she would bring down shame on him and kill him.

Can anyone possibly build his happiness on the unhappiness of another? Happiness is more than a matter of enjoying the fruits of love; happiness depends on a higher spiritual harmony. But what remains to console the spirit, when one commits a dishonest, pitiless, inhuman act? Should Tatyana run off with Onegin simply because happiness seems so close? And what sort of happiness can there be, if it is built on another's unhappiness? Imagine yourself erecting the edifice of human destiny with the ultimate aim of making men happy, of giving them peace and rest. And then imagine that in order to do this you must torment just one human being—someone who is not a particularly worthy person, someone people may even laugh at, certainly not a Shake-speare, just an honest old man who is married to a young woman and has blind faith in her love. Though he does not know her heart at all, he respects her, is proud of her, happy with her, and at peace. All you have to do is disgrace and torment this one man, and you can erect your edifice on his tears! Under these conditions would you consent to be the architect? That is the question. And could you entertain, even for a moment, the idea that the people for whom you erected this edifice would agree to accept such happiness, if they knew that it was built on the suffering of even one contemptible individual who had been cruelly and unjustly tormented? And if they were to accept this happiness, could they remain happy forever? Tell me: could Tatyana have acted otherwise, given her lofty soul, given that heart which had known such suffering? No, the pure Russian soul resolves the matter in this way: 'Even if I alone am deprived of happiness, even if my unhappiness is infinitely greater than the unhappiness of this old man, even if no one, not even this old man, ever learns of my sacrifice or appreciates it, I do not want to obtain happiness at another's expense!' Herein lies the tragedy, and it is complete. The line cannot be crossed. It is too late, and so Tatyana sends Onegin away. It will be said: 'But Onegin is unhappy too. Although she saves one man, she ruins the other!' Permit me to point out that this is an entirely different question, perhaps the most important one in the entire poem.

Incidentally, the question of why Tatyana does not run off with Onegin has a long history in our critical literature, which is very typical of us Russians, and that is why I have discoursed on it at such length. And it is also extremely characteristic of us that the moral answer to this question remained in doubt for so long a time. Here is what I think: Even if Tatyana were to become free, even if her old husband were to die and she were to become a widow, even then she would not run off with Onegin. One needs to understand Onegin's true character! She sees him for what he is: an eternal wanderer who suddenly meets a woman he once disdained in a glamorous new setting where she is inaccessible. Yes, it all seems to be in the setting. Society now bows to the girl he had all but scorned. Society remains the supreme authority for Onegin despite his universal aspirations, and that is why, dazzled, he throws himself at her feet. 'Here is my ideal,' he exclaims. 'Here is my salvation, a way to escape my ennui. I failed to see it then, but happiness was so close, so possible.' And just as Aleko was drawn to Zemphira, so Onegin is attracted to Tatyana, seeking in this new, whimsical fantasy a solution to all his problems. Surely Tatyana realizes this, surely she saw through him long ago. Undoubtedly, she knows that he really loves a new fantasy of his own invention and not her, the ever humble Tatyana! She knows that he takes her for someone else and not the person she really is, that he does not love her, that perhaps he does not love anyone and is incapable of loving anyone, despite the fact that he suffers so! Yes, he loves a fantasy and is himself a fantasy. Even if she were to run off with him, the very next day he would become disillusioned and look mockingly on his infatuation.

Onegin is not rooted in the soil. He is like a blade of grass, carried hither and yon by the wind. Tatyana is quite different. Even though she is in despair and realizes that her life is ruined, she still possesses something firm and unshakable which sustains her soul: memories of childhood, memories of Russia, her native land, and the countryside where her pure, humble life began, where "cross and swaying branches grace her poor Nanny's final resting place" [VIII, 46]. Oh, these memories, these images of her former life are even dearer to her now; they are all that she has left, and somehow they save her soul from total despair. This is most important; here is an unshakable, an indestructible foundation. There is an indissoluble bond between Tatyana and her native land. She is joined to her people and what they hold sacred. What does Onegin have and who is he? Tatyana feels great compassion, great pity for Onegin, but she does not follow him. She knows that she could amuse him, make him think for one brief moment that he was happy, but she also knows that the very next day he would mock this happiness. No, there are profound and resolute individuals who cannot consciously dishonor that which they deem sacred, even if they are filled with boundless compassion. No, Tatyana could never have followed Onegin.

And so in *Eugene Onegin,* in that immortal poem which has yet to be surpassed, Pushkin revealed himself to be a great national writer, greater than any writer who had come before him. Incisively and perspicaciously he grasped the very essence of our being. He delineated the Russian wanderer as a type. With the sensitivity born of genius, he intuited the wanderer, divined his historical destiny and his enormous significance for our future. Next to him Pushkin placed a type of positive and indisputable beauty in the person of the Russian woman.

Not only was Pushkin the first Russian writer to delineate these two types, but also he introduced a whole series of positive, beautiful Russian types, drawn from the Russian people, in other works of this same period. The principal beauty of the latter lies in their truth, a truth so unquestionable, so tangible, that it is impossible to deny their significance. They stand firm, like pieces of sculpture. Once again I remind you that I am speaking not as a literary critic, and therefore I will not elaborate on my idea, discussing in detail these great works. One would have to devote an entire book to that Russian monk and chronicler in *Boris Godunov,*[7] for example, in order to show the whole importance, the whole significance for us Russians of this majestic Russian type which Pushkin found on Russian soil. He portrayed, sculpted, presented this type to us for eternity with its meek, majestic, indubitable spiritual beauty as testimony to that mighty spirit in our national life which has the ability to produce images with such indisputable truth. This type is now known. It exists. No one can dispute it, claiming that it is mere invention, that it is only a fantasy, an idealization on the poet's part. Look at it yourselves and you will agree that it exists. Hence the spirit of the people which created it also lives. And the strength of this spirit lives, and it is both mighty and boundless. In each of Pushkin's works one senses faith in the Russian character, faith in

Russia's spiritual might, and where there is faith, there is hope, great hope for each and every Russian. On the occasion of the accession of Nicholas I to the throne, the poet said:

> In hopes of fame and bliss to come
> I gaze ahead with resolution.[8]

These words, however, are applicable to all his national Russian works. Never was there a Russian writer so closely linked with his people as Pushkin. To be sure, many of our writers are connoisseurs of the people and have written about them accurately and lovingly, but they never cease being "gentlemen." Even our most talented writers sometimes display haughtiness, as if they were from a different world, from a different way of life, and wanted to raise the people up to their level and in this way make them happy. Pushkin is *truly* linked to the people. He is genuinely moved by and open to even the most artless emotions.

All the treasures, all the insights that our great poet left as a legacy have pointed the way for future writers, for future laborers in that same vineyard. We can say with absolute certainty that had it not been for Pushkin, the gifted writers who came after him could not have been. At least these writers would not have manifested such power, such clarity—no matter how gifted they were. It is not merely a matter of poetry or of literature, however. Had it not been for Pushkin, our faith in our distinctive Russianness, our confidence in our own powers, our belief in Russia's future mission to the family of European nations would not be so strong, so unshakable. This great achievement of Pushkin's becomes particularly evident when we examine what I will call the third period in his literary development. To repeat: these periods I define do not have rigid boundaries. For example, some of the works which actually belong to this third period could just as easily have appeared at the very beginning of Pushkin's career. Pushkin was always, so to speak, a whole, unified organism. He bore within himself all of his future works in "embryonic" form. He did not ingest any of them from without. Outside influences merely awakened in him what was already present in the depths of his soul. But, like any organism, he kept developing, and in this development one can discern definite stages. One can also observe the specific character of each stage and the gradual transition from one to another.

In the final stage of his development our poet becomes a near-miraculous phenomenon, something without precedent in world literature. There have been, of course, an enormous number of geniuses in European literature— Shakespeares, Cervantes, Schillers. But none of these great geniuses possessed the empathy, the all-embracing responsiveness of our Pushkin. And that trait, which Pushkin shares with the Russian people, is the principal trait of our national character; this explains why Pushkin is a national poet. Even the greatest European poets were never able to embody so powerfully the genius of another people, even a neighboring people, incarnate its very soul and all the anguish of its calling, as does Pushkin. On the contrary, when European poets write about other nationalities, more often than not they recreate them in their own national image, understand them in their own way. Even Shakespeare's Italians, for example, are virtually Englishmen. Pushkin alone of all the great world poets possesses the ability to reincarnate himself fully in the spirit of another people. Reread *Don Juan,* for example; were it not signed by Pushkin, you would assume that it was written by a Spaniard.[9]

No, I can say with absolute certainty that there has never been another poet like Pushkin, that there has never been another poet who possessed such empathy, who was so universally responsive. And it is not simply responsiveness *per se.* It is the amazing profundity of that empathy, it is Pushkin's ability to reincarnate his own spirit in the spirit of other peoples and to do so in a way that is so perfect it seems miraculous. No other poet in the whole world has been able to do this. Pushkin alone has this ability, and for this reason he is a unique phenomenon and a prophetic one. In the works of his third period his specifically Russian strength and the national character of his poetry find their fullest expression; it is a prophetic one, for the national character as it promises to be is revealed, the national character of our future implicit in the present. Wherein lies the strength of the Russian national character if not in the striving for universality and for the brotherhood of all mankind? No sooner had Pushkin become fully a national poet, no sooner had he formed an indissoluble bond with the Russian people, than he intuited their great destiny. In this sense he is a seer and a prophet.

And in fact what do the reforms of Peter the Great mean to us? What do they now portend for our future, and what significance did they have for our past? What did these reforms really signify? Surely, it was not simply a matter of adopting European dress, customs, inventions, European science. Let us look more closely at what happened. It may well be that originally Peter initiated these reforms for purely utilitarian reasons. But in further developing his idea, undoubtedly he heeded some sixth sense, which drew him on toward much greater goals than narrow utilitarianism. And so it was with the Russian people. They did not accept the reforms for their utilitarian value alone. Undoubtedly they sensed an incomparably higher goal. Naturally, they relied on intuition; it was not a conscious perception. Their reaction was spontaneous, pulsating with life. Even then we longed for the reunion, for the unity of all mankind! Not in a spirit of enmity (as it seems should have been the case) but in a spirit of love and friendship, we took unto ourselves the geniuses of foreign nations. We accepted them all, making no distinctions. We instinctively reconciled differences and contradictions, and in doing so we showed our willingness and our inclination to join with all the nations of the great Aryan race to form a union of all mankind. Yes, undoubtedly the Russians have been chosen for a pan-European, for a universal destiny. Perhaps to become a true Russian, to become fully Russian, means simply (in the final analysis, and I stress this) to become brother to all men, to become a *universal man*.

Oh, the argument between Slavophiles and Westernizers is the result of a terrible misunderstanding, although historically the clash was inevitable. Europe and the destiny of the whole great Aryan race are as dear to a true Russian as Russia itself, as the destiny of his own land, because Russia's destiny is universality, won not by the sword but by the power of brotherhood and our brotherly aspiration for the reunion of all men. If you look closely at our history after the reforms of Peter the Great, you will find evidence to support this idea, this dream of mine if you will, in our relations with European nations, even in the policies of our state. For what course has Russian policy followed during these two centuries, if not one beneficial to Europe—perhaps even more beneficial to Europe than to Russia herself? Surely this has not happened simply because our statesmen have been inept. Oh, the peoples of Europe have absolutely no idea how dear they are to us! Later on, I really believe this, we—not we of course but future Russians—will all, to the very last man, understand that to be a true Russian means to reconcile once and for all the contradictions of Europe, to show Europeans how to escape their ennui in the all-encompassing Russian soul, to embrace all our fellow men in the spirit of brotherly love, and ultimately perhaps to utter that final Word which will bring great, universal harmony and brotherly love to all nations in accordance with the teachings of Christ and the Gospels! I know only too well that my words may seem excessively fervid, exaggerated, fantastic. Be that as it may, I do not regret having uttered them. They needed to be said, especially now during our celebration, as we pay homage to our great poet, who so powerfully embodied this idea in his works. And I am not saying anything new, since this view of Pushkin has been set forth more than once. Nonetheless people will say that I am presumptuous. 'Is this really the destiny of our wretched and uncouth land? Are *we* really destined to utter this new word for mankind?' Do I speak of economic glory or the glory of the sword or the glory of science? No, I speak only about the brotherhood of men and about the Russian heart being destined perhaps to bring about the all-embracing, brotherly union of all mankind. I see signs of this in our history, in our gifted individuals, in the artistic genius of Pushkin. Our land may be wretched, but "Christ traversed this wretched land in the garb of a slave and blessed it."[10]

And is there any reason why Christ's final word should not be embodied in us? Was not He Himself born in a manger? To repeat: at least we can point to Pushkin, to that universal and all-embracing quality of his genius. After all Pushkin's soul could encompass foreign geniuses as if they were his own. In his poetic works he revealed the Russian spirit's longing for universality, a trait that points to our future. If our view seems fantastic, at least there is in Pushkin a basis for this fantasy. Had he lived longer, perhaps he would have disclosed great, immortal images of the Russian soul more intelligible to our European brothers. He would have drawn them much closer to us. Perhaps he would have succeeded in explaining to them the whole truth about our aspirations. They would have understood us better than they do and thus would no longer be inclined to look down on us, to view us with suspicion. Had Pushkin lived longer, perhaps too there would have been fewer misunderstandings among us and fewer arguments. But God willed otherwise. Pushkin died at the peak of his development. Unquestionably he took with him to the grave a great secret. It is up to us to divine this secret without his help.

Twentieth-Century

Views

On the Composition of
Eugene Onegin

YURY TYNYANOV
(1921–22)

1

All attempts to demarcate poetry from prose on the basis of sound texture are
frustrated by facts which contradict the widespread notion that phonic organi-
zation is present in verse and absent in prose.[1] On the one hand, there is *vers
libre* and *freie Rhythmen,* which have absolutely free prosody, and, on the other,
there is rhythmically and phonically organized prose, such as that of Gogol and
Andrey Bely[2] in Russia and Heine and Nietzsche in Germany. Both these
phenomena attest to the fact that we are on very shaky ground when we talk
about phonic organization being present in poetry as distinct from prose and
demonstrate that no clear boundary can be drawn between poetry and prose on
the basis of this principle. Yet these very same literary phenomena attest to the
surprising stability and distinguishability of poetic and prose forms. No matter
how well organized prose is rhythmically and phonically (in the broad sense of
the word), it will not be perceived as verse.[3] On the other hand, no matter how
much verse sounds like prose, it will not be equated to prose—except in the
heat of literary polemics.

Here we should take note of the fact that modern Russian prose, from its
very beginnings in the eighteenth century, is no less carefully organized with
respect to sound than is verse. The prose of Lomonosov, father of modern
Russian literature, developed under the influence of the theory of eloquence,
for he applied the rules of oratorical rhythm and euphony to prose. His *Rhetoric*
(1748), which established stylistic norms and played such an important role in
the development of Russian literature, dealt equally with poetry and prose.
However, the distinguishing phonic features of Lomonosov's and Karamzin's
prose, which were perceptible to their contemporaries, in time lost their
perceptibility. Today we tend to regard the endings of particular rhythmic
divisions (clauses) in their prose as syntactic and semantic phenomena rather
than as phonic ones,[4] and we have difficulty responding to the phenomenon of
euphony in their prose.

Translated and published with the permission of the Copyright Agency of the USSR. Some
lines of Walter Arndt's translation of the verse have been modified to conform with Tynyanov's
remarks about particular words.

On the other hand, in poetry another aspect of the word loses its perceptibility over time. Groups of words, word combinations which are constantly used together, lose their semantic perceptibility and remain linked principally by sound association (resulting in the petrification of epithets).

However, it would be premature to conclude that what distinguishes prose and verse forms is the fact that in verse the outward sign of the word plays a decisive role, while in prose it is meaning that plays this role. This is corroborated by what I shall call the phenomenon of *semantic threshold*. The *exclusive* orientation toward intrinsic sound texture in poetry (transrational language,[5] *Zungenrede*) gives rise to a particularly intense search for meaning and thus calls attention to the semantic aspect of the word. Conversely, the complete disregard for the phonic dimension in prose may evoke phonic phenomena (special confluences of sounds, etc.), which then pull the center of gravity onto *themselves*. Moreover, it is indisputable that phonic organization is present in prose and that poetry influences it in this regard. On the other hand, the semantic principle not only has bearing on the poetic word but is even normative for one of the traditions in Russian poetry.

In the eighteenth-century theory of the ode, formulated by Lomonosov and Derzhavin, the poetic word was assigned the emotional and persuasive functions of oratorical speech. Therefore, poetry was constructed in accordance with the articulatory and auditory characteristics of the word. Words entered into emotional and phonic bonds. In tropes *rather remote* ideas were joined together, and they were joined not by a logical thread (words were not linked on the basis of primary meaning) but by an emotional one (oratorical unexpectedness and strikingness). Subsequently, however, literary warfare erupted as Lomonosov and Derzhavin's theory of the word came into conflict with the antagonistic principles of a second, younger tradition, represented by such poets as Karamzin and Batyushkov, who were drawn to small genres and fugitive themes. In their poetry the semantic aspect of the word began to play an important role. They opposed Lomonosov's theory of the emotional and persuasive poetic word and championed the theory of the logical and clear word. In tropes they strove not to distort the semantic line but to achieve greater clarity. Consequently, in their poetry words were joined not according to emotional coloring or phonic characteristics but according to primary semantic usage (as given in a dictionary). And their theory of the poetic word approached the theory of the word in prose. Poetry began to learn from prose. Apropos of Karamzin's lyrics, Prince Vyazemsky wrote: "One would think that Karamzin adhered to the famous expression 'c'est beau comme de la prose.' He demanded that everything be said succinctly and with absolute precision. He gave full play to imagination and feeling but not to expression."[6] And Batyushkov made a similar observation: "In order to write well in verse, no matter what the genre, to write with variety, with a style both forceful and pleasing, with original ideas, and with feeling, one must write a great deal in prose—not for the public but simply for oneself. I have often found that this method worked well for me. Sooner or later what one writes in prose proves useful. 'Prose is the nourisher of verse,' said Alfieri—if my memory serves me right."[7] Pushkin wrote prose plans and programs for his verse; clearly here prose was the nourisher of verse.[8] As if retorting to Batyushkov, the Wisdom-Lover Ivan Kireevsky, who was akin to the archaic, older tradition, the "lofty" (emotional and persuasive) tradition, wrote to a friend: "Do you know why it is you've produced nothing yet? It's because you do not write verse. If you wrote verse, then you would enjoy expressing even idle thoughts, and any word well said would have the value of a good idea. This is essential if one is to write from the heart. One only feels like writing when one enjoys writing. To be sure, he who does not delight in expressing himself elegantly, independent of his subject, will not enjoy writing. And so, if you want to be a good prose writer, write verse."[9]

Thus, both prose (for Batyushkov) and verse (for Kireevsky) were sources of new meaning, ways of making a kind of semantic shift within prose and within poetry. Apparently there is no inherent difference between poetry and prose. We cannot say that poetry is oriented toward sound texture and prose toward semantics. Rather what distinguishes poetry and prose is the way these elements relate to each other. In prose the phonic aspect is deformed by the semantic aspect (the orientation toward semantics), and in poetry the meaning of the word is deformed by the verse.[10]

The deformation of sound by meaning is the constructive principle in prose; the deformation of meaning by the sound texture is the constructive principle in poetry. Changes in the correlation between these two elements play a decisive role in both prose and poetry.

If phonic organization as it exists in verse is introduced into a prose construction, it is deformed by the orientation toward meaning. If the principle of linking verbal quantities on the basis of semantics is applied to a verse construction, then it too inevitably is deformed by the principle of sound texture.

Because of this, prose and poetry are closed semantic categories. Meaning in prose is always different from meaning in poetry. The fact that both the syntax and the vocabulary of poetry and prose are substantially different accords with this.

When, however, constructive principles of prose are introduced into verse (or, conversely, when verse principles are introduced into prose), the correlation between the deforming and the deformed elements changes somewhat, even though the closed semantic categories of poetry and prose are not disturbed. In this way prose is enriched with new meaning thanks to poetry, and poetry is enriched with new meaning thanks to prose. (Cf. Ivan Kireevsky's letter, quoted above.)

Thus, sound texture and meaning do not have equal value in prose and in poetry. If we attempt to isolate either the semantics or the sound texture in either poetry or prose (although this may be necessary initially and is useful for pedagogical purposes), in reality we split up elements which mutually condition each other and which, moreover, do not have the same significance. When we examine sound texture in prose, we must never forget that it is deformed by semantics. When we talk about the semantics of poetry, we must remember that we are dealing with deformed meaning. We can see this most clearly if we take a poetic style which is rich in prosaisms and a prose style in which verse devices have obviously been introduced. Prose ingredients, which are incorporated into a verse construction, become elements of meter, orchestration, etc., and are subordinated to its principle—to the deformation of meaning by sound. Thanks to the fact that prosaisms undergo a remarkable phonic rejuvenation when they enter into phonic bonds with neighboring words, lines, etc., words and expressions which are completely colorless and indistinguishable in prose become extremely perceptible semantic elements in poetry.[11] Likewise, when rhymes and the like are introduced into prose, their phonic perceptibility is heightened precisely because of semantic expectation. Thus, rhymes which seem trite in poetry will not seem so in prose. In this way poetry and prose mutually enrich each other.[12]

However, as soon as a prosaism, which has been introduced into a poetic category, is completely drawn into it, that prosaism begins to be deformed by the sound texture *to the same degree* as the elements of poetic speech. It loses its semantic *freshness* and moves totally into the poetic category, becoming an element of poetic speech. Conversely, certain rhymes may become so tightly knit into the phonic fabric of prose that they no longer stand out and lose their phonic freshness. Therefore, the historical approach to the problem assumes particular importance here.

And so, we have no right to treat semantic elements in verse speech the same way we treat semantic elements in prose speech. *Meaning* in poetry is not the same as *meaning* in prose. It is easy to confuse the two, however, when a type of literature which is common in prose (the novel, for example), one which is closely identified with the constructive principle of prose, is incorporated into verse. Here first and foremost the semantic elements are deformed by the verse.

In the prose novel the most important semantic unit is the *hero*—whereby heterogeneous dynamic elements are joined and marked by one outward sign. But in the *verse* novel these elements are deformed, and the sign itself acquires a different nuance than it has in prose. Therefore, the hero of a verse novel is not the hero of the same novel, were it to be shifted into prose. While recognizing that he is still the most important semantic unit, we must not forget that this unit is subjected to a peculiar kind of deformation once it is incorporated into verse. *Eugene Onegin* is such a verse novel, and all its heroes are subjected to such deformation.

2

When Pushkin spoke about those literary genres where it would seem that verse was supposed to play a secondary, subordinate role—for example, drama—he always emphasized the primacy of the verbal or the verse aspect in such works. Commenting on an inferior translation of Racine's *Phèdre,* he wrote:

Apropos of muck, I have been reading Lobanov's *Phèdre.* I wanted to write a critique of it, not for Lobanov's sake, but for the sake of the Marquis Racine—but I just couldn't. Where you are they are making a noise about it, and journalists are calling it a most beautiful translation of Mr. Racine's famous tragedy! *Voulez-vous découvrir la trace de ses pas*—do you hope to find
Theseus' hot trace or dark paths—
the rhyme fucker! That's how it's all translated! And what is Ivan Ivanovich Racine characterized by if not verses full of meaning, precision, and harmony! The plan and characters of *Phèdre* are the acme of stupidity and insignificance in invention. Thésée is nothing but Molière's first cuckold. Hippolyte *le superbe, le fier Hippolyte*—*et même un peu farouche, Hippolyte* the stern Scythian bastard—is nothing but a well-bred child, polite and respectful—
D'un mensonge si noir. . . , etc.
Read all that belauded tirade, and you will be convinced that Racine had no understanding of how to create a tragic character. Compare Hippolyte's speech with the speech of the young lover in Byron's *Parisina,* and you will see the difference between minds. And Thérèmene the abbot and pimp—*Vous-même où seriez vous,* etc. . . .—here is the acme of stupidity![13]

There is no reason to think that this is a negative evaluation. Pushkin recognizes in Racine that law which Racine himself recognized and by which he should be judged—that is, the genre in which Racine wrote (not genre in the traditional sense of the word but genre as the dominance of a certain aspect of form). In Racine the dominant element was style—more specifically, verse.

In much the same way Pushkin insists that a poet is entitled to an "insignificant plan" and to a "lack of events." Reviewing a Russian imitation of Byron's *The Corsair,* he observes: "Bryon worried little about the plans of his works, or he didn't even think about the arrangement at all. A few weakly connected scenes sufficed him for this multitude of thoughts, emotions, and tableaux. . . . But what will we think about a writer who takes from Byron's poem *The Corsair* the plan alone, worthy of an absurd Spanish tale, and composes a dramatic trilogy using this childish plan, replacing the enchanting, profound poetry of Byron with stilted and deformed prose worthy of our unfortunate imitators of the late Kotzebue? . . . The question arises: what was it in Byron's poem that struck him—can it really have been the plan? *o miratores!* . . ." [Proffer, pp. 64–65].

Thus, "a few weakly connected scenes," "a plan, worthy of an *absurd tale*" are quite sufficient for "enchanting and profound *poetry*" [the italics are Ty-nyanov's]. Pushkin's opinion of Baratynsky's *Eda* is even more emphatic: "Reread his *Eda* (which our critics found *insignificant,* for, like children, they demand events from a poem) . . ." [*PSS*, 11, 186]. Pushkin is not simply offering a critical opinion here but waging battle. Willingly he advances to meet the charges of critics that his "characters" are inconsistent, his "heroes" pallid, his plans imperfect. Apparently for him the center of gravity rested elsewhere in a poem. Apparently he felt that the *verse* plan and the *verse* hero should be judged differently from the plan and the hero of a tale or novel.

In *Eugene Onegin* the "imperfection" of the plan and the characters is no longer justified as a distinguishing characteristic of the verse form but becomes itself a compositional element. It would be a mistake to assume that Pushkin was really trying to excuse or justify this "imperfection," that he indicated omitted stanzas and lines because he did not want to disrupt the *coherence* of the novel, that he sensed the incompleteness of his plan and aspired to *complete* the novel. In the preface to Chapter I of *Onegin* (written in 1825, when *three* chapters were already completed) Pushkin speaks about the "imperfection" in the plan half-ironically: "No doubt farsighted critics will notice the imperfec-tion in the plan. Everyone is free to judge the plan of a whole novel after reading the first chapter of the latter." At the same time the author admitted that "the first chapter constitutes a certain whole." Just how serious Pushkin was here is revealed by comparing this preface with the final stanza of Chapter I:

> I've thought about the hero's label
> And about what form the plan should take;
>
> . . . .
>
> And contradictions there are clearly
> Galore, but I will let them go,

(I, 60)

This statement about what form the plan should take is connected with analogous digressions in which the novel itself is the subject of the novel (from this standpoint *Eugene Onegin* is not a novel but a novel about a novel). The line "I've thought about the hero's label," after the hero's name has been mentioned numerous times, is an ironic introduction to the line, "And contradictions there are clearly/ Galore." We find the same sort of play on contradictions in the final stanza of Chapter VII:

> But here, with bows before this feather
> In Tanya's cap, *we turn away,*
> *Lest we abandon [forget] altogether*
> *The one I sing, and go astray . . .*

(VII, 55) [the italics are Tynyanov's]

Thus, it is easy to *forget* about the hero, and returning to him is also a digression in a novel of digressions *("we turn away")*. Here Pushkin's ironic note to Chapter III is also relevant: "A misprint in the earlier edition [of the chapter] altered 'homeward they fly' to 'in winter they fly' (which did not make any sense whatsoever). Reviewers, not realizing this, saw an anachronism in the following stanzas. We venture to assert that, in our novel, the chronology has been worked out calendrically" [Nabokov, 1, 316n17].

In a preface to Chapters VIII and IX,[14] drafted in November 1830, Pushkin is openly ironic: "Here are two more chapters of *Eugene Onegin*—the last ones, at least for publication. Those who would seek entertaining events in them may rest assured that there is *even less action in these chapters than in all the preceding ones*. I had all but resolved to abolish altogether Chapter VIII ["Onegin's Journey"] and to replace it with a Roman numeral; *the fear of criticism,* however, stopped me. Moreover, many excerpts from it had already been published" [Nabokov, 3, 127; the italics are Tynyanov's].

The question of the omitted stanzas is of particular interest here. It should be pointed out that *several numbers,* which are supposed to designate *omitted* stanzas, stand as it were on an empty spot, for these stanzas were never written. Pushkin himself explains the omission of stanzas in the following way: "The fact that *Eugene Onegin* contained stanzas that I could not or did not wish to publish should not be deemed surprising. But since their exclusion *disrupts the coherence of the story,* it is necessary to indicate the place where they ought to have been. It might have been better to replace those stanzas by others, or to rework and recombine those I kept. But pardon me, I am much too lazy. Moreover, I humbly submit that two stanzas are left out of *Don Juan*" [Nabokov, 3, 127–128; the italics are Tynyanov's].

This note was also written in the autumn of 1830, and, after what Pushkin said earlier about the plan and coherence of the novel, this explanation sounds ironic. But Pushkin goes further and underscores the irony by citing laziness and a literary source in which omissions play exactly the same compositional role. If we recall that in the draft preface to the final chapter and to the "Fragments from Onegin's Journey," Pushkin talks about omitting an *entire chapter,* then it becomes even more obvious that what is at issue is not really *coherence* or harmony of plan. Here is what Pushkin writes in the preface to Chapter VIII, when it was published separately in 1832: "Pavel Katenin (whom a fine poetic talent does not prevent from being also a subtle critic) observed to us that this exclusion [that is, the exclusion of "Onegin's Journey"], *though perhaps advantageous to readers,* is, however, detrimental to the *plan* of the entire work, since, through this, the transition from Tatyana the provincial miss to Tatyana the *grande dame* becomes too unexpected and unexplained: an observation revealing the experienced artist. The author himself felt the justice of this but decided to leave out the chapter *for reasons important to him but not to the public*" [Nabokov, 1, 323–324; the italics are Tynyanov's].

Thus, the omission of an entire chapter, which really did evoke an astute comment from Katenin[15] regarding the unmotivated and sudden change in the heroine (reminding one of a theatrical transformation), is explained as being *"advantageous to readers"* and is not in fact motivated at all. At this point Pushkin's meticulous concern for *the coherence of the story,* which prompted him to use numbers—in some instances "empty" ones—to indicate omitted stanzas, begins to seem strange. Having analyzed these stanzas, we are convinced that there was no need to indicate even one of these omissions, for the omitted stanzas all relate either to digressions or to minutiae and details of everyday life, and only a few introduce new elements into the action, into the *plan.* The very fact that there are "empty" numbers, *unwritten* stanzas, means that there is no need to indicate any special role that might have been played by the omitted stanzas, no need to assume that lines and stanzas were eliminated because of imperfections or for personal reasons or out of fear of the censor.

The matter becomes clearer, although no less complex, if we look upon these omissions as a compositional device, whose entire significance—significance of extraordinary weight—rests not on the *plan,* or on the matter of *coherence,* or on the *events* (the story), but on the verbal dynamics of the work.

It is as if these numbers represent equivalents of stanzas and lines which can be filled with any content whatsoever. Instead of verbal matter, there is a dynamic sign pointing to it. Instead of a definite semantic weight, there is an indefinite, enigmatic semantic hieroglyph, which serves to complicate and semantically impede the following stanzas and lines. No matter how compelling the omitted stanza (artistically speaking), it is weaker than the sign of omission and the dots—if we view the matter from the standpoint of semantic complication and the intensification of verbal dynamics. This is perhaps even truer when an individual line is omitted, since the omission is emphasized by metric phenomena.[16]

The same orientation toward the *verbal* plan is found both at the end of *Eugene Onegin* and in the so-called attempts to continue it.

As a matter of fact, the real ending to *Eugene Onegin* is not stanza 51 of Chapter VIII, but "The Fragments from Onegin's Journey," which follow Chapter VIII and which are not in any way connected to the action or integrated into the novel at all. Not only Chapter VIII of *Eugene Onegin,* which was published in 1832, but also the first full edition of the novel, published in 1833, concluded with these "Fragments." Their inclusion was motivated by a preface, part of which we had reason to quote above: "The author candidly confesses that he omitted from his novel a whole chapter in which Onegin's journey across Russia was described. It depended upon him to designate this omitted chapter by means of dots or a numeral; but to avoid ambiguity he decided it would be better to mark as number eight, instead of nine, the last chapter of *Eugene Onegin,* and to sacrifice one of its closing stanzas" [Nabokov, 1, 323]. (Then follows reference to Katenin's remark about this exclusion being detrimental to the plan, since the resulting transition from Tatyana provincial miss to Tatyana *grande dame* is too sudden and unmotivated.) This preface, in which the renumbering of the chapters is carefully explained ("to avoid ambiguity") and the unmotivated change in the heroine is emphasized, was particularly ironic because it did not justify at all the inclusion of the "Fragments" after Chapter VIII. Here again Pushkin emphasized the verbal dynamics of his novel. Without question, the ending to *Eugene Onegin* is "The Fragments from the Journey," whose inclusion can only be explained in this way.[17] In these fragments the digressions are extremely condensed and concentrated, pushed to the limit—encompassed in a single sentence, a single phrase. Moreover, the digressions extend all the way from line 63 to the very end (line 203):

> 63.   I lived then in Odessa dusty . . .

> (J, 20)

> 91.   But let me take my ramble farther . . .
>   I called Odessa dusty then;
>   I might have called it muddy rather

> (J, 22)

> 109. But then another, hardly lesser,
>   Defect bedevils moist Odessa.

> (J, 23)

And finally, the concluding line of the entire novel (for *Eugene Onegin concludes* with it), line 203 of the "Fragments":

> 203. And so, I lived then in Odessa . . .[18]

> (J, 30)

This is the culmination of the whole novel. Here Pushkin realized what he had emphasized in the last stanza of Chapter VIII:

> And, loath to finish life's long story,
> *Abruptly* made his parting bow,
> As I to my Onegin now.

> (VIII, 51) [the italics are Tynyanov's]

Here the digressions are condensed to their compositional essence, pushed to the very limits of linguistic and syntactic play, and the purely verbal dynamics of *Onegin* are emphasized to an extraordinary degree.

Pushkin did everything possible to emphasize the *verbal* plan of *Eugene Onegin*. By publishing the novel one chapter at a time, with one or more years intervening, he quite obviously eliminated any possibility of focusing on the plan of *action*, on the *plot* as a *story*. The work is propelled not by semantic signs but by the dynamics of the *word* in its poetic meaning, not by the development of action but by the development of the *verbal* plan.

3

With regard to the *verbal* plan, what was decisive for Pushkin was the fact that *Onegin* was a *novel in verse*. When he first began work on *Onegin* in 1823, Pushkin wrote Prince Vyazemsky: "As for what I am doing, I am writing, not a novel but a novel in verse—a devil of a difference! It's in the genre of *Don Juan*. There's no use even to think of publishing; I am writing the way I feel like writing" [Shaw, p. 141].

Here an entire prose genre was to merge with verse, and Pushkin vacillates. Sometimes he regards *Eugene Onegin* as a novel, sometimes as a poem. The chapters in the novel become cantos in the poem. The novel, which parodies the conventional plot schemes of novels by means of compositional play, undergoes changes and intertwines with the mock epic.

December 1, 1823, Pushkin writes: "I am writing a new *poem*. . . . Two *cantos* are already finished" [Shaw, p. 146]. June 13, 1824: "I shall try to knock at the holy gates of the censor with the first *chapter* or *canto* of *Onegin*" [Shaw, p. 160]. March 24, 1825: "You compare the first *chapter* with *Don Juan*. . . . Wait for the other *cantos*. . . . The first *canto* is simply a rapid introduction" [Shaw, pp. 209–210]. June 8, 1825: "Send me Zhukovsky's opinion of the second *chapter* of *Onegin*" [Shaw, p. 225]. September 14, 1825: "I have four *cantos* of *Onegin* ready. . . . I am glad the first *canto* is to your liking" [Shaw, p. 253]. May 27, 1826: "In the fourth *canto* of *Onegin* I have depicted my own life" [Shaw, p. 311]. December 1, 1826: "In Pskov, instead of writing the seventh *chapter* of *Onegin*, I am losing the fourth at shtoss" [Shaw, p. 336]. March 10, 1828: "I am taking the liberty of sending you the last three *cantos* of *Onegin*" [Shaw, p. 352]. At the end of March 1828: "You would not want . . . to make me, your peace-loving friend, include hostile stanzas in the eighth *chapter* of *Onegin*, would you?" [Shaw, p. 352]. In October and November 1830: "The first hostile articles began to appear after the publication of the fourth and fifth *cantos* of *Eugene Onegin*. The critique of these *chapters* printed in the *Athenaeum*. . . . In the journal which he started to publish, Mr. Fedorov, examining the fourth and fifth *chapters* rather favorably. . . . No critique was written on the sixth *canto*. . . . I ran through the criticism of the seventh *canto* in *The Northern Bee* when I was visiting someone."[19] In a note Pushkin jotted down the same fall, he divided *Eugene Onegin* into three parts, each containing three *cantos* [Nabokov, 3, 255].

4

The verse form made itself felt in the oscillations between poem and novel, canto and chapter. But precisely because of this, in the verse text Pushkin emphasized the word *novel*,[20] which, in combining with verse (and thus being altered), became particularly perceptible:

> Tatyana was her name . . . I grovel
> That with such humble name I dare
> To consecrate a tender novel.

(II, 24)

> Allow me, with no cautious feeler
> Or foreword, to present at once
> The hero of my new romance [novel]:

(I, 2)

> Meanwhile, it seems, my present fable [novel]
> Has grown as far as Chapter One.

(I, 60)

> I started, early in my story [novel],
> To conjure up (see Chapter One)

(V, 40)

This *novel* is literary through and through. The heroes and heroines are presented against the backdrop of old novels as if they were parodistic shadows. *Onegin* is, as it were, a novel about imagination: Onegin imagined himself to be Childe Harold, Tatyana—a whole gallery of heroines, her mother—likewise. In addition, there are stereotyped characters like Olga, whose literariness is also underscored.

ONEGIN:

> Wry, gloomy, with Childe Harold vying,
> He seemed to languish in *salons,*

(I, 38)

> Onegin lived just like a hermit
>
> . . . .
> In tribute to Gülnare's singer
> He swam his Hellespontus too,
> Then drank his coffee, ...

(IV, 37)

OLGA:

> Gay as the morning sky, compliant
> And modest ever like the dove,
> Pure-minded like the Muse's client,
> Dear as the kiss of youthful love,

All flaxen-ringleted and smiling,
Celestial blue of eyes, beguiling
By grace of movement, form, and voice,
Thus Olga . . . Novels (take your choice)
All paint the type to satisfaction:
She's an engaging little elf.
I once was fond of her myself,
But now she bores me to distraction.

(II, 23)

TATYANA: But novels, which she early favored,
Replaced for her all other treats;

(II, 29)

Her fancy-fed imagination
Casts her in turn as heroine
Of every favorite creation,
Julie, Clarissa, or Delphine.

(III, 10)

THE MOTHER: . . . had a crush herself
On Richardson—still on her shelf.

(II, 29)

Here the close relationship between the initial portrayal of Tatyana, in love
with Richardson, and the portrayal of her mother should be noted.

All the clichés associated with the novel are parodistically underscored:

The hall, well sheltered from intrusion
Of world and wind, stood in seclusion
Upon a stream-bank; . . . .
. . . .
The park, far-rambling and unkempt,
Where pensive dryads dwelt and dreamt.

(II, 1)

The stately manor was constructed,
As manors always should be built

(II, 2)

And immediately, in the following stanza, in parodistic opposition:

For his own use Eugene selected
The room where till his late demise

> The laird had cursed his cook, inspected
> The same old view, and swatted flies.
>
> (II, 3)

Further examples:

> Bored in his lordly isolation,
> . . . .
> The backwood wiseacre commuted
> The harsh *corvée*. . . .
> . . . .
> The serf called blessings on his head.
>
> (II, 4)

> At every step, at every glance
> Your fateful tempter's countenance.
>
> (III, 15)

> Eugene in person, glances sparkling,
> Portentous like a shadow darkling,
> And she, as though by fire seared,
> Shrank and stood rooted as he neared.
>
> (III, 41)

> The moon behind the hills descended
> Before our fair young pilgrim found
> She should long since be homeward bound.
> . . . .
> But first requested free permission
> The manor empty to explore
>
> (VII, 20)

> Back home toward those lowly hovels,
> That pastoral sequestered nook
> A-murmur with its limpid brook,
>
> (VII, 53)

> She cannot hope to see him ever,
> And for her brother's death should sever
> All traffic with his slayer. . . .
>
> (VII, 14)

(Tatyana provides the motivation for the last two examples, which are presented from her perspective.)

The plan for a *lofty* novel is combined with the plan for a novel about everyday life, which is rendered through conversations and narrational devices.

On more than one occasion Pushkin confronted the problem of the prose substratum of the poem. Apropos of *The Prisoner of the Caucasus,* he wrote: "The description of Circassian customs, the most tolerable passage in the entire poem, is not connected with any of the events and is nothing more than a geographical *article or the account of a traveler.* The personality of the main character (it would be better to say, of the only character)—in all there are actually two characters—is *more suited to a novel than to a poem*" [*PSS,* 6, 371; the italics are Tynyanov's]. Regarding *The Fountain of Bakhchisaray* he wrote: "I superstitiously set to verse the story of a young woman" [Shaw, p. 151].

And here if we recall that many poets of the period drafted prose plans and programs for their verse, it becomes obvious that for Pushkin too prose programs were *primary* (in comparison with verse). The fact that we have Pushkin's programs and plans proves that the general compositional structure of his works harks back to a prose scheme. Thus, the digressions in *Eugene Onegin* are undoubtedly fundamental to the compositional design and are not a secondary phenomenon evoked by the verse. But this phenomenon never becomes an independent, perceptible element in the work; it always remains a part of the *substratum.*

5

The coupling of prose with poetry, which in *Eugene Onegin* constituted the compositional design, was made perceptible in and of itself and in the course of the work became a source of important effects. I will cite several examples of its dynamic utilization. The novel begins with a speech by Onegin:

> "But what a bore, I ask you, brothers,
> To tend a patient night and day
> And venture not a step away:
> Is there hypocrisy more glaring
> Than to amuse one all but dead,
> Shake up the pillow for his head,
> Dose him with melancholy bearing,
> And think behind a public sigh:
> 'Deuce take you, step on it and die!' "

(I, 1)

That a novel would open with a character's direct speech is interesting, but it is even more interesting because this direct speech opens a *novel in verse.* The flow of the colloquial intonation intrudes into the verse. What in prose would be perceived exclusively from the standpoint of meaning, in verse is perceived precisely as the consequence of the unusual combination of colloquial intonation with *verse.* Pushkin develops intonational devices in more and more striking ways, once that intonation has become perceptible:

"Come, introduce me!" "You're jesting." "No!"   (III, 2)

(Here within the limits of a single line there are three intonations.)

"There'll be a frightful crowd and babble,
A crush of every kind of rabble . . ."
"Oh, nonsense, not like that at all!"   (IV, 49)

"Why, Tanya, hush! We did not bother
With suchlike notions in my day;"   (III, 18)

(Striking colloquial intonation, introduced by the interjection *i*.[21])

"You must be taken sick, my baby;
May Heaven keep you and preserve!
See what you want, and let me serve . . .
I'll sprinkle Holy Water on you,
You're burning up with fever . . ." "No,
Not fever . . . I'm . . . in love, you know."   (III, 19)

(The jerky intonation of dialogue with repetition.)

"Take this, then, let your grandson bear it,
This note, I mean, to O. . . . , you know,
Our neighbor . . . only, tell him so,
He mustn't breathe a word about it,
Nor let my name be mentioned, pray . . ."   (III, 34)

(Even jerkier intonation with an unfinished word.)

The prince looked puzzled. "Aha [*aga*]!
You've long been out of circulation. . . ."   (VIII, 17)

(An intonational gesture.)

"I dandled you when you were small!"
"I had to cuff you, I recall . . ."
"I stuffed you full of ginger cookies!"   (VII, 44)

(Uniform, crescendoing intonation.[22])

Pushkin utilizes these colloquial intonations, which arise naturally in dialogue and become particularly significant in *verse,* for other goals as well. He uses them in narration to create a thin intonational "layer," in order to make the narrative itself a kind of indirect speech:

> And in her [Tatyana's] bearing they detected
> Something provincial and affected,
> They found her somewhat pale and small,
> But quite attractive, all in all.

(VII, 46)

> Who would have ventured to conjecture
> That she, who penned in tender youth
> That note, all candor and all truth,
> Which he still kept, a declaration . . .
> That same Tatyana—had he dreamed
> All this?—to whom it must have seemed
> That he disdained her age and station,
> Could face him now without a qualm,
> So blandly self-assured and calm?

(VIII, 20)

> . . . Ugh! No look or greeting crossed
> That zone of January frost!

(VIII, 33)

> Amazing! Not the slightest tremor,
> Her diction never halts or trips;
> No change of color, frown or stammer,
> No faint compression of the lips.

(VIII, 19)

The last example is a borderline case. We are not certain whether it is presented from the perspective of the hero or is introduced without any motivation as authorial speech.

In prose, authorial comments, addresses, etc., were a common device. Sometimes the author attained the status of a character. Sometimes he was a character, but remained inactive;[23] sometimes he served as the narrating character. In prose this device is hardly noticeable (for example, the "I" in Dostoevsky) given the intensity of the semantic principle. In verse, however, this device is extremely prominent, thanks to the fact that the authorial comments, which are set out as discrete clauses, violate the customary intonational structure of the verse and so become forms of intonational play:

The Latin vogue has now receded,
And I must own that, not to brag,
He had what knowledge may be needed

(I, 6)

All poets—*while I'm on these subjects*—
Are given to daydreaming love;

(I, 57)

On which, *ye gods,* she starts to strum;
"Into my golden chamber come!"

(II, 12)

What foes he had, what friends he had
(Same thing, perhaps, on close inspection)
Befouled him, each in his own way.

. . . .
What friends they were to me, my friends!

(IV, 18)

And thus he mourned; we call Romantics
Bards of this dark and languid strain.
(Though how this name describes such antics
I cannot see; but why explain?)
Not long before the dawn was shining,   (VI, 23)
                [all italics are Tynyanov's]

(In this case an entire sentence is set off.)

That London's fashionable classes
In their fastidious slang decry
As *vulgar.* (And I vainly try . . .

I'm very fond of this locution,
And vainly try to render it;

(VIII, 15–16)

The last example is especially interesting because the interruption occurs on the boundary of two stanzas, and this creates a kind of gesture at the end of VIII, 15.

Pushkin goes even further, introducing colloquial interjections into authorial addresses:

"Whom did your verse immortalize?"
Why, nobody, my friends, I swear it [*ei-bogu*]!

(I, 58)

But fie on me [*T'fu*]! What prosy blather,

(J, 19)

H'm! H'm! [*Gm! Gm!*] . . . Sweet reader, let me question,
How is your family? All well?

(IV, 20)

In the last example the interjections are especially perceptible, since the verse and the meter make them equivalents of actual words. The device is condensed to the point that it becomes a gesture:

Tatyana, "*oh* [*akh*]!" He [the bear] stretches forth

(V, 12)

What in a prose novel would have purely semantic significance, what would be perceived as an important moment in the development of the plot, becomes in verse a perceptible concrete motor image:

> All of a sudden, hoofbeats! Quaking,
> She strains . . . Yes, closer . . . In a chaise [comes]
> Eugene! "Oh [*akh*]!" Like a shadow fleeting
> Tatyana crossed the hall, retreating
> Past landing, stairs, and courtyard, right
> Into the park in headlong flight;
> Without a backward glance, she rounded
> The pleasance, bridgelets, formal lawn,
> Pond-lane and grove, and like a fawn
> Broke through the lilac screen and bounded
> Through flower beds toward the bank,
> And there, her bosom heaving, sank

(III, 38)

> Upon a bench . . .

(III, 39)

In this fragment the dynamic power of the verse is revealed most clearly of all. Here enjambment acquires the primitive meaning of a motor image: "In a chaise comes" (a rise and a pause, which is made more perceptible precisely because it is not supposed to be here, because the preceding line is linked with the following one)—"Eugene" (a fall and then again a pause). Here the verses acquire a remarkable dynamic power from enjambment:

> Without a backward glance, she rounded
> The pleasance,

all the way up to

> Upon a bench . . .

It is not meaning that is perceived here. Rather these verses form a kind of obstacle for the motor image, and, therefore, "sank"[24] acquires the concreteness of a verbal gesture, a concreteness achieved solely because of the dynamics of the verse.

Even the simplest phenomena associated with the prose novel are deformed by the verse to such a degree that they become comic (precisely as a consequence of the fact that a prose phenomenon is transformed into a verse phenomenon, that phonic elements replace semantics as the organizing principle).

We can see this, for example, in III, 34, where the colloquial intonations seem to destroy a word. But the destroyed element, which in prose would not assume the role of an independent word but would only stand in for it, in verse becomes a full metrical member, a verse word:

> This note, I mean to O. . . , you know,
> Our neighbor . . .

In stanza 37 of the same chapter:

> And lost in thought; and there, dear heart,
> Her dainty finger, idly wand'ring,
> Upon the clouded window traced
> An "E" and "O" all interlaced.

Here the device is condensed, but the concreteness of the image recedes into the background because the verse acts to make the letters resemble full-fledged words (even ones that rhyme[25]).

Even words with secondary meaning, expressing the category of grammatical relationships (particles, etc.), are raised by the *verse,* by their metrical role in the verse, to the status of full-fledged words. It is this in part that determines the difference between the language of poetry and the language of prose. Poetic language has difficulty coming to terms with secondary words.

Likewise, the device of enumeration, which in prose plays the role of differentiation, acquires quite another meaning in verse:

> The entries: Bear, Bench, Blizzard, Briar,
> Bridge, Dagger, Darkness, Feasting, Fire,
> And so on. . . .

> (V, 24)

> Across Tverskaya's holes and cobbles,
> Past shops and lanterns, crones and youths,

By convents, gardens, mansions, booths,
Bokharans, sleighs, muzhiks in blouses,
By cossacks, merchants, kitchen yards,
Past battlements and boulevards,
Parks, pharmacies, and fashion houses,
Past gates where guardian lions rear,
While daws about the crosses veer.

(VII, 38)

Here the enumeration is particularly humorous because the disparate objects that are enumerated are equated not only by the intonation (that happens in prose as well) but by the uniform pulse of the verse.

6

The deformation of the novel by verse manifested itself in the deformation of small units and in the deformation of large groups, and finally as a result the entire novel was deformed. Out of the merging of two elements, out of their mutual struggle and interpenetration a new form was born.

In *Eugene Onegin* the deforming element was the verse. The word as an element with meaning yielded to the verse word, was eclipsed by it. Thanks to the power of the verse, secondary words, interjections expressing relationships of grammatical categories, were equated with full-fledged words. The same thing happened to conventional designations (abbreviated words, initials) as well. In prose they always stand in for reality, but in verse, where they play the role of metric and sometimes rhyming words, they are deformed even with regard to their own *meaning,* and, by being adjacent, they acquire a semantic (comic) coloring. When colloquial interjections are introduced into the verse mechanism, they are concretized to the point of becoming phonic gestures.

In a prose novel one has the impression that the segments are motivated by actual reality. These segments may not always correspond to the development of the story, but, because of the close resemblance between prose fiction and prosaic speech, it is inevitable that the essential will be distinguished from the less important (if only in the conventional sense of this word). Verse segments are perceived precisely as verse. Their uniformity is sanctioned by the verse; the essential is equated with the nonessential. The dynamics of Sterne's *Tristram Shandy* is the digression. In *Eugene Onegin,* where the digressions are equated to the "action" by the verse itself, this does not happen. An emotional shift in a prose novel is always perceptible; in verse segments such a shift is created naturally by the verse itself.

As we have stated, in *Eugene Onegin* the deforming element was the verse. In this order: the metrical character of the verse; then the phonic character of the verse in the narrow sense of the word; and, finally, the stanza.

The Structure of
Eugene Onegin

YURY LOTMAN
(1966)

The literary character of Pushkin's novel in verse has repeatedly been discussed in scholarly literature.[1] In the mid-1940s Grigory Gukovsky proposed a penetrating and fruitful definition of realism, a definition which then took hold in a wide range of scholarly works. Gukovsky pointed out that *Eugene Onegin* was the first work in Russian literature to give expression to the idea that character is determined by environment and historical factors and that this is reflected in the way the heroes are constructed. "Pushkin applied the same method he had worked out in his lyric poetry and drama of the 1820s to his verse novel. He no longer saw man as a metaphysical entity but as a historical and national phenomenon, as a type."[2]

A wide circle of scholars accepted Gukovsky's view that a man's character is determined by his environment and that this social determinism, as it were, forms the basis of nineteenth-century Russian Realism. At the time this seemed to be the correct way to approach the problem. However, scholarship has moved forward, and now it is obvious that in and of itself this concept does not fully explain the literary significance of realistic works. It does not adequately define Realism as a literary phenomenon, since we arrive at the same definition whether we consider literary, publicistic, or philosophical texts. Furthermore, we know that in the history of philosophy this concept was formulated prior to the time it was embodied in literary works; so this was really a case of art's moving to "appropriate" a concept that was set forth outside it. It is no accident that this interpretation of Realism jibes best with those historical and literary periods in which the literary practice of the writer followed the theoretical constructs of the critic and publicist (i.e., the "Natural School"[3]).

Perhaps I am not above reproach either, for the article I published on *Eugene Onegin* in 1960[4] was also based on the assumption that literature is an illustrative activity whose value is defined by the degree of accuracy with which it embodies extrinsic ideas. (The purpose of that article was to elaborate on Gukovsky's view of *Eugene Onegin*.) The formulas I used, such as "a man is

Translated and published with the permission of the Copyright Agency of the USSR.

defined by the extent to which he is enlightened," "by whether or not he is numbered among 'intelligent' skeptics or naive enthusiasts," "by his relationship to his people, history, and social milieu," can tell us a great deal about the general concept of Pushkin's novel, but they are equally applicable to other art forms (prose, drama, painting) and in themselves are extraneous because they are philosophical concepts. References to these formulas do not really help us understand the specific nature of literary realism, which is created strictly by the verbal text—specifically by this particular verbal text.[5]

In my earlier article I attempted to show how Pushkin's ideas about what determines a man's character changed during the years he was working on the text of *Eugene Onegin,* and that, correspondingly, the literary plan of the novel underwent evolution. However, even if one assumes that I succeeded in showing that the evolution in literary principles was in accord with the evolution in Pushkin's ideas, the question still remains: Why does the novel exist in the reader's consciousness as a whole, given such a clear shift in the author's aesthetic position? To put it differently: Why didn't Pushkin, who was such a severe critic of his own work, make changes in chapters which were written from a position he no longer espoused? Or why didn't he abandon the novel? Often Pushkin did abandon unfinished sketches of stories and novels which lagged behind the tempo of his literary development, but with *Eugene Onegin* he proceeded differently. Over the years he stored up chapters, he "garnered the stanzas"[6] of his "motley"[7] novel and created an organic whole from heterogeneous parts. The inevitable contradictions which arose as a result of this process did not disturb him at all. To the contrary, as if fearing that the reader would not notice them, he hurried to report at the end of Chapter I:

> I have gone over it severely,
> And contradictions there are clearly
> Galore, but I will let them go,

(I, 60)

And, in fact, contradictions are evident in the characterization of the hero, even within Chapter I. From studying Pushkin's evolution as a poet it is quite easy to explain why he altered the ironic characterization of Onegin's disenchantment (cf., for example, the mocking note to I, 21, where Onegin's exclamation that the ballet leaves him cold is labeled "A trait of chilled sentiment worthy of Childe Harold" [Nabokov, 1, 313n5]), making that disenchantment appear tragic in I, 44–46: "He who has lived and thought can never/ Look on mankind without disdain" [I, 46]. It is equally easy to explain why the characterization of Tatyana changed. From "She knew our language only barely/. . . In her own language she was slow/ To make her meaning clear"

[III, 26], she became "Tatyana—Russian in her feeling" [V, 4]. It is considerably more difficult, however, to explain why Pushkin did not eliminate these and other contradictions when he compiled the stanzas and chapters into a single text. When we attempt to list these "contradictions," we become convinced that they occupy a very significant place in the literary fabric of the novel. This makes us wonder if what we perceive to be a "contradiction" is not really a significant structural element.

In order to resolve this question let us introduce the concept "point of view." This concept manifests itself as the relationship of a system to its subject ("system" in a given context may be realized either on the linguistic level or on some other higher level). By "subject of a system" (whether ideological, stylistic, or whatever) we mean a consciousness capable of generating such a structure and, consequently, a consciousness which can be reconstructed in the process of reading the text.

A literary system is constructed as a hierarchy of relationships. The very concept "to have meaning" implies the presence of a certain attitude, that is, of a definite orientation. But since the literary model, in its most general form, reproduces an image of the world for a given consciousness, that is, models the relationship between the individual and the world (in particular, between a cognizing individual and the cognizable world), then this orientation will be both subjective and objective in nature.

In Russian poetry before Pushkin typically all the subjective and objective relationships expressed in the text converged in a single fixed focus. In eighteenth-century literature, which we know as Classicism, this single focus transcended the author's personality and coincided with the concept of Truth, in whose name the artistic text spoke. The relationship of truth to the world represented became the artistic point of view. The fixed and monosemantic nature of these relationships, their convergence toward a single center, corresponded to the notion that Truth was eternal, indivisible, and immutable. Though indivisible and unchanging, Truth was at the same time hierarchical—that is, it revealed itself to different consciousnesses in differing degrees. Hence the corresponding hierarchy of points of view, which formed the basis of the rules governing the various genres.

In Romantic poetry the points of view also converged toward a firmly fixed center, and the relationships themselves were monosemantic and highly predictable (this explains why the Romantic style is so easy to parody). The center, which was the subject of the poetic text, coincided with the author's personality, becoming his lyrical double.

However, a text may be structured in such a way that the points of view are not focused in a single center but form a diffused subject made up of different centers. The relationships between these centers create additional meanings. For example:

In vain I hasten on to Sion's heights; I feel
Sin ravenously racing close upon my heel;
Thus, dusty nostrils down the shifting sand-trail bent,
The hungry lion tracks a fleeing roebuck's scent.

[*PSS*, 3, 419]

Clearly one cannot attribute both "dusty nostrils" and "fleeing roebuck's scent" to a single point of view. The first has as its subject the man observing the lion; the second, the lion itself, since man is incapable of perceiving the track of a roebuck as something which gives off an odor, to say nothing of a pungent scent.[8] But "hungry lion" and "dusty nostrils" do not have a single subject center either, since one implies an observer who is not concretized in space, while the other implies the contemplation of the lion at close range, at a distance which would permit the observer to discern the dust covering the lion's nostrils. Thus, even if we restrict ourselves to the final two lines, we observe not one focal center for the points of view but a kind of diffused subject embodying a series of viewpoints. The relationships between them become an additional source of meanings. Obviously, if one is striving to create an illusion of reality, to endow certain combinations of words with the character of the reproduced object, one will find that this second structural principle opens up greater possibilities.

As we noted, in Russian literature before Pushkin typically the point of view expressed in a work was fixed. In this sense the multiplicity of viewpoints in the genre system of Classicism and the singleness of viewpoint (based on philosophical subjectivism) in the lyrics of Zhukovsky were phenomena of the same sort. The number of possible viewpoints was small, determined for the reader by his previous literary experience. Inevitably, if the reader found that a literary text diverged from some point of view, he assumed that this was a sign that the text belonged to another system with another fixed structure.

Ruslan and Lyudmila marked an important stage in the development of Pushkin's own literary system. Here the innovation was largely negative in character. Taken as a whole the poem did not fit any one of the canonical points of view. The mechanism used, which posed such difficulties for critics at the time, was relatively simple. Each of the individual fragments constituting the text easily accorded with traditional notions. However, the commingling of points of view, which would have been unthinkable in the preceding period, transformed the world of Pushkin's poem into a kingdom of relativity. The fixed nature of the relationships between the work and its subject was undermined by play, which ironically revealed the conventionality of all the viewpoints ascribed to the author.

Eugene Onegin marked a new stage in text construction.

In a well-known note, "On Prose" (1822), Pushkin explicitly opposes expression and content in purely semiotic terms. He condemns periphrastic prose (most notably the school of Karamzin) because it is not truthful. And here the criteria for truthfulness are very interesting. Pushkin rejects the notion that a text should be constructed according to conventional rules. To the structurally organized text ("glittering expressions") he opposes "simple" content, conceived of as life itself. Now "life" in a literary work is non-aestheticized speech; it is a text which is artistically unorganized and therefore true. But naturally, any text, once it is incorporated into a literary work, becomes a literary text. Thus we are confronted by the problem of constructing a literary (i.e., organized) text, which will imitate a nonliterary (unorganized) one, of creating a structure which will be perceived as the *absence* of structure.

In the course of this article we will attempt to show how such a textual structure is generated in Pushkin's novel. As we will see, in order to evoke in the reader the feeling that the text is simple, its language colloquial, its plot lifelike and spontaneous, and its characters natural, a far more complex literary construct was required than any known at that time. The effect of *simplification* was achieved at the price of greatly *complicating* the structure of the text.

In the 1822 note Pushkin expresses the conviction that only by renouncing the false conventionality of existing literary styles can one achieve artistic truth. To tell the truth means to state things simply. Pushkin writes: "One day d'Alembert said to La Harpe: 'Don't extol Buffon to me. The man writes: "The Noblest of all the acquisitions of man was this proud, fiery creature!" etc. Why not simply say "horse"? . . . I read some theater-lover's review: "This youthful nurseling of Thalia and Melpomene, generously gifted by Apol. . . ." My God, just put "this good young actress" and continue; be assured no one will notice your expressions'. . ." [Proffer, p. 18].

Thus, Pushkin opposes one way of constructing a text (a false, literary way) to another which is true and "simple." It should be emphasized that here "simple" content is not understood to be diverse reality at all, but ideas. It is ideas that Pushkin opposes to the conventionality of literary expression: prose "demands ideas—and then more ideas; without them glittering expressions serve no purpose" [Proffer, p. 19]. The notion that ideas can be best expressed in simple language, that they are antithetical to the artificiality of conventional literary speech, emerged more than once at moments of crisis in Romanticism. It is no accident that Belinsky called the era of Romanticism "the century of phraseology" and that Lermontov wrote:

> When will at last we barren Russians
> All specious trumpery outreach,
> And find for thought a simple speech,
> And noble voices for the passions.9

In 1822 Pushkin thought that "simple speech" was essential for prose but that "poetry was another matter" [Proffer, p. 19]. However, subsequently his understanding of "prose" (prose conceived of as simplicity, the rejection of literary conventions, the movement of content into an extra-literary series— i.e., realia) expanded to embrace poetry as well. And here the process of prosifying poetry was viewed as a struggle for truthfulness and pithiness.

One of the most widespread devices used in *Eugene Onegin* is that of exposing the real-life content of romantic expressions when brought face to face with the "prose" of reality. This device is particularly obvious in passages where the author's style is formed in opposition to the system of conventional literary expressions. The text that emerges consists of two paired parts, where one of the parts—the "simple" one—acts as the *meaning* of the other, exposing its literary conventionality:

> He thinks: "I will be her redeemer,
> Will not permit the shameless schemer
> With sighs and praise and sultry art
> To tempt the inexperienced heart,
> That noisome gnawing worm shan't slither
> Near the young lily's tender stem
> Oozing his poison, to condemn
> The yet half-open bud to wither."
> *And all this meant was, in the end:*
> *I shall be shooting at my friend.*

(VI, 17) [the italics are Lotman's]

Here the "simple" part of the text, which is constructed of extrasystemic vocabulary (extrasystemic from the standpoint of the conventional first part), is perceived to be prose or, what in this case is equivalent, content, the *meaning* of Lensky's monologue. The specific rhythmic organization of the text ceases to be relevant. It is not significant since it is characteristic of both opposing texts, and therefore it does not preclude our thinking that the final two lines lack structural organization. The rhythmically organized text becomes a re-creation of colloquial prose. Everything that distinguishes the text from colloquial prose loses significance, and everything that coincides with it becomes a sign of differentiation.

In using this kind of construction, the author must constantly cite an "antisystem" of style in order to create models of literary "veracity." Pushkin does this extensively in *Eugene Onegin*. For example:

> The moon, celestial luminary,
> . . . .
> But now we only see in her
> But one more lantern's tarnished blur.

(II, 22)

Upon the fashion [modish] word "ideal,"
Did dreamless sleep upon him steal;

                                                                    (VI, 23)

Blest they who can, their doubts suspended,
All frigid reasoning dismiss,
And find an ease as all-consoling
As travelers drunk on inn-beds lolling,
Or, gentler, butterflies that cling
To honeyed blossoms in the spring.

                                                                    (IV, 51)

Since only the "false" plane has structure, the "true" plane can only be characterized negatively as the *absence* of any marked structural quality. Similarly, Tatyana shapes her own personality in correspondence with the system of expression she has assimilated:

. . . and in herself discovers
Another's glow, another's smart,

                                                                    (III, 10)

Her real personality is the living equivalent of the conventional romantic heroine she perceives herself to be:

Her fancy-fed imagination
Casts her in turn as heroine
Of every favorite creation,
Julie, Clarissa, or Delphine.

                                                                    (III, 10)

Here we are not talking about any concrete system of consciousness, although in this cluster of ideas one can easily detect elements of Romanticism. What we have in mind is much broader: it is the conventional bookish model of the world, encompassing the *sum total* of literary traditions present in Pushkin's time. This unified structure, wherein are joined the conventional image of the heroine and the conventional system of expression, also determines the type of hero. In this system Onegin can be perceived only when translated into Tatyana's conventional language. To her, he is "dear hero" [III, 10], "guardian angel," or "demon of temptation" [Tatyana's letter]. If he is "dear hero," he will be "perfection come to earth," endowed "With soul so tender, intellect,/ Abetted by attractive looks" [III, 11]. If he is a "tempter," he will be "a brooding Vampire,/ Or wandering Melmoth, dark of brow" [III, 12]. In Tatyana's mind each of these variants of the hero will decisively determine the development of the love affair. Either vice will inevitably be punished ("by the end of the final quire"—III, 11) and true love triumph, or the seduced heroine will perish ("She murmurs: 'I shall be undone' "—VI, 3). For Tatyana, the traditional norms of plot construction in the novel become a ready-made pattern for comprehending real-life situations. In order to expose the falsity of this (romantic) model of the world, an inverted system is constructed. Instead of "art reproducing life," "life reproduces art."

Tatyana is more inclined to see Onegin as a "tempter": ". . . before her loomed/ Eugene in person, glances sparkling,/ Portentous like a shadow darkling" [III, 41]. That there is no third possibility is evident from the fact that the romantic Lensky thinks in the very same categories: "redeemer—seducer" [VI, 17]. Pushkin affirms the falsity of this interpretation of the hero and, consequently, the falsity of this entire structure. However, when it comes to giving a true characterization of the hero, he can speak only in negative terms:

> But hers [our hero], whatever type you guessed,
> *Was not a Grandison, at best.*
>
>   (III, 10) [the italics are Lotman's]

Thus, when a style is called for that is not simply polemically opposed to literary clichés but completely independent of them, this system is no longer satisfactory.

Let us consider the stylistic structure of two stanzas from Chapter IV in the novel:

IV, 34

> As freedom's lover, glory's gallant,
> His mind on stormy fancies fed,
> Vladimir might have tried his talent
> On odes—which Olga never read.
> Your elegist, now, must be fearful
> To face his love and read his tearful
> Effusions [creations] to her! Yet than this,
> They say, there is no higher bliss.
> Yes—count the modest lover blessed
> Who may recite [his dreams] beneath the eyes
> Of Her for whom he sings and sighs,
> Young beauty, languorously placid!
> Though this, when all is said and done,
> May not be her idea of fun.

IV, 35

My own harmonious contriving
I bring to my old Nanny's ears,
A crop of dreams for the surviving
Companion of my childhood years.
To chase a dull meal, I belabor
A stray and unsuspecting neighbor
By seizing hold of his lapel
And spouting blank verse by the ell,
Or else (and here the joke is over)
Beset by heartache and the Muse,
I wander by my lake and choose
To flush a flock of ducks from cover,
Who, hearing those sweet stanzas ring,
Break from the shoreline and take wing.

In these stanzas one and the same situation—"the poet reading his verses to his beloved"—is repeated over and over in stylistically contrasting systems. Each of the three components in the situation—"poet," "verses," "beloved"—is transformed:

I	Vladimir	odes	Olga
II	elegist	creations	love
III	modest lover	dreams	Her for whom he sings and sighs, Young beauty, languorously placid
IV	I	crop of dreams	old Nanny
V	I	blank verse	neighbor
VI	I	sweet stanzas	flock of ducks

Correspondingly, each time the act of reading the verses is designated in a particular way: "I read," "I spout," "I flush." And the reaction of the one being read to undergoes the same sort of "transformation":

. . . Odes—which Olga never read.

. . . Yet than this,
They say, there is no higher bliss.

Blessed . . .
Though this, when all is said and done,
May not be her idea of fun.

Who, hearing those sweet stanzas ring,
Break from the shoreline and take wing.

The meaning of these lines is constructed according to a complex system. Each separate lexical unit acquires additional stylistic meaning depending on

the nature of the structure into which it is incorporated. Here the immediate
environment of a given word plays a particularly important role. The act of the
poet in III and IV is characterized almost identically: "Who may recite [read] his
dreams . . ." [III]; "Crop of dreams . . . and / My own harmonious contriving
/ I bring [read] . . ." [IV]. But since in III this act links "the modest lover" and
his "young beauty, languorously placid," while in IV it links the "I" and his
"old Nanny," identical words are endowed with profoundly different stylistic
meaning. "Dreams" in III is incorporated into a conventional (in the literary
sense) phraseological structure and correlates with IV according to the princi-
ple of false expression—true content. "Old Nanny" relates to "young beauty,
languorously placid" in exactly the same way. But the antithesis, "conventional
poetry—true prose," is complicated by the fact that the "old Nanny" is
simultaneously "companion of childhood years," and this combination is
presented not as an ironic juncture of different styles but as a monosemantic
stylistic group.

In place of the antithesis "poetry—prose," there emerges the antithesis
"false poetry—true poetry." "Freedom's lover, glory's gallant" and his "odes"
acquire special meaning from the fact that "Olga never read them." (In this
case the relationship works both ways: Olga's indifference reveals the bookish
nature of Lensky's "stormy fancies" since the line ". . . odes—which Olga
never read" sounds like the voice of sober prose, which in the structure of the
novel is invariably associated with truth. But, at the same time, the indisputa-
ble poetic charm of "glory" and "freedom" and "stormy fancies" underscores
Olga's mundaneness.) In the lines "Yet than this,/ They say, there is no higher
bliss" the combination of two units which are equated—one colloquial, the
other conventional and literary—results in a "deflating" stylistic effect.

However, meaning in these stanzas is not generated simply by syntagmatic
linkage. The words arranged vertically in columns are perceived as variants of
single invariant meanings. And not one of them relates to another as content to
expression: they are superimposed one on the other, producing complex mean-
ing. The incorporation into a single paradigm of such remote and seemingly
incompatible notions as "Her for whom he sings and sighs," "old Nanny,"
"neighbor," "flock of ducks" is an important means of semantic intensification.
The result is a unique kind of semantic suppletion, where words which are
disparate and remote are perceived at the same time to be variants of a single
concept. This makes each variant of the concept difficult to predict and,
consequently, particularly significant. And here it is essential to note some-
thing else. Not only do remote lexemes converge in a complex arch unit, but
elements from different (often opposing) stylistic systems are incorporated into
a single stylistic structure. Such an equation of different stylistic levels leads to
the realization of the relativity of each separate stylistic system and to the
emergence of irony. The dominant role irony plays in creating the stylistic
unity of *Eugene Onegin* is obvious and has been noted by critics.

In Wilhelm Küchelbecker's diary we find a definition of humor which helps us understand the stylistic function of irony. Küchelbecker writes: "The biting satirists Juvenal and Persius limit themselves to a single feeling—indignation, anger. The humorist is just the opposite: he is open to all feelings but he is not their slave. They do not rule him; he rules them and plays with them. By the same token it is this that distinguishes him from the elegist and the lyricist, who are completely carried away and enslaved by feelings. The humorist amuses himself at their expense and even makes fun of them."[10] In Küchelbecker's view irony is the transcendence of any definite "feeling." It is the systematic toleration of any value judgment, any "feeling," and thereby it offers the writer the possibility of standing above them (making fun of them). If we consider that "feelings" in Küchelbecker's terminology closely corresponds to our notion of systemic orientation ("point of view"), then the implication of his statement for a writer who seeks to build a literary structure that will transcend the subjectivism of one or another system and move in the direction of extrasystemic reality becomes obvious. Moreover, as we have had occasion to note, the principle of a multiple recoding of systems[11] can serve both Romantic irony, where the poet seeks to demonstrate that each of the systems is relative but to transcend their limits is to step into emptiness, and realistic irony, where the writer seeks to recreate the essential character of reality by superimposing different stylistic structures, thereby canceling out the very principle of subjectivity.

In the 1822 fragment "On Prose," Pushkin demanded "ideas—and then more ideas." (This principle could be realized not only in prose but also, for example, in satire, in a political comedy like Griboedov's *Woe from Wit,* which was written from the point of view of a man who had "become enlightened.") Subsequently Pushkin advanced a new principle, which surprisingly he defined as "chatter" [*boltovnia*]. In a letter to Anton Delvig dated November 16, 1823, he confessed: "I am now writing a new poem [*Eugene Onegin*], in which I chatter to the limit" [Shaw, p. 143]. Later, in the summer of 1825, he admonished Alexander Bestuzhev: "Enough of your writing *rapid* tales with romantic transitions—that is all right for a Byronic poem. But a novel requires *chatter*" [Shaw, p. 224]. As critics have repeatedly noted, what Pushkin had in mind here was the "narrative quality" which he felt the novel called for. However, it would seem he had something else in mind as well: that stylistic diversity which prompted Nikolay Polevoy to compare Chapter I of *Onegin* to a musical "capriccio."[12] And, in I, 34, precisely at the point where the author feigns to have digressed accidentally, he terms his own lyre "garrulous" [*boltlivyi*].

The mechanism of irony constitutes one of the fundamental keys to the novel's style. Let us examine it on the basis of the following examples:

II, 36

So they grew old like other mortals.
At last a final mansion drew
Asunder its sepulchral portals

Before the husband [spouse], wreathed anew.
Near dinnertime he died, contented,
By friends and neighbors much lamented,
By children, faithful wife, and clan,
More truly mourned than many a man.
He was a simple, kindly *barin,*
And where his earthly remnant rests,
A graven headstone thus attests:
"A humble sinner, Dmitri Larin,
God's servitor and brigadier,
Found peace beneath this marble here."

                    II, 37

To his ancestral hall returning,
Vladimir Lensky sought the plot
Of his old neighbor's [humble] last sojourning
And sighed in tribute to his lot.
And long he mourned for the departed:
"Poor Yorick!" quoth he, heavy-hearted,

In these stanzas the stylistic breaks are produced not by a system of transformations of one and the same extrastylistic content, but by a succession of different stylistic modes, one replacing the other. The first line, "So they grew old like other mortals," is clearly neutral. What is striking here is the marked absence of any signs pointing to a particular poetic style. Stylistically speaking, this line is *without point of view.* The next three lines are characterized by a sustained lofty (in the spirit of the eighteenth century) style and by a corresponding point of view. The periphrases "a final mansion drew/ Asunder its sepulchral portals" and "wreathed anew" (instead of "he died") and vocabulary like "spouse" and "wreathed" could not have evoked in Pushkin's reader any other literary associations. However, in the following line the solemn periphrases are translated into another system: ". . . he died." The style of the subsequent lines is not neutral at all because of its prosaic character, which is achieved by linking accurate prosaic expressions. In the given textual construct, these endow the style with a tinge of veracity and hence poeticality, which then combines with the elements that deflate the style. The detail "near dinnertime" in combination with "a final mansion drew/ Asunder its sepulchral portals" gives a slightly comic tinge to the old-fashioned rural naiveté. The time of death is reckoned by the time of eating. Compare:

                    . . . I like to tell
          The hours' advancing, like the locals.
          By luncheon, dinner, tea; we yokels

Keep track of time without much fuss;
Our stomachs watch the clock for us.

(V, 36)

The same comic effect is created by combining the solemn "much la-
mented" and "neighbors," since the character of the neighboring country
landowner was familiar to the reader of *Eugene Onegin* and had already been
sketched out earlier in the same chapter [II, 4–6]. In light of this, "children"
and "faithful wife," who "much lamented" the deceased, can only be perceived
as archaic and pompous stock phrases. All of this sheds light on the point of
view in lines 2 to 4. The lofty poetics of the eighteenth century is perceived as a
string of clichés, behind which lies an old-fashioned and naive consciousness,
provincial culture, simple-mindedly experiencing the yesteryear of the nation's
intellectual development. However, the line "More truly mourned than many a
man" reveals that these archaic clichés contain an element of truth. Although
they remain clichés, obligatory in epitaphs of the high style, and, although
they bear the imprint of clumsy provincialism, they do not prevent the text
from being a bearer of truth. The line "He was a simple, kindly *barin*"
introduces a completely unexpected point of view. The semantic orientation
suggests that the subject of this system is a serf. For the subject of the text, the
object (Larin) is a *barin*[13] and *from this point of view* appears "simple" and
"kind." In this way the contours of patriarchal relationships ruling in the
Larins' household continue to be outlined. All these repeated stylistic and
semantic switches are synthesized in the concluding lines of the stanza—in the
text of the epitaph (which simultaneously is both solemn ["humble sinner,"
"found peace"] and comic ["God's servitor *and* brigadier"]), with its naive
equation of earthly and heavenly powers.

In the following stanza we encounter a new group of switchings. The
conventionally poetic (in the tradition of the familiar epistle) "To his ancestral
hall returning" gives way to information about Lensky's visit to Larin's grave.
To Lensky, the "last sojourning of his old neighbor" seems "humble," that is,
prosaic ("humble prose"—III, 13). (From the naive point of view, realized in
the epitaph, it is grand.) "And sighed in tribute to his lot" takes us into
Lensky's view of the world, which fittingly concludes with the exclamation
"Poor Yorick!" Lensky constructs his "I" on the model of Hamlet and recodes
the whole situation in images of Shakespearean drama.

These examples have demonstrated (any of the novel's stanzas could have
been analyzed in an analogous manner) that the succession of semantic and
stylistic breaks creates not a focused but a diffused multiple point of view,
which thus becomes the center of a supersystem perceived to be an illusion of
reality itself. Moreover, what is important to the realist, who seeks to tran-
scend the subjectivism of semantic and stylistic "points of view" and to
recreate objective reality, is the nature of the relationships between these

multiple centers, these diverse (adjacent or superimposed) structures. None of
them cancels out any of the others; they all correlate. Consequently, the text
means not only what it means but something else as well. The new meaning
does not cancel out the old but correlates with it. Because of this, the literary
model reproduces an extremely important dimension of reality—that aspect
which attests to the impossibility of giving any definitive and final interpreta-
tion.

The principle of the semantic and stylistic break is only one manifestation
of the general structural design of *Onegin*. On a lower level it is manifested in
the intonational diversity of the novel. Different intonations coexist and,
consequently, are equated on a scale of artistic values, and all this is organically
linked with the principle of "chatter"—transcending the limits of any fixed
literary structure.

Since the lexical and semantic structure of the verse influences the style of
recitation, the equivalence of different types of intonation is determined by the
breaks analyzed above. However, there is also another aspect to the "melod-
ics": its link with the rhythmic and syntactic texture of the verse.

On the level of intonation, the reproduction of reality is in large measure a
matter of re-creating the illusion of colloquial intonations. This does not mean
that constructions borrowed directly from everyday speech are simply trans-
ferred into the text of the novel. After all, the structure of the verse and the
specific manner in which it is recited are given; therefore, "colloquiality" is not
a rejection of them but a matter of building a superstructure over them. Thus,
on this level too the aim of imitating a free and easy manner of speaking turns
on the creation of a "superstructure." And here again objectivity (perceived as
being "beyond structure") results from increasing both quantitatively and
qualitatively the structural bonds and not from weakening them—not from
destroying structures but from creating a structure of structures (systems).

Obviously, a verse text divided into stanzas (what is more, into stanzas
with an intricate rhyme scheme), is more removed from "simple" (non-verse)
speech then is a nonstrophic poetic text. The structural quality of the text is
more evident. In the history of Russian literature there have been instances
where poets have sought to make verse prosaic by eliminating the external
signs of verse structure: rejecting rhyme, rejecting poeticisms, creating an
abundance of enjambments (what could be called "the minus device"). In the
present case, however, we are dealing with a phenomenon that is exactly the
opposite.

It is remarkable that a whole series of European poets—Byron, Pushkin,
Lermontov—all turned to a stanzaically constructed text at the very moment
they rejected the subjective construct of the Romantic poem. As it turns out,
the imitation of the diversity of living speech, of colloquiality, the intonation

of "chatter" is linked with the uniformity of strophic divisions. This paradox
requires an explanation.

The fact of the matter is that prosaic intonation (like any other) is defined
not by the presence of any particular elements but by the relationship between
structures. To make verse sound like unorganized speech, one must not only
give it the structural features of a nonpoetic text but recall in the mind of the
person who is reciting the verse both the cancelled-out and the cancelling
structures simultaneously.

In the case of *Onegin* the principal means of depoetization is the noncoinci-
dence of syntactic and metrical units. It is their relationship (in this case, one of
noncoincidence) that becomes the significant sign of the structure. However,
the significant noncoincidence of syntactic and rhythmic units (experienced by
the reciter as the triumph of language over verse, that is, as "naturalness") can
only occur when there are uniform and fixed boundaries marking the rhythmic
divisions of the text. In Pushkin's "southern," Romantic poems with their free
stanzas—that is, stanzas of varying lengths—the relationship between su-
pralinear syntactic and rhythmic units could not become a semantically dis-
tinguishing element.

In *Eugene Onegin* the text of the chapters (on a supralinear level) is strictly
divided into stanzas and within the stanzas, thanks to a constant rhyme
scheme, into discrete parts—three quatrains and one couplet—which sym-
metrically repeat from stanza to stanza. For example:

> Those albums of a country maiden
> You all have met with, I'll be bound:
> Front, back, and sides scrawled up and laden
> With sayings of perfervid sound.
>
> There, all orthography defying,
> Parade, unscanning but undying,
> Those rhymes of faithful friendship's pledge,
> Sprawled out or squeezed along an edge.
>
> Atop page one you will find written
> *Qu'écrirez-vous sur ces tablettes?*
> Beneath it: *t. à v. Annette;*
> And on the last by this you're smitten:
>
> "She who loves you more must then sign
> Her name and pledges under mine."

(IV, 28)

It is quite obvious that the stanza is divided into well-defined parts not only by
the system of rhymes but also by the syntactic structure which fully corre-
sponds to it.

We see that the rhythmic boundaries which divide the stanza (between the first and second quatrains, between the second and third quatrains, and between the final quatrain and the couplet) coincide with the syntactic boundaries and that consequently distinct separating pauses occur. These divisions within the stanza are maintained throughout the entire novel. The work is constructed this way so as constantly to renew and sustain in the reader the feeling that the text is being intersected by boundaries.

According to Grigory Vinokur, there are 260 instances in the novel where the rhythmic and syntactic units coincide at the end of the first quatrain and only 75 where they do not because of enjambment (to the former must be added another 32 instances where the quatrains are linked syntactically, but the link is optional, so that here too we note the absence of enjambment).[14] Less often the second quatrain is separated from the third. This can be explained by the specific character of the thematic construction of the stanza. However, here too, syntactic and rhythmic units coincide in the vast majority of cases (187+45 instances where the link with the third quatrain is optional, as opposed to 134). Correspondingly, for the third group we find 118+119, as opposed to 127.[15] On the basis of this count we can conclude that the bulk of the text of the novel is constructed this way to make the reader constantly anticipate pauses in certain structurally programmed places. It is the presence of this expectation that makes its violation significant, and such violation is practiced extensively in the novel: after the first quatrain in the stanza, almost 25% of the time; after the second, 57.75% of the time; after the third, more than 53% of the time.

The correlation between violations and observances of the rhythmic boundary is like this so that the reader will be constantly aware of the boundary and therefore recognize the significance of boundary violation. At the same time, this correlation makes the reader feel that these violations occur sufficiently often that they cannot be accidental. Here, obviously, the reader is confronted not by one poetic structure but by two interrelated structures—one affirming certain regularities, the other violating them. Moreover, it is the relationship between the two (one structure perceived against the background of the other) that is the bearer of meaning.

In order to understand the substantive nature of this relationship, it is essential to focus on its effect on the "melodics" of the verse. We will use this term, which Boris Eikhenbaum introduced into the study of Russian verse,[16] in two ways—distinguishing the melodics of the verse formed by the relationship of rhythmic and syntactic units (that is, "syntactic melodics," hereafter designated SM) from the melodics of the verse formed by the relationship of the vocabulary used by the poet to stylistic norms, according to a scale of lofty, low, poetic, nonpoetic (that is, "lexical melodics," hereafter designated LM). The relationship between SM and LM forms the intonation of any given verse line. And here, examining SM, we must abstract ourselves from the words of which the line is constructed and, examining LM, we must abstract ourselves from the relationship between rhythmic and syntactic units. In the latter case syntactic constructions interest us only insofar as they influence the stylistic meaning of one or another lexeme or group of lexemes.

Let us consider several aspects of SM in *Eugene Onegin*. Eighteenth-century verse did not permit the divergence of syntactic and rhythmic units. Thus, for example, alexandrine verse consisted of a fixed rhythmic group of two lines, divided internally into verses and joined together by paired rhymes. It has been demonstrated that the rhythmic divisions (lines, couplets) and syntactic divisions almost always coincided in this kind of verse. Therefore, the relationship between them could not be a bearer of meaning. It was not significant in a poetic sense, since divergence was taken as evidence of low quality. Such SM formed the basis of a measured and unchanging intonation; it was a sign that the text belonged to poetry. Any other kind of intonation was taken as a sign that the text was not a poetic one.

The principle of the coextensiveness of syntactic and rhythmic boundaries was so universal that, in those genres in which freer syntactic constructions were called for (genres which stood counter to "high," "lofty" poetry), "free verse" became firmly established. This allowed the poet to extend or shorten the rhythmic unit according to the length of the syntactic unit, but it did not permit the two to diverge. Something analogous happened in the strophic division of Pushkin's "southern," Romantic poems. The length of the stanza was free, determined by the length of the utterance (a phenomenon analogous to the line in "free verse" and to the paragraph in prose). Therefore, the relationship between these two units, which always coincided, could not be a bearer of meaning. Consequently, SM was a constant quantity. Of course, the SMs of a poem written in alexandrine verse, the SMs of a poem written in "free verse," and the SMs of one of Pushkin's "southern" poems were all different, but within each of these text types the quantity was constant.

The text of *Eugene Onegin* is constructed in a totally different manner. The structure, which implies both the presence of clear-cut rhythmic boundaries and the possibility of significantly violating them, creates a large number of semantically distinctive differentiations. In the abstract, the stanza (broken down by quatrains) contains sixteen possible relationships between syntactic and rhythmic units [see table next page].

However, this does not exhaust the variety of relationships possible between syntactic and rhythmic units. Each of the lines can end in a long pause with the intonation of syntactic completion (represented graphically by a period or some other sign equal to it); in a short pause, marking the end of an elementary syntactic unit with the intonation of incompleteness (most often represented graphically by a comma); in a pause intermediate in length with the intonation

	Presence of Enjambment	Absence of Enjambment
Stanza	+	−
	−	+
First quatrain	+	−
	−	+
Second quatrain	+	−
	−	+
Third quatrain	+	−
	−	+

in all   16   possibilities

of continuation, but where this continuation is not as obligatory as in the previous case (this intermediate pause is represented graphically by a semicolon or the conventional equivalent, a colon or a dash). Finally, a line can conclude with the absence of a syntactic pause, the pause coming in the middle of the following line or at the end of it. The *last two cases* should be carefully distinguished, since the first permits maximal intonation of noncoincidence, the second minimal.

Thus, five different syntactic endings are possible for each line in the stanza. And, since order also influences the number of intonational possibilities, this produces 5^{14} varieties. It is not important that not all of the possible relationships between the rhythmic and syntactic divisions are actually encountered in the text of the novel or that some of them are encountered only rarely, since, in the first place, rarity only increases significance, and, in the second, the actual text is perceived in relationship to a great number of possibilities just as a concrete speech act is perceived in relationship to language.

In actual fact, since each of these possible relationships has its own SM, the number of intonational types is inexhaustibly rich. Moreover, because the reader constantly feels that this abundance violates the intonation dictated by the rhythmic structure, he has the impression that the intonation has been liberated, that a free intonation has been created which overcomes the conventionality of poetic speech. By complicating the structure, an illusion is created that it has been destroyed, that non-verse speech has triumphed over verse. And here the general SM of a stanza results from the juxtaposition of the SM of its separate parts. Thanks to the variety of relationships, parts of the stanza almost always carry different intonations, but the information which the intonation of the entire stanza carries does not result from the sum of perceptions formed in succession but from their interrelationship.

In this way the stanza takes shape as an intonational whole. But it too is perceived in relation to other stanzas. And that law of breaks—of the juxtaposition of different intonations—which reigns within the stanza also defines strophic composition.

The same can be said of LM as well. In eighteenth-century poetry there was unity of intonation not only because syntactic and rhythmic units were not permitted to diverge but because the type of vocabulary permissible in each poetic genre was strictly governed. Thus, the general character of LM was predetermined by the genre itself, well before the reciter turned to a concrete text. The classification of specific groups of vocabulary according to "poetic–nonpoetic" was preserved in Romantic poetry as well.

In *Eugene Onegin* not only was the vocabulary permissible in poetry enlarged, but diverse and opposing stylistic layers were treated as equivalents. (It was this principle that shaped LM, as well as the style of Pushkin's novel in general.) The kind of play that this entailed was based on the assumption that any words could turn up side by side and any stylistic antinomy could be presented as an isomorphism. For example:

> At last a crackling frost enfolded
> Fields silvered o'er with early snows:
> (All right—who am I to withhold it,
> The rhyme you knew was coming—ROSE)

> (IV, 42)

In this case the conventionality of the literary cliché is exposed by putting words that belong to the same stylistic level and are in this sense equivalents into different categories. "Snows" signifies a phenomenon of the real world, while "rose" is only a rhyme.

Thus, the general principle shaping the construction of Pushkin's novel in verse is realized on this level as well.

In my earlier article on *Eugene Onegin,* I attempted to outline the principles which shaped the construction of character in the novel.[17] Now I would like to ascertain the means used to unite such diverse literary constructs into a single structural whole. One of the distinguishing features of character construction in the novel is the fact that the novel can very easily be divided into distinct synchronic sections (chapters). Pushkin conceived of the chapter as the natural unit of construction—moreover, a unit of considerable independence.[18]

As a rule, the chapter initiates a new turn in the plot and, as I tried to show in my earlier article, a new type of character construction as well. The chapter, taken as a separate unit, is a synchronically organized system, in which each literary character is only one component of the function, the correlation of characters. As Grigory Vinokur noted: "The relationships between the author and his hero are fully formulated, and, in order to understand the meaning of *Eugene Onegin* as a whole, one must recognize that these relationships are no less important than the plot. . . . Pushkin's objective was not simply to portray a typical individual. Alongside the portrait of the hero there emerges a self-portrait of the narrator, so that each illuminates the other."[19]

In each synchronic section not only the author and the hero but all the characters form a correlated system. Moreover, what is given, what is primary, is not the characters themselves but the functions (the relations between characters). Thus, for example, the plan for Chapter I assumed a relationship between a moral ideal (approximating the aims of the Union of Welfare[20]) and a superficial young man, outwardly in contact with progressive circles (like Repetilov in Griboedov's play *Woe from Wit*). This opposition is manifested in the following antitheses:

	A	B
I	true education "lofty mind"	superficial, shallow education
II	civic-mindedness "lofty labors"	idleness empty pursuits superficial Byronism
III	true love	worldly love-making
IV	lofty art	light poetry voluptuous, base art

Outwardly the hero belongs to the author's circle. He is capable of carrying on a "learned conversation" with the ladies and "even a manly argument," just as Repetilov can talk about "Byron, as well as important matters." The real difference between the author and the hero—i.e., their true functional relationship—is revealed through the ironic tone of the narration.

However, in the second synchronic section of Chapter I, the functional correlation between characters breaks down. Onegin acquires significance; his character gains depth. He draws closer to the sphere of values esteemed by the author. Simultaneously, changes in the conceptual field take place. Disenchantment and skepticism, which were treated as signs of worldly eccentricity, move over into column A, becoming the sign of a "lofty mind" ("He who has lived and thought . . ."—I, 46). Both inwardly and in terms of the plot, Onegin and the author find themselves side by side. With the function broken, the irony disappears.

In each new synchronic section it is the *relationship* established between characters that is most important. The intelligent skeptic (Onegin) versus the youthful enthusiast (Lensky); the sister Olga—ideal of the "romantic" poet, a hackneyed literary character (". . . Novels [take your choice]/ All paint the type to satisfaction"—II, 23) who is most ordinary versus the sister Tatyana with a provincial name and original character; "contemporary man" (Onegin) versus the girl (Tatyana) who believes "in simple folkways of the past" [V, 5]. The most complicated antitheses are found in Chapter VIII. However, within each synchronic section the antithesis does not emerge by itself but derives from a general notion of what contemporary man is like. Moreover, the traits of the hero are not presented as a list of individually named qualities but as a sum total of oppositions. In the course of working on the novel Pushkin evolved. A number of his ideological and artistic principles changed, and, correspondingly, his notion of what constitutes the essence of character changed. This is illustrated by the following diagram:

I	Intellect	Ignorance
	Education	Superficiality
II	Intellect	Enthusiasm
	Skepticism	Naiveté
	Sobriety	Romanticism
III	Intellect	Naiveté
	Spiritual weariness	Capacity for pure feeling
IV	Intellect	Naiveté
	Egoism	*Narodnost'* [national character]
V	Striving for	Fulfillment of duty
	happiness	Intellect

Depending on the nature of the principal antithesis (and we are only pointing out the principal ones; in the actual fabric of the work each synchronic section is represented not by one antithesis but by a hierarchy of semantic oppositions), the hero type also changes. In each case the heroes—i.e., the intersecting functional relationships within each synchronic section—acquire distinct characteristics and different motivations. Thus, if in Chapter I superficial education, ignorance of the achievements of enlightenment, was perceived as an obstacle separating the hero from the positive ideal, then in Chapter V the very same thing (in combination with naiveté and spiritual purity) is perceived as a positive factor.

In this way, one and the same character may in different chapters be characterized in very different—at times, totally opposite—ways. Compare the assessment of Onegin in Chapter VII, 24, which is offered as the opinion of the author (and Tatyana), to that in Chapter VIII, 12, which is presented as the opinion of "sensible men." The number of such breaks in the construction of character is very large. However, while the adoption of new principles of constructing the artistic model was prompted by changes in Pushkin's literary method and inevitably led to contradictions in the text of the novel, the refusal to eliminate them immediately acquired something of a programmatic character. Moving through the text, the reader passed from one synchronic section to another, and each of them created its own particular image of the functional relationships. But, even though in the separate publications of Chapter I (1825), Chapter VII (1830), and Chapter VIII (1832), Onegin seemed to represent totally different characters belonging to different systems, when brought together in the indivisible text of the novel, all these Onegins took on a certain unity.

A paradigm of the character emerges where very different functional intersections, designated within each individual section by the name "Onegin," come together vertically to form a system of variants joined by invariant unity. Because of this, the new literary principles do not cancel out the old ones but join with them to form a functional whole. Thus, instead of affirming the idea that there is only one possible way to represent an object by literary means, it is suggested that there are many ways to re-create an object in its different states.

Because the poetics of the novel establishes a new paradigm of characters for each chapter and, simultaneously, makes the novel an unfinished construct, one permitting continuation, the heroes acquire the character of complex structures, which in principle can be interpreted in an infinite number of ways. This reveals yet another structural principle of Pushkin's novel. Not only is it constructed as a system of correlated heterogeneous structures and parts, but it *has an open character.* In terms of plot it can go on; it can be extended in other respects as well. It is a literary system, a construct which is designed in principle to be extended. With this is linked the novel's special fate, for its open character makes it correlate with the *entire* subsequent tradition of Russian literature and not simply with some of its individual trends. The deliberately polemical plot construct is also linked with this. The novel—and Belinsky pointed out this peculiarity[21]—is not finished by anything. The usual novel construct, which Pushkin sensed to be a jumping-off point, implied the presence of a plot ending. Addressing his friends, Pushkin wrote ironically:

> You are quite justified in saying
> That it is strange, in fact betraying

Bad form, to break the novel off
With half already set in proof;
And that the least one ought to do
Is get the hero duly married,
Or if he can't do better, buried,
And with a cordial adieu
Deliver the supporting cast
Out of the labyrinth at last.

(*PSS,* 3, 1, 397)

"To break the novel off," to leave it unfinished, is a conscious literary principle. The novel "with an ending" (a "marriage" or a "burial") gives a finite model of infinite life. Pushkin consciously constructs his text as a re-creation of the very principle of infinity. At the same time we should point out something else: the finite model relates to the infinite as *langue* to *parole* (to use the terminology of Ferdinand de Saussure). The novel "with an ending" relates to real life the same way (this, of course, does not preclude the fact that within the text of such a novel levels of language and speech can and should be distinguished). Pushkin's novel is an unfinished text which reproduces another unfinished text (reality). Consequently, the language (the finite system) is not given; it must be deduced. And the test of the truth of this language will be whether it can serve to describe the speech act (the text) accurately. But one and the same text can be described in different ways. And it is precisely this that constitutes the profound literary significance of Pushkin's novel in verse. The author gives the reader complexly structured language which the reader must take for speech (language acts as imitation of the speech of another system). The complex structural construction becomes a re-creation of extrastructural reality.

The reader himself must create a model which will be both more defined and, inevitably, more impoverished than Pushkin's text. Precisely this was the subsequent fate of Pushkin's novel. It nourished different interpretations—very often ones that distorted its meaning and were polemical. All too often the interpretations oversimplified the novel. But it was this breadth of possible interpretations that permitted the novel to exert such a long influence on subsequent literature. And this also makes it rich material for proving the thesis that only a work which has lost its literary significance can be exhaustively interpreted.

Often we hear complaints that critics and literary scholars are too inclined to contradict each other when they give interpretations of great works of literature. This is taken as a sign of scholarly weakness. Of course, one can do nothing but deplore those cases where disagreement results from a lack of honesty or insufficient erudition on the part of the critic. But we should not forget that a literary work is a special structure capable of storing information. It "transmits" new interpretations as long as it enjoys artistic life. This is characteristic of every significant work of literature and of *Eugene Onegin* to the highest degree.

Discourse in *Eugene Onegin*

MIKHAIL BAKHTIN
(1940)

[The uniqueness of speech in the novel as a special literary genre has been far from adequately researched.[1] The majority of works analyzing language and style in the novel are] to a greater or lesser degree remote from those peculiarities that define the novel as a genre, and they are also remote from the specific conditions under which the word lives in the novel. They all take a novelist's language and style not as the language and style of a *novel* but merely as the expression of a specific individual artistic personality, or as the style of a particular literary school or finally as a phenomenon common to poetic language in general. The individual artistic personality of the author, the literary school, the general characteristics of poetic language or of the literary language of a particular era all serve to conceal from us the genre itself, with the specific demands it makes upon language and the specific possibilities it opens up for it. As a result, in the majority of these works on the novel, relatively minor stylistic variations—whether individual or characteristic of a particular school—have the effect of completely covering up the major stylistic lines determined by the development of the novel as a unique genre. And all the while discourse in the novel has been living a life that is distinctly its own, a life that is impossible to understand from the point of view of stylistic categories formed on the basis of poetic genres in the narrow sense of that term.

The differences between the novel (and certain forms close to it) and all other genres—*poetic* genres in the narrow sense—are so fundamental, so categorical, that all attempts to impose on the novel the concepts and norms of *poetic* imagery are doomed to fail. Although the novel does contain poetic imagery in the narrow sense (primarily in the author's direct discourse), it is of secondary importance for the novel. What is more, this direct imagery often acquires in the novel quite special functions that are not direct. Here, for example, is how Pushkin characterizes Lensky's poetry [*Eugene Onegin* II, 10, ll. 1–4]:

> Of love he sang, love's service choosing,
> And limpid was his simple tune [song]

As ever artless maiden's musing,
As babes aslumber, as the Moon

(a development of the final comparison follows).

The poetic images (specifically the metaphoric comparisons) representing Lensky's "song" do not here have any direct poetic significance at all. They cannot be understood as the direct poetic images of Pushkin himself (although formally, of course, the characterization is that of the author). Here Lensky's "song" is characterizing itself, in its own language, in its own poetic manner. Pushkin's direct characterization of Lensky's "song"—which we find as well in the novel—sounds completely different [VI, 23, l. 1]:

Thus he wrote *murkily* and *limply* . . .

In the four lines cited by us above it is Lensky's song itself, his voice, his poetic style that sounds, but it is permeated with the parodic and ironic accents of the author; that is the reason why it need not be distinguished from authorial speech by compositional or grammatical means. What we have before us is in fact an *image* of Lensky's song, but not an image in the narrow sense; it is rather a *novelistic* image: the image of another's [*chuzhoi*] language, in the given instance the image of another's poetic style (sentimental and romantic). The poetic metaphors in these lines ("as babes aslumber," "as the Moon" and others) in no way function here as the *primary means of representation* (as they would function in a direct, "serious" song written by Lensky himself); rather they themselves have here become the object of representation, or more precisely of a representation that is parodied and stylized. This novelistic image of another's style (with the direct metaphors that it incorporates) must be taken in *intonational quotation marks* within the system of direct authorial speech (postulated by us here), that is, taken as if the image were parodic and ironic. Were we to discard intonational quotation marks and take the use of metaphors here as the direct means by which the author represents himself, we would in so doing destroy the novelistic image [*obraz*] of another's style, that is, destroy precisely that image that Pushkin, as novelist, constructs here. Lensky's represented poetic speech is very distant from the direct word of the author himself as we have postulated it: Lensky's language functions merely as an *object* of representation (almost as a material thing); the author himself is almost completely outside Lensky's language (it is only his parodic and ironic accents that penetrate this "language of another").

Another example from *Onegin* [I, 46, ll. 1–7]:

He who has lived and thought can never
Look on mankind without disdain;
He who has felt is haunted ever
By days that will not come again;

No more for him enchantment's semblance,
On him the serpent of remembrance
Feeds, and remorse corrodes his heart.

   One might think that we had before us a direct poetic maxim of the author
himself. But these ensuing lines:

All this is likely to impart
An added charm to conversation

(spoken by the posited author to Onegin) already give an objective coloration
to this maxim. Although it is part of authorial speech, it is structured in a realm
where Onegin's voice and Onegin's style hold sway. We once again have an
example of the novelistic image of another's style. But it is structured some-
what differently. All the images in this excerpt become in turn the object of
representation: they are represented as Onegin's style, Onegin's world view. In
this respect they are similar to the images in Lensky's song. But unlike Lensky's
song these images, being the object of representation, at the same time repre-
sent themselves, or more precisely they express the thought of the author, since
the author agrees with this maxim to a certain extent, while nevertheless seeing
the limitations and insufficiency of the Onegin-Byronic world view and style.
Thus the author (that is, the direct authorial word we are postulating) is
considerably closer to Onegin's "language" than to the "language" of Lensky:
he is no longer merely outside it but in it as well; he not only represents this
"language" but to a considerable extent he himself speaks in this "language."
The hero is located in a zone of potential conversation with the author, in a
zone of *dialogical contact*. The author sees the limitations and insufficiency of the
Oneginesque language and world view that was still fashionable in his (the
author's) time; he sees its absurd, atomized and artificial face ("A Muscovite in
the cloak of a Childe Harold," "A lexicon full of fashionable words," "Is he not
really a parody?"[2]); at the same time however the author can express some of
his most basic ideas and observations only with the help of this "language,"
despite the fact that as a system it is a historical dead end. The image of
another's language and outlook on the world [*chuzhoe iazyk-mirovozzrenie*],
simultaneously represented *and* representing, is extremely typical of the novel;
the greatest novelistic images (for example, the figure of Don Quixote) belong
precisely to this type. These descriptive and expressive means that are direct
and poetic (in the narrow sense) retain their direct significance when they are
incorporated into such a figure, but at the same time they are "qualified" and
"externalized," shown as something historically relative, delimited and in-
complete—in the novel they, so to speak, criticize themselves.
   They both illuminate the world and are themselves illuminated. Just as all
there is to know about a man is not exhausted by his situation in life, so all
there is to know about the world is not exhausted by a particular discourse

about it; every available style is restricted, there are protocols that must be observed.

The author represents Onegin's "language" (a period-bound language associated with a particular world view) as an image that speaks, and that is therefore preconditioned [*ogovorennii govoriashchii*]. Therefore, the author is far from neutral in his relationship to this image: to a certain extent he even polemicizes with this language, argues with it, agrees with it (although with conditions), interrogates it, eavesdrops on it, but also ridicules it, parodically exaggerates it and so forth—in other words, the author is in a dialogical relationship with Onegin's language; the author is actually *conversing* with Onegin, and such a conversation is the fundamental constitutive element of all novelistic style as well as of the controlling image of Onegin's language. The author represents this language, carries on a conversation with it, and the conversation penetrates into the interior of this language-image and dialogizes it from within. And all essentially novelistic images share this quality: they are internally dialogized images—of the languages, styles, world views of another (all of which are inseparable from their concrete linguistic and stylistic embodiment). The reigning theories of poetic imagery are completely powerless to analyze these complex internally dialogized images of whole languages.

Analyzing *Onegin,* it is possible to establish without much trouble that in addition to the images of Onegin's language and Lensky's language there exists yet another complex language-image, a highly profound one, associated with Tatyana. At the heart of this image is a distinctive internally dialogized combination of the language of a "provincial miss"—dreamy, sentimental, Richardsonian—with the folk language of fairy tales and stories from everyday life told to her by her nurse, together with peasant songs, fortune telling and so forth. What is limited, almost comical, old-fashioned in Tatyana's language is combined with the boundless, serious and direct truth of the language of the folk. The author not only represents this language but is also in fact speaking in it. Considerable sections of the novel are presented in Tatyana's voice-zone (this zone, as is the case with zones of all other characters, is not set off from authorial speech in any formally compositional or syntactical way; it is a zone demarcated purely in terms of style).

In addition to the character-zones, which take up a considerable portion of authorial speech in the novel, we also find in *Onegin* individual parodic stylizations of the languages associated with various literary schools and genres of the time (such as a parody on the neoclassical epic formulaic opening, parodic epitaphs, etc.). And the author's lyrical digressions themselves are by no means free of parodically stylized or parodically polemicizing elements, which to a certain degree enter into the zones of the characters as well. Thus, from a stylistic point of view, the lyrical digressions in the novel are categorically distinct from the direct lyrics of Pushkin. The former are not lyrics, they are the novelistic image of lyrics (and of the poet as lyricist). As a result, under careful analysis almost the entire novel breaks down into images of languages that are connected to one another and with the author via their own characteristic dialogical relationships. These languages are, in the main, the period-bound, generic and common everyday varieties of the epoch's literary language, a language that is in itself ever evolving and in process of renewal. All these languages, with all the direct expressive means at their disposal, themselves become the object of representation, are presented as images of whole languages, characteristically typical images, highly limited and sometimes almost comical. But at the same time these represented languages themselves do the work of representing to a significant degree. The author participates in the novel (he is omnipresent in it) with *almost no direct language of his own*. The language of the novel is a *system* of languages that mutually and ideologically interanimate each other. It is impossible to describe and analyze it as a single unitary language.

We pause on one more example. Here are four excerpts from different sections of *Onegin:*

> (1) Thus a young [*molodoi*] good-for-nothing muses,
>
> (I, 2, l. 1)
>
> (2) . . . Our youthful [*mladoi*] singer
>   Has gone to his untimely end!
>
> (VI, 31, ll. 10–11)
>
> (3) I sing of a young [*mladoi*] friend, his checkered
>   Career in fortune's cruel coil.
>
> (VII, 55, ll. 6–7)
>
> (4) What if your pistol-shot has shattered
>   The temple of a dear young [*molodoi*] friend,
>
> (VI, 34, ll. 1–2)

We see here in two instances the Church Slavonic form *mladoi* and in two instances the Russian metathesized form *molodoi*. Could it be said that both forms belong to a single authorial language and to a single authorial style, one or the other of them being chosen, say, "for the meter"? Any assertion of the sort would be, of course, barbaric. Certainly it *is* the author speaking in all four instances. But analysis shows us that these forms belong to different stylistic systems of the novel.

The words *"mladoi pevets"* [youthful singer] (the second excerpt) lie in Lensky's zone, are presented in his style, that is, in the somewhat archaicized style of Sentimental Romanticism. The words *"pet'* " [to sing] in the sense of *pisat' stikhi* [to write verses] and *"pevets"* [singer] and *"poet"* [poet] are used by Pushkin in Lensky's zone or in other zones that are parodied and objectified (in

his own language Pushkin himself says of Lensky: "Thus he wrote. . . ."). The
scene of the duel and the "lament" for Lensky ("My friends, you mourn the
poet. . . ." [VI, 36, l. 1] etc.) are in large part constructed in Lensky's zone, in
his poetic style, but the realistic and sober-minded authorial voice is forever
breaking in; the orchestration in this section of the novel is rather complex and
highly interesting.

The words "I sing of a young friend" (third excerpt) involve a parodic
travesty on the formulaic opening of the neoclassical epic. The stylistically
crude link-up of the archaic, high word *mladoi* with the low word *priiatel'*
[acquaintance, friend] is justified by the requirements of parody and travesty.

The words *molodoi povesa* [young good-for-nothing] and *molodoi priiatel'*
[young friend] are located on the plane of direct authorial language, consistent
with the spirit of the familiar, conversational style characteristic of the literary
language of the era.

Different linguistic and stylistic forms may be said to belong to different
systems of languages in the novel. If we were to abolish all the intonational
quotation marks, all the divisions into voices and styles, all the various gaps
between the represented "languages" and direct authorial discourse, then we
would get a conglomeration of *heterogeneous* linguistic and stylistic forms
lacking any real sense of style. It is impossible to lay out the languages of the
novel on a single plane, to stretch them out along a single line. It is a system of
intersecting planes. In *Onegin,* there is scarcely a word that appears as Pushkin's
direct word, in the unconditional sense that would for instance be true of his
lyrics or Romantic poems. Therefore, there is no unitary language or style in
the novel. But at the same time there does exist a center of language (a verbal-
ideological center) for the novel. The author (as creator of the novelistic whole)
cannot be found at any one of the novel's language levels: he is to be found at
the center of organization where all levels intersect. The different levels are to
varying degrees distant from this authorial center.

Belinsky called Pushkin's novel "an encyclopedia of Russian life." But this
is no inert encyclopedia that merely catalogues the things of everyday life. Here
Russian life speaks in all its voices, in all the languages and styles of the era.
Literary language is not represented in the novel as a unitary, completely
finished-off and indisputable language—it is represented precisely as a living
mix of varied and opposing voices [*raznorechivost'*], developing and renewing
itself. The language of the author strives to overcome the superficial "liter-
ariness" of moribund, outmoded styles and fashionable period-bound lan-
guages; it strives to renew itself by drawing on the fundamental elements of
folk language (which does not mean, however, exploiting the crudely obvious,
vulgar contradictions between folk and other languages).

Pushkin's novel is a self-critique of the literary language of the era, a
product of this language's various strata (generic, everyday, "currently fashion-
able") mutually illuminating one another. But this interillumination is not of

course accomplished at the level of linguistic abstraction: images of language are inseparable from images of various world views and from the living beings who are their agents—people who think, talk, and act in a setting that is social and historically concrete. From a stylistic point of view we are faced with a complex system of languages of the era being appropriated into one unitary dialogical movement, while at the same time separate "languages" within this system are located at different distances from the unifying artistic and ideological center of the novel.

The stylistic structure of *Eugene Onegin* is typical of all authentic novels. To a greater or lesser extent, every novel is a dialogized system made up of the images of "languages," styles and consciousnesses that are concrete and inseparable from language. Language in the novel not only represents, but itself serves as the object of representation. Novelistic discourse is always criticizing itself.

In this consists the categorical distinction between the novel and all straightforward genres—the epic poem, the lyric and the drama (strictly conceived). All directly descriptive and expressive means at the disposal of these genres, as well as the genres themselves, become upon entering the novel an object of representation within it. Under conditions of the novel every direct word—epic, lyric, strictly dramatic—is to a greater or lesser degree made into an object, the word itself becomes a bounded [*ogranichennii*] image, one that quite often appears ridiculous in this framed condition.

The basic tasks for a stylistics in the novel are, therefore: the study of specific images of languages and styles; the organization of these images; their typology (for they are extremely diverse); the combination of images of languages within the novelistic whole; the transfers and switchings of languages and voices; their dialogical interrelationships.

The Stylistic World
of the Novel

SERGEY BOCHAROV
(1974)

> Pushkin, too, belongs to the same epoch, and that is why he
> was the first to speak as an independent and *conscious* Rus-
> sian. . . . Yes, here is a child of his epoch; here is the whole
> epoch, consciously looking at itself *for the first time*.
> —Dostoevsky on *Eugene Onegin*

> Belinsky called Pushkin's novel an "encyclopedia of Russian
> life." But this is no inert encyclopedia that merely catalogues
> the things of everyday life. Here Russian life speaks in all its
> voices, in all the languages and styles of the era.
> —Mikhail Bakhtin[1]

1

When Chapter I of *Eugene Onegin* first appeared in 1825, it was published along
with the poem "Conversation between Bookseller and Poet."[2] The latter
served as a kind of introduction and was perceived as such by the first readers.
In the final reply of the "Conversation," the Poet shifts from poetic reminis-
cences couched in suitable language directly into prose. It is as if this move-
ment from poetry to prose were transmitted to Chapter I of *Onegin,* which
followed the "Conversation." The same kind of stylistic progression is con-
stantly reproduced in the text. Consider, for example, the following stanza:

> To hold life cheap for Sound, he never
> Experienced the sacred curse:
> Do what we would, he took forever
> Iambic for trochaic verse.

> (I, 7)

In the first two lines of this quatrain poetry is described figuratively
through refined periphrasis; in the second couplet poetry is presented from a

Translated and published with the permission of the Copyright Agency of the USSR. Some
lines of Walter Arndt's translation of the verse have been modified to conform with Bocharov's
remarks about particular words.

prosaic point of view, as an empirical fact—as iambs, trochees, and rhyme. By laying bare the mechanism of the verse the "lofty" image of poetry is systematically destroyed in the novel in verse. It should be pointed out that the very emphasis on "verse" in Pushkin's definition of the genre—"not a novel but a novel in verse"[3]—indicates a detached view of verse. "Novel in verse" is not simply a complex definition. It signifies duality, a counterpoint of diverse principles, "indivisible yet ununitable."

While the quatrain is clearly divided into two equal parts, the second two lines not only add a new dimension but *translate* what has been said from "poetic" into "simple" language. As a result not only the "sacred curse" but also the hero, who does not experience it, are deflated. Thus a theme is introduced which will be significant both in terms of the plot and in terms of the novel's stylistic development: namely, that the hero of the novel, who on one compositional plane is a "friend" of the poet–author and on another a friend of the poet Lensky, is himself *no poet*.

In Chapter III we find another quatrain constructed in a similar manner:

> The secret miscreant's perdition,
> His terrors, shall be left untold,
> But soberly [simply] I will unfold
> Old Russia's family tradition;

(III, 13)

In the transition signaled by the word *prosto* [simply], content and expression merge completely. "Simply" switches the speech[4] exactly in the middle of the quatrain into another register, from the sphere of "style" into what seems to be life itself. Within the rhythmic syntactic unit there is movement toward reality and "prose."

The two stylistic poles of Chapter I are found in adjacent stanzas 35 and 36:

> The peddler struts, the merchant dresses,
> The cabman to the market presses,
> With jars the nimble milkmaids go,
> Their footsteps crunching in the snow.
> . . . .
> But, worn-out by the ballroom's clamor,
> And making midnight out of dawn,
> The child of luxury and glamour
> Sleeps tight, in blissful shade withdrawn.

These two stylistic poles are also the two poles of the Petersburg world depicted in Chapter I. Not surprisingly, they are completely separate in terms of time. Onegin, "making midnight out of dawn," and the characters in stanza 35 (the merchant, the peddler, and others) move in different orbits and never

meet. The hero of the novel sleeps, but the course of the story is not inter-
rupted because of this. Completing its twenty-four-hour circle, it captures *in a
single stanza* all the remaining life of the capital, which marches on without
Onegin and apart from him. By means of this one stanza Pushkin sketches the
whole of life surrounding his hero and allows us to experience him as a small
part of this whole.

The other verbal reality, the other stylistic pole corresponds to a different
Petersburg time, to a different side of life. For "the child of luxury and
glamour" who sleeps in "blissful shade" belongs to a different *stylistic reality*
from that of "the merchant [who] dresses and the peddler [who] struts." One
of these stylistic realities is characterized by glittering periphrasis, "the over-
refinement of delicate phrases";[5] the other by the simple, direct, "bare" word.

"Child of luxury and glamour" is part of a whole *figurative reality* which is
unfolded in Chapter I and which forms the world of the hero. This purely
stylistic reality is constituted first and foremost by the hero's verbal masks. In
Chapter I Onegin periphrastically appears as "no mean economist" [I, 7]; "the
stage's arbiter, exacting," "established freeman of the wings" [I, 17]; "fashion's
acolyte," "philosopher at age eighteen" [I, 23]; "child of luxury and glamour"
[I, 36]; and a little later, conversely, as "apostate from the whirl of pleasure" [I,
43]. Stylistically, each of these characterizations is closed in itself and at the
given moment periphrastically replaces the hero. Thus, instead of one Onegin,
there appear a whole series of "characters," each of whom possesses a purely
verbal reality and nothing more. "Established freeman of the wings," for
example, ceases to exist if one tries to phrase it differently. Outside the given
combination of words it is not real. In and of itself the manner of expression
creates its own reality, apart from the real person who is the subject of the
story.

Such a periphrastic treatment of character is associated with a genre tradi-
tion that Pushkin knew well—the language of the familiar epistle, which masks
the addressee and presents him periphrastically.[6] In a certain sense the pe-
riphrastic descriptions of Onegin in Chapter I are closely linked to the lan-
guage of Pushkin's own verse epistles to friends. After all Onegin too is his
"friend." Thus a whole series of periphrases drawn from the rough draft of
Pushkin's 1821 epistle to the members of the Green Lamp[7]—for example,
"and, you freeman of the wings" [*PSS*, 2, 776]—are transferred to Onegin. But
before our very eyes such periphrases are objectified and distanced, as they
move from the uniform stylistic milieu of the verse epistle into the open and
diverse world of the novel, where they become a verbal guise for the novel's
hero.

The figurative reality is also constituted by the everyday objects which
surround the hero. These objects are glorified: the truffle called "youth's
delight" [I, 16] and perfume in crystal bottles termed "able/ To soothe the
brow with scented cool" [I, 24]. The word as an object, the name plus a "halo

of glory," the *apposition* which erects a figurative superstructure over the word as a term—this is the usual manner of storytelling and "description" found in Chapter I.[8] Both hero and objects are treated periphrastically. This puts them on an equal footing and makes the hero blend with his milieu. Bestuzhev expressed this very well when he observed: "Nowadays coldness, misanthropy, and eccentricity are numbered among toilet articles" [*PSS*, 13, 149]. And, in fact, the various periphrases of the hero in Chapter I are numbered among his costumes; words become clothing, a mask. In these glittering characterizations Onegin also "dresses, undresses, and dresses again" [I, 23].

The words "the peddler struts, the merchant dresses" are not only direct but also "bare." If Onegin's story is richly "dressed" and adorned with periphrasis, then this manner of speaking is deliberately stripped down to simple, elementary sentences where the substantives are abstract lexical terms— "merchant" as such and "peddler" as such—and the predicate is an indicator of their monosemantic function. According to Lydia Ginzburg, "A prosaism is first and foremost a *nonstylistic* word, that is, one which is aesthetically neutral and is not known to belong to any poetic style."[9] "The peddler struts, the merchant dresses" are nonstylistic words completely stripped of any and all stylistic elaboration, as if absolutely equal to that reality of which they speak. Compare them to "child of luxury and glamour," a phrase luxurious in and of itself, which relates freely and capriciously to its reality because it has grown distant from it and become enclosed in a separate reality of its own.

It is between these poles that the reality of Chapter I is situated and the narration and authorial speech are constructed. At one extreme there is simple naming, using lexical terms which are absolutely necessary. At the other, there is verbal prodigality. Here the relationship to the object is not fixed, but in return figurativeness is compulsory. That is why young Onegin multiplies in periphrastic variants.

When Chapter I of *Onegin* appeared, critics immediately began to debate the question of its "national character." In a rejoinder to Polevoy's review, the poet Venevitinov wrote, "I don't know what is national here except the names of Petersburg streets and restaurants. In France and in England, too, corks pop to the ceiling, devotees go to theatres and to balls."[10] Polevoy answered, "Mr. [Venevitino]-v himself calls Pushkin's poem a *complete picture of Petersburg life.* Surely he who has *portrayed Petersburg completely* has portrayed the national character."[11] And, in fact, the stratification and polarity of national life are expressed *stylistically* in Chapter I of *Onegin.* Thanks to stanza 35, there is a "complete picture" of Petersburg, the focus of this stratification and polarity. At the same time the stylistic stratification gives expression to an important problem in the national life: namely, the relationship between "native" and "foreign." The lexical barbarisms in Chapter I and the circumlocutory periphrases constitute a single stylistic layer. The phraseological masquerade constitutes a single context with *"pantalons, gilet,* and *frack"* [I, 26]. The hero appears in his stylistic masks "like playful Venus from her bower,/When in a man's disguise arrayed,/The goddess joins a masquerade" [I, 25]. In December 1823, immediately after finishing the first two chapters of *Onegin* one after another, Pushkin wrote Vyazemsky: "I hate to see in our primitive language traces of European affectation and French refinement. Rudeness and simplicity are more becoming to it. I preach from internal conviction but as is my custom I write otherwise" [Shaw, p. 146].

The stylistic contrasts in Chapter I play with this contradiction between "native" and "foreign":

> What London makes for cultured whimsy
> Of novelties polite and flimsy,
> And ships upon the Baltic brine
> To us for tallow and for pine,
> All that Parisian modish passion
> And earnest industry collect
> To tempt the taste of the elect
> With comfort and caress of fashion,
> Adorned the boudoir of our green
> Philosopher at age eighteen.
>
> (I, 23)

"Tallow and pine" are the very same "basic staples" that Onegin, "no mean economist," knew how to assess in I, 7. But "basic staples" is a fashionable quotation from Adam Smith. Stylistically, it is in accord with the ephemeral role of "no mean economist" [I, 7] and more broadly with the entire figurative reality of the hero in Chapter I, including the florid stylistic context of "the philosopher at age eighteen" (another role of the same "no mean economist"). "Tallow and pine," like foreign bodies, stratify this impenetrable, stylized environment. "Tallow and pine" are raw, crude words—real Russian raw materials, basic staples in the true sense.

Obviously, in the debate about national character Polevoy was closer to the truth. However, only through proper stylistic analysis can we adequately explain how a "complete picture of Petersburg life" is realized in the text of Chapter I. And it is through stylistic means that the contrasts in Chapter I are linked in the subsequent development of the novel with such "national" declarations as the famous passage from "Onegin's Journey," which concludes: "Now my ideal is the *khoziaika* [housewife],/My wish, just to be left alone:/'A pot of *shchi* and me my own'" (J, 18).[12] In the 1820s a system of oppositions is present in Pushkin's thinking. It is manifested in both his poetic and his theoretical reflections: in the 1822 note "On Prose," in the letter to Vyazemsky dated December 1823, and in the text of *Eugene Onegin*. Within this system pull in one direction is exerted by "conventional, select language,"[13] the cult of periphrasis in which "traces of European affectation" are perceived, and by the seemingly artificial reality of the "young good-for-nothing" Onegin [I, 2]. The derivative character of this reality is in accord with its figurative manner of expression. At the other pole is simple reality—specifically, Russian reality, simple modes of expression, simple language. It is with the latter that a broader understanding of prose is linked.

Stanzas 35 and 36 in Chapter I constitute one of the passages in the text of *Eugene Onegin* where these poles are presented. Another such passage is the poetic declaration in "Onegin's Journey" [stanzas 17 and 18]. To be sure, these passages are quite different in terms of content. But in a broader sense they are connected and set off in the text of the novel by their "polar" construction. In both instances two different kinds of content, two totally opposed contexts, two clusters of images, two worlds, and two languages—two *stylistic realities* (this is the way we tried to characterize I, 35–36)—are strictly demarcated and presented as isolated poles. In I, 35–36, this stylistic polarity clearly portrays the character of the Petersburg world itself. It can be said that here the poetic world of the novel and its stylistic laboratory are one. As we shall see, this is characteristic of the text of *Onegin* as a whole. The stylistic play is intertwined with the development of the novel, with the story of the heroes; and reality, the world of the novel, is a stylistic laboratory. In some passages, as in our example, this characteristic of the text is laid bare.

The poles of the "programmatic" passage from "Onegin's Journey" no longer characterize the reality of the novel but the poetic world of the author himself: specifically, his evolution, the transition from one poetic world to another which is its polar opposite. To put it differently, it is a transition from the "poetic" world, now perceived to be conventional, to the real world, to life itself. Despite these differences, however, in both instances the poles of the conventional and "simple" world and of conventional and "simple" language are opposed to one another. (In "Onegin's Journey" they are opposed strictly in a theoretical sense; in I, 35–36, they are opposed by means of juxtaposition.) It is as if such passages indicate the range in which the text of *Onegin* is constructed. We are shown the naked "lines of force" which operate in the "real field" of the novel in verse.

However, this "field"—reality, the world of the novel, its stylistic world, its text—is situated *between* the poles. In the text of the novel the polar stylistic principles interact in a complex and very lively manner. Unanticipated, living contexts are formed where principles can unite—principles which in other contexts of that same novel are at opposite poles.

In the Petersburg chapter of *Onegin*, "the peddler struts, the merchant dresses" is opposed to "child of luxury and glamour [who] sleeps tight, in blissful shade withdrawn." In this novel, however, defined modes of expression are not tied to defined realia. In "Onegin's Journey" the merchant is "on the move" again:

> The child of pluck and calculation,
> The merchant, scans the mooring station

(J, 25)

The very same word, which in the context of Chapter I was an absolutely simple, "bare" word, now also receives a figurative double, acquiring, as it were, a halo: the merchant, too, becomes a "child." This example may not appear to be very significant, but it demonstrates the significance of small stylistic changes. It shows how the world of the novel is constructed through the manner of expression. The interesting stylistic situation that results from the parallel between the passage in Chapter I and the passaage in "Onegin's Journey" reveals both the difference between the Petersburg and Odessa spheres of the novel and that "difference between Onegin and me" [I, 56], which is so important in the novel. For if the "bare" merchant is totally divorced from the Petersburg atmosphere of the hero, then the Odessa atmosphere of both the "I" and the "merchant" is one and the same. And in the description of everyday life the periphrases—halos for objects presented directly by the "I"—are more spontaneous, intimate, and more organically connected ("To swallow from the sea-wet shell/ The chubby hermit, live and well"—J, 26) than in the descriptions of Chapter I.

The poles of Chapter I (and other similar passages) provide the key to the stylistic stratification of the text of the novel as a whole. The line "The peddler struts, the merchant dresses" forms one context, one stylistic cluster and, as it were, one reality with such verses as "the hungry wolf emerges/ Upon the highway with his mate" (IV, 41—the same "bare" behavior of the "bare" wolf) and with many others which are also narrated in the simplest, absolutely "barest" of words. If we recall the 1822 note "On Prose," it is obvious that this stylistic layer corresponds to its program: "Why not simply say horse." According to this program "simplicity" is "truth," but the matter is not nearly so simple in the stylistic world of the novel in verse. The enormous difference between a theoretical program like that set out in the 1822 note, which is monosemantically oriented, and an artistic text, particularly the text of a *novel*, is revealed in this comparison.

There is no way that the reality of *Eugene Onegin* can be reduced to monosemantic relationships and to the "simple word." If we were able somehow to isolate the so-called simple reality where the peddler struts, the merchant dresses, and the wolf emerges upon the highway from the context of the entire work, it would appear abstract and bare, simply unreal. For this stylistic layer is only one aspect of the much more complex world of the novel; it is precisely one pole in a vast and varied "field." Let us examine the context in which the "wolf" appears in Chapter IV:

Through frigid haze the dawn resurges,
Abroad the harvest sounds abate;
And soon the hungry wolf emerges
Upon the highway with his mate.

(IV, 41)

Everything is very simple. However, while the last two lines of this quatrain
do not have any stylistic antecedents and are therefore "bare," the first line
cannot be divorced from its stylistic background: namely, the diverse ways of
expressing the event, dawn, elaborated in the poetry of the period. Recall the
1822 note: "One should say 'early in the morning,' but they write: 'barely had
the first rays of the rising sun illumined the eastern edges of the azure sky'"
[Proffer, p. 18]. And in the text of *Onegin* there are a number of parodic
variants: "When with the morrow's ray of dawning" [VI, 22]; "The day by Eos'
rosy fingers/ From vales of dawn. . ." [V, 25]. In the latter case the parodied
model (Lomonosov) is clearly indicated in one of Pushkin's notes to the novel
[note 34].

Further in the same stanza [IV, 41] we read:

No longer are the cattle chased
Out of the byre at dawn, the thinning
Horn-notes of cowherds cease the tune
That rounds them up again at noon.
Indoors [in a hut] the maiden sings at spinning
Before the crackling pine-flare light,
Companion of the winter night.

Possibly the following verses from Batyushkov provided the stylistic back-
ground for the last three lines:

Beneath the sheltering eaves, as winter blizzards roar,
The dear companion in the dark of night will kindle
Bright lights, and calmly turning in her hand the spindle,
Relate the happenings and yarns of days of yore.

—"Elegy from Tibullus"[14]

The sign of this speech structure in Pushkin's text is the word "maiden"
[*deva*[15]] and "companion of the winter night," the periphrastic apposition with
pine-flare light, which, as Irina Semenko has noted, is "a Karamzinian
periphrasis through and through."[16] (Cf. Batyushkov's "bright lights" and also
his periphrastic designation of dwelling, "beneath the sheltering eaves," with
Pushkin's "in a hut.") "Maiden" provoked *Athenaeum*'s critic to complain: "Say
what you will, but *maiden in a hut* is the same as *maiden on a cliff*."[17] "Maiden on

a cliff" is an allusion to Pushkin's lyric "Buria" ["Tempest"]: "You saw perched on a cliff a maid [*deva*]. . ." [Arndt, *PuCP*, p. 70]. In *Onegin* "maiden" does arise later in the same context with "cliffs" in the author's poetic declaration:

> I felt I had to pay addresses
> To pearly wave-crests, wildernesses,
> What ocean voice and cliffs reveal,
> And that proud maiden [*deva*], my ideal,

(J, 17)

But this maiden-*cum*-cliffs is poles apart from the "peasant hut" ("Two rowans by a peasant hut"—"Onegin's Journey," 18), where "maiden" is translated into another language:

> Now my ideal is the *khoziaika* [housewife],

(J, 18)

Thus, "maiden in a hut" unites into a single context both poles, those two contexts which are diametrically opposed to each other in the "programmatic" passage of the same work. And this indicates the difference between the stylistic poles of the novel and its stylistic "field"—its real world, its text.

Apropos of the word "maiden" in IV, 41, Pushkin commented in a note: "Reviewers wondered how one could call a simple peasant girl *maiden* when, a little further, genteel misses are called *young things* [*devchonki*]"[18] [Nabokov, 1, 317n23]. Here Pushkin is responding to *Athenaeum*'s criticism of the line "The girls [*devchonki*] already skip with rapture" [V, 28], apropos of which the critic complained: "How ludicrous these young things getting ready for the ball are in comparison to the *maiden* spinning in a hut."[19] From the point of view of the old-fashioned critic, for whom certain names were associated with certain objects in certain situations, this was obviously an improper renaming of objects. We will find not only that the *renaming of reality*—glorifying or, conversely, disparaging, debunking, trying new names on objects, playing intensively with synonyms—occurs continually in the stylistic world of the author of *Eugene Onegin,* but that in the author's stylistic world this play re-creates what is taking place in the world of the heroes and in their consciousnesses.

In large measure this process of naming and renaming reality constitutes the very reality of the novel in verse. Even Mother Larin sometimes calls Praskovya by the name Paulina [II, 33] and later calls Selina by the name Akulka [II, 33]. Of course, these are the most primitive metamorphoses, but similar transformations of Onegin and Tatyana in the novel, although incomparably more complex and subtle, are essentially of the same nature.

By calling attention, in the wake of *Athenaeum*'s criticism, to the synonyms "maiden" [*deva*] and "young things" [*devchonki*], Pushkin also called attention to the significance of this stylistic difference in the text of the novel. Here it should be pointed out that of all these synonyms "maiden" itself is primary. Tatyana is most often called "maiden"; moreover, elements of the high style, corresponding to her state of mind, merge here with the simple appellation. In *Onegin,* in the majority of cases—although not in all—a "poeticism" is not the lofty variant but the *norm* of naming a given content, in relation to which other synonyms appear to have a deflating effect.

The way synonyms are used is stylistically significant in Pushkin's mature works. Take, for example, the 1829 lyric, "Zima. Chto delat' nam v derevne?" ["Winter. What's There for Us in the Country?"], where first we find the archaic form *devitsa* ["girl"] in an everyday context:

> But if at evenfall our sleepy rustic station,
>
> . . . .
>
> Stirs to a two-in-hand or sledge and cob in shafts
> And springs some guests on us, a matron and two girls
> A shapely pair of sisters, trim and fair of curls,

and then the poetic Slavonic form *deva:*

> At sundown then the maid steps on the porch
>
> . . . .
>
> How fresh the Russian maid blooms in the powdery snows!
>
> (*PSS,* 3, 181–182)

We can see here how poeticization is achieved simultaneously with generalization. In the transformed and generalized "Russian maid" [*deva*] of the last line it is difficult to recognize the same "girl" [*devitsa*], although according to the lyric's plot this after all is she. And in *Onegin,* too, the lofty word "maiden," used as a stylistic norm, generalizes and unites Tatyana with the "maiden" spinning in the peasant hut [IV, 41]. They are essentially one and the same. The stylistic significance of this word *deva* as a "norm" is particularly apparent in the last chapter. In comparison with the "new" Tatyana, the "former" Tatyana conjured up in Onegin's memories consistently appears as a "little girl" [*devochka*] or a "young thing" [*devchonka*]:

> That same Tatyana [*devochka*]—had he dreamed
> All this?—to whom it must have seemed
> That he disdained her age and station,
>
> (VIII, 20)

> Not of poor shy Tatyana [*devochka*]—trusting,
> In love, obscure, and unrefined,

> But of the princess who serenely,
> Like sheltered godhead, ruled the queenly,
> The lush imperial Nevá.

(VIII, 27)

> Who dared to seek the tender young thing [devchonka]
> In this assured, decorum-laden
> High Priestess of the polished floor?

(VIII, 28)

By means of the same word, Tatyana herself conveys Onegin's former view of her:

> Confess: a little girl's [devochka] affection,
> Shy worship, was no novel thrill!

(VIII, 43)

However, while Tatyana is uttering this,

> . . . The simple maiden [deva],
> With heart of old and dreams that were,
> Rose up to live again in her.

(VIII, 41)

Not the "little girl" but the "simple maiden" rose up in her. "Simple maiden" cancels out the opposition developed in Chapter VIII between "little girl" and "lady," "princess," "goddess," "high priestess of the polished floor." "Simple maiden" restores unity to Tatyana's image and conveys Onegin's altered view of the former "little girl." We see how the synonyms of this word are used to express the situation of the former and then the new Tatyana, and the former and then the new Onegin in the novel's final chapter. Whereas in the "programmatic" passage in "Onegin's Journey," "maiden" is associated with the "nonsimple" pole, in VIII, 41, "simple maiden" unites the lofty and the simple.

Returning to stanza 41 in Chapter IV, we see that here the heterogeneous stylistic elements are united differently than they were in Chapter I. In this stanza we find "cattle chased out of the byre" [iz khleva], where khleva rhymes with deva ["maiden"]. Here the "lofty" and "low" elements seem to neutralize *each other,* thereby creating a stylistically smooth context, a unified stylistic reality. The hierarchy of words with differing degrees of loftiness is canceled out, but this does not mean that the stylistic *differences* are smoothed away. These differences remain very active. At certain points in conjunction with particular problems they are concentrated as poles; in the stylistic "field" of the novel they are dispersed as its living reality. In the case of IV, 41, elements

embedded in rich stylistic traditions and "bare" lines without any stylistic
antecedents ("And soon the hungry wolf emerges/ Upon the highway with his
mate") are joined to form a single reality. It was because of these "bare" lines
that we turned to IV, 41. Other similar "bare" lines in Chapter I led us to these
lines. What produced first and foremost a *contrast* in Chapter I (these contrasts
also impart to Chapter I its special "brilliance") manifests itself differently in
subsequent chapters. We should not forget that Baratynsky made his remark
about the "lofty poetic simplicity" of *Onegin* precisely in connection with
Chapters IV and V.[20]

2

In the final stanzas of Chapter I the author talks about his poetic evolution:

> All poets—while I'm on these subjects—
> Are given to daydreaming love;
> [It used to be] My soul, too, harbored charming objects
> Whom I at times did daydream of,
> And kept an image of their features;
> The Muse breathed life into these creatures,
> Then I, carefree, did serenade
> Both my ideal, the mountain maid,
> And the Salgir's fair slaves admire.

(I, 57)

This is the way "it used to be" [*byvalo*]. "These days" [*teper'*][21] things have
changed, and personal experiences and poetry correlate differently:

> The Muse appeared, past Love's intrusion,
> The mind was cleared in darkness bound,
> And free once more, I seek the fusion
> Of feeling, dream, and magic sound.

(I, 59)

This is the way it is for the poet–*author.* But for the poet *Lensky,* within the
novel itself, the correlation between love and poetry is quite different, as is the
correlation between "clarity" [*iasnost'*][22] and "murkiness" [*temnota*] in Lensky's
poetry. Lensky "sang of love, love's service choosing"—like "all poets," like
the poetic "I" "used to do":

> And limpid [*iasnyi*] was his simple tune
> As ever artless maiden's musing,
> As babes aslumber, as the Moon

(II, 10)

This is a characterization of Lensky's song in its own language. The author characterizes it quite differently:

Thus he wrote *murkily* [*temno*] and *limply*

(VI, 23)

Thus in the context of the novel a curious situation is created by the concepts "clarity" and "murkiness." In the lines "the mind was cleared in darkness bound" [I, 59] and "limpid was his simple tune" [II, 10], one and the same concept suggests opposite things. What in the author's language corresponds to the "clarity" of Lensky's poetry is his own "dark mind," which now "has cleared."

If we turn to Pushkin's lyrics from the 1820s, we encounter both "clarity" in this sense and another kind of "clarity." One of them is a word replete with special meanings associated with the Sentimental and Romantic traditions. (Lensky's song possesses this kind of clarity, but, of course, its "lucidity" is simplified and parodic.) These meanings—purity, bliss, happiness, peace—are usually linked with innocence, with youth (or infancy), with "spring,"[23] and with dreaming, which is the realm of this "clarity," for in life it disappears with youth.

Zhukovsky in particular cultivated this word in his poetry, where it is replete with such meanings. In his poetry "clarity" is a leitmotif, a key word. The same word, imbued with an aura of similar meanings, is used widely by poets of the period, including Pushkin. He employs it as a general poetic word. In his poetry it lacks the metaphysical character Zhukovsky gave it. Usually it is motivated by the context: for example, by the address to youth in the draft "Mladentsu" ["To the Babe"]: "May limpid [*iasnyi*] be your days to come,/ As your dear gaze is limpid now" [*PSS*, 2, 351]. (Compare the characterization of Lensky's song: "As babes aslumber"—II, 10.) The poet sends this word as a "consolation" to the exiled Decembrist Ivan Pushchin in 1826:

And bear into your prison station
Of bright [*iasnyi*] Lyceum days a ray![24]

(Arndt, *PuCP,* p. 77)

But in the critical year 1823, when *Onegin* was begun, another kind of "clarity" appears in Pushkin's poetry:

I scanned the world with gaze unclouded [*iasnyi*]
And in a mute soliloquy:
"Had it in truth appeared to be
So grand and splendorous?" I doubted.

—"My Carefree Ignorance"[25]

These lines, the first variant of the lyric poem "Demon" ["The Demon"], were written shortly after Pushkin's epistle to Vladimir Raevsky and echo lines from it:

> Could it [i.e., the world] have played for me in former time
> So splendorous and grand a part,
> Could I in that abyss of vice and slime
> Have really reveled, pure [*iasnyi*] of heart?[26]

In one and the same context the new sense of clarity has canceled out and supplanted the former understanding of clarity, which now is viewed as "carefree ignorance." In his commentary to "The Demon," Pushkin explained this new clarity as the knowledge "of the eternal contradictions of being" which destroys "the poetic predilections of the soul" [*PSS*, 11, 30]—that is, destroys precisely what is expressed in the characterization of Lensky's song: "And limpid [*iasnyi*] was his simple tune" [II, 10]. The cycle linked with "The Demon" and work on the first two chapters of *Eugene Onegin* intersected not only chronologically but also thematically and textually. As Boris Tomashevsky pointed out, "The verses which characterize Lensky echo themes stated in the epistle to Vladimir Raevsky."[27] It is as if the "I" of that lyrical cycle were in the position of Lensky—"reveling, pure of heart"—before the onset of the new clarity: "I scanned the world with gaze unclouded."

The lines from Chapter I of *Onegin*—"The Muse appeared, past Love's intrusion,/ The mind was cleared in darkness bound" [I, 59]—emerged out of the same context. But this new "lucidity" differs, in both creative and poetic terms, not only from the naive clarity of Lensky's song but also from the purely negative clarity of disillusionment found in "The Demon" and in the poetry linked with it. Compare the lines in Chapter VI of *Onegin* where the author consciously reconciles himself to the passing of youth: "Enough! And now I set, untroubled [literally—"with a clear heart"],/My course for quite another shore" [VI, 45].

In June 1824 Zhukovsky wrote to Pushkin: "I embrace you for your 'Demon.' Send the devil to hell! For the time being that should be your motto. You are destined to find yourself among the gods. Upward! Your soul has wings! It should not fear heights since that is its true element! Give those wings freedom to soar, and the heavens are yours. That is my belief. . . . Farewell, little devil; be an angel" [*PSS*, 13, 94–95]. The letter expresses Zhukovsky's "belief" more than it does reality, for Zhukovsky interprets Pushkin's lyric his own way ("send the devil to hell!") and beckons Pushkin to his own realm—to "heaven" and to the "angels."

Pushkin re-created Zhukovsky's world in an 1818 lyric addressed to the poet:

> When to the world of dreamy fancies
> Aspiring with exalted soul. . . .
>
> .   .   .   .
>
> When visions follow one another
> Before you in a magic mist.

(PSS, 2, 59)

Here Zhukovsky's "world of dreamy fancies" appears as a "magic mist," whereas in Zhukovsky's own poetry this world is "clear." But in the 1820s whenever Pushkin depicts and stylizes the "world of dreamy fancies" associated with Zhukovsky and his school, this world is presented in images of magic twilight and mist, in images which are the exact opposite of "clarity."

In the 1818 lyric the word "clarity" appears. However, it is not the property of Zhukovsky's world but an indication of the way the author of the poem, Pushkin, perceives that world:

> And grasped your rapturous delight
> With rapture flaming and pellucid [*iasnyi*].

It is as if the word *iasnyi* portrays the moment when this world is "grasped" by another poetic consciousness, one that is different in terms of structure.[28] The difference between one "rapture" and the other—that perceived ("yours") and that perceiving—is signified by this word.

In 1822 Pushkin composed lines which he later (1825) reworked into a separate lyric:

> I worship your uncertain gloaming,
> Your blossoms nursed in secrecy,
> O you, the blessed dreamy roaming
> Of captivating poetry![29]

The "blossoms nurtured in secrecy" denotes the poetic myth of the shades of the dead who "like an airy multitude" visit familiar places and friends. This motif, in both its light and its somber variants, is found in the poetry of Batyushkov, Zhukovsky, and Baratynsky. Pushkin also used it to re-create an appropriate poetic world in his lyrics "K Ovidiiu" ["To Ovid"—1821] and "Andrei Shené'e" ["André Chénier"—1825]. The "uncertain gloaming" simultaneously expresses both the atmosphere of such poetry and the problem of the immortality of the soul to which Pushkin's lyric is addressed. At the same time the poetic "gloaming" and "blossoms," which the poet "worships," are opposed to "clarity": "But idle daydreams, they may be. . . ."[30]

The theme of immortality, of belief and disbelief, runs through all of Pushkin's lyrics in the 1820s, and the same questions preoccupied the poet when he was writing *Eugene Onegin*. It is remarkable that in the letter which caused Pushkin to be exiled to his mother's estate Mikhaylovskoe, he mentions *Onegin* and these questions in the same breath: "I am writing the motley stanzas of a Romantic poem, and I am taking lessons in pure atheism" [Shaw, p. 156]. In the novel several passages bring these motifs to mind—passages which characterize the "poetic predilections of Lensky's soul" and his relations with Onegin, with whom the author sides at times to form a skeptical "we": "With rosy dreams he [Lensky] would belittle/ His spirit's dubious surmise;/ The goal of life was to his eyes/ A species of alluring riddle;/ On it he exercised his mind/ And nameless marvels there divined" [II, 7].

In the lyric poem "Fontanu Bakhchisaraiskogo dvortsa" ["To the Fountain at the Bakhchisarayan Palace"—1824], the atmosphere of poetic mists and "dimness" [*neiasnost'*] characterizes Pushkin's own poetry in the recent past:

> Did but my fancy's dream creation
> In mists of solitude outline
> A momentary emanation,
> A dim [*neiasnyi*] ideal of soul and mind?

> (*PSS*, 2, 343)

Compare, in "Onegin's Journey": "Was this my way when sap was mounting?/ Speak up, Bakhchisarayan Fountain!" (J, 19).

Pushkin persistently linked personal recollections with his southern poem *The Fountain of Bakhchisaray:* "I superstitiously set to verse the story of a young woman" [Shaw, p. 151]. And he termed the poem's epilogue, which he refused to publish during his life, "love's delirium" [Shaw, p. 136]. The poem is alluded to in *Onegin*, Chapter I, 57 ("And the Salgir's fair slaves"[31]), where the period in Pushkin's poetry which has just ended or is ending is characterized in a deprecating manner. This period is described as if it were one in which love and poetry are identical—where the intensely personal feelings of the poet, his recollections of "charming objects," are directly elevated into an "ideal." But the situation has changed. Now love and poetry part ways, and in conjunction with this the "mind in darkness bound" is cleared.

The situation depicted at the end of Chapter I indicates the difference between the poet–author and the poet Lensky. Lensky is like "all poets" ("All poets—while I'm on these subjects"—I, 57). This generalization refers both to the "style of the period," as it was expressed in the works of major poets, and to the wide currency enjoyed by that style in everyday life. Lensky combines both.

Lensky is a poet not only in his verses but also in life. In everyday life he behaves like a "poet." He is *always* a poet, just as his heroine Olga is "always modest, always docile" [II, 23] and as the hero of a novel is "always ecstatic" [III, 11]. It is as if the person is identical with the poet and the poet with his poetic images. But, conversely, these images encompass only Lensky the person. Lensky's poetry is unconsciously fused with his spiritual life. The latter is formulated "ideally," but it is easy to detect behind every poetic image its "real basis" in simple everyday life and natural young feelings. After all, Lensky is in love. The detached observer can immediately spot this "stylistic contradiction." Thus, the "poet" lives as if in darkness, although his song is "clear" and its tone lucent.

In the novel there is an episode in which the stylization of Lensky the person ironically affects his fate at a decisive moment. On the eve of the duel at the Larins' he is distracted, agitated, pensive, melancholy: "But then, he whom the Muses foster/ Is always so; . . ." [VI, 19]. At this final moment the person is not recognized in his guise as "poet."

One of Zhukovsky's precepts was "to write and to live as you write, so that your works will be not a mask, but a mirror of your soul and deeds. . . ."[32] "To write so as to speak to the heart and elevate it, and while you live, to live, think, and feel as you write."[33] Here it is assumed that one achieves sincerity in poetry not simply by "writing as you live" but by "living as you write"—by writing in such a way that you elevate your own image as a person and thereby bring it into accord with the image in your poetry. Nonetheless, this poetry is perceived to be a sincere "mirror of the soul and deeds"—as if it were a mirror of that which in itself is a mirror of this poetry.

The notion that a poet's life and his poetry are identical was widespread in the literature of the period. Along with it went the practice of "*creating life out of art*—of deliberately realizing in life artistic images and aesthetically organized plots."[34] In the minds of readers (both contemporary and subsequent generations) the poets became legendary figures. As Grigory Gukovsky observes: "The image readers had of Zhukovsky, the way he was perceived from the 1820s up to the end of the nineteenth century, the image readers had of Denis Davydov, of Venevitinov, were all similar—in the sense of being an amalgam of fact and fiction given a certain unity."[35] Here the image created by the poet and the image of the poet coalesced. Typically, in life the poet adapted his behavior to the poetic image he himself had created, as if imitating it, but this image in poetry was experienced by the author and perceived by his readers to be a "mirror of the soul and deeds" of the person qua poet, his poetic other self, his alter ego.

The moment Pushkin realized that such a poetic structure—it could be called the "poetics of oneness"—was alien to him is recorded in his correspondence: "The character of the Prisoner is unsuccessful; this proves that I am not cut out to be the hero of a Romantic poem" [Shaw, p. 105].[36] Pushkin wrote this at the end of 1822, and in Chapter I of *Onegin,* written soon after, he returns to the same theme: "As though we were by now unable/ On any subject to intone/ A song, but on ourselves alone" [I, 56]. It is no accident that the story of the author's poetic evolution vis-à-vis "love" [I, 57], which we examined above, comes directly after these lines.

In 1816 Pushkin composed a lyric poem "Pevets" ["The Bard"] in the manner of Zhukovsky, modeled on the latter's "Pevets" ["Piteous bard!"]. In Zhukovsky's lyric, the bard's fate and feelings are the content of his "song." Pushkin summarizes this in a single line, which is repeated three times as a refrain:

> The bard of love, the bard of his own sorrow

> (*PSS*, 1, 211)

By means of this formula Pushkin *defines* the very poetic structure which he himself *re-creates* in the lyric. Thus, while appearing to follow a particular style, at the same time he seems to see it objectively and to formulate its principles in the very poem. If we correlate "bard of his own sorrow" with later and more candid Pushkinian definitions, we see that this bard is precisely the one who is unable "on any subject to intone a song, but on himself alone" [I, 56].

Increasingly in his poetry Pushkin draws a line of demarcation between himself and other poets, and he presents this through a series of opposing motifs. "The bard of his own sorrow" is also "bard of love": "Of love he sang, love's service choosing" [II, 10]; "All poets . . ./ Are given to daydreaming love" [I, 57]. The "dreamy world" is associated with poetic twilight, magic mist, and the "dim ideal of soul and mind." But love passes, the Muse appears, and the dark mind is cleared. And in conjunction with this comes the ability to write—and not to "sing"—about "another" and not simply about oneself and "one's own sorrow."

In Lensky, characteristics of a poet "almost turned eighteen" and characteristics of "all young people," who find in such a poet "*almost* their own thoughts and feelings clothed in brilliant colors,"[37] are combined and mixed together. "Almost" points to the atmosphere which is created when the "human" and the "poetic" mingle. This comes about when style and life are perceived to be identical, a situation which is always ambiguous. Lensky is an example of such commingling. We can assume that he is a true poet but "eighteen," and we can regard him as a "poet," a widespread and commonplace phenomenon. The two variants of Lensky's possible fate projected in Chapter VI, stanzas 37 and 39, correspond to the two possibilities that are commingled in him.

The author of the novel constructs an image of a particular poetics from which here in the novel he disassociates himself. This image is constructed very broadly. It embraces both phenomena in real poetry and the poetics of everyday life predetermined by that poetry—from Zhukovsky and the young Pushkin to Lensky and the provincial Svetlana. In the stylistic world of the novel these phenomena from different realms are deliberately brought together and mixed. Thus the poetic "I's" own Romantic period, the period of the southern poems, is subjected to deflation in I, 57, where "My ideal, the mountain maid," is explained "humanly" as the recollection of "charming objects." The personal impressions of youth are "almost" the same as those of "all young people" clothed in "brilliant colors." "All poets" are like that.

The author's own recent poetic condition is equated with Lensky's condition. In IV, 31, Lensky's elegies are equated with the elegies of Yazykov on the basis of the alleged identity of this poetry with the poet's own life: "And may imagine you have captured/ In that rare elegiac freight/ The sum and essence of your fate." Here poetry is identified with "love." "Love" is the sign of this poetics. But the poetic "I's" new state of mind runs counter to this poetics. Compare I, 59: "The Muse appeared, past Love's intrusion. . . ."[38] Even Onegin, whose distinguishing characteristic is the fact that he is not a poet, almost becomes a poet in the last chapter, when he is "magnetically fired" by love for Tatyana: "What figure, come to think, could better/ Suggest a poet . . ./ Than in his chimney-nook Eugene" [VIII, 38]. But Onegin's love is different from that of Lensky, about whom it is said: "Of love he sang, love's service choosing" [II, 10]. Such stylization of man turned "poet" is only contemplated in Onegin's case, for we are told: "And he did not become a poet" [VIII, 39].

The typical figure of the "poet" is portrayed in "Onegin's Journey":

> Our friend Tumansky has depicted
> Odessa in resounding rhyme,
> But he must clearly be convicted
> Of being partial at the time.
> For he arrived fresh from Parnassus[39]
> And wandered with his spying-glasses
> Alone above the sea, and then
> With his intoxicating pen
> Extolled "the gardens of Odessa."
> But he ignored the facts: to wit,
> There's naked steppe surrounding it;

(J, 21)

Actually there is only one line about "gardens" in Tumansky's lyric poem "Odessa," an imitation of Pushkin's lyric "To Ovid":

> Beneath the airy shade of vesper clouds
> The breath of gardens intoxicates one here.[40]

Pushkin, however, portrays the "typical situation." Here in the text of the novel he seems to reduce to a single common denominator Tumansky, Yazykov, Küchelbecker, Baratynsky, his own recent self, the "average romantic" Vladimir Lensky, and all the phenomena of "poetic" stylization in life and in human relations which occupy so much space in the reality of the novel in verse.

For "our friend Tumansky," the image of the real Odessa is fused with its "ideal" image, just as his own image is fused with the ideal of the "true poet," "fresh from Parnassus." And in both respects the "I" of the novel stands in opposition to the "true poet," the one "fresh from Parnassus." The "I" lives "in Odessa dusty," "in Odessa muddy" [J, 22]—in the real Odessa—and the life he leads is far from being that of a "true poet." To the contrary, that way of life is depicted empirically with its bathing, oysters, and trips to the theater. The *poet* portrays in a detached manner the very ordinary existence of the *man*. The author can talk about "himself" as "another." In *Onegin* the author of the novel, the poet, is shown in life to be an ordinary person. The author of the novel is categorically opposed to the idea that the life of the poet and his poetry are identical. The author is not the sort of poet "all poets" are.

3

> "Yet it's the younger you admire?"
> "Why not?" "Your Olga's face lacks fire;
> If I wrote poetry like you,
> I'd choose the elder. . . ."

(III, 5)

It is remarkable that Onegin does not simply judge his friend's choice on the basis of ordinary life but judges the poet's choice on aesthetic grounds. He puts himself in Lensky's position and judges from Lensky's point of view—from the point of view of the supposed identity of poet with man, of poetry with the life of the poet. At the same time, since he himself is "not a poet," he judges dispassionately; he detects in Lensky's choice, instead of the alleged "stylistic unity," a stylistic contradiction, a "misalliance." The misalliance is not in life, where Olga and Lensky appear to be well matched, but in that realm where Lensky's poetic consciousness mingles with his empirical life—his ordinary, everyday existence. The critical view of the friend and "realist" destroys this idyll of oneness, separates the "real" from the "ideal."

However, Onegin does not confine his judgment to Lensky's choice. He involves both Tatyana and himself in the comparison he draws: "If I wrote poetry like you,/ I'd choose the elder." In this hypothetical situation the novel's two pairs of heroes are joined. Moreover, the real relations are mediated through the peculiar stylistic relations of these heroes. Onegin's remark shows how stylistics and reality look in the pair Lensky and Olga. But with these words the relationship between Tatyana and Onegin is also set in motion [*zaviazyvat'sia*] for the first time.

The subjunctive mood used by Onegin points to an ideal obligation, corresponding to the point of view of "poet" which Onegin has assumed. Ideally, the poet *should* choose the "other," the "objectively poetic" Tatyana, meaning that there is an "objective," a marked "stylistic difference" between Tatyana and her sister. The subjunctive mood, however, also points to the opposite—to the discrepancy between the ideal and life. Through this discrepancy that Onegin remarks, the novel's two pairs of heroes are joined.

The relationship between Onegin and Tatyana is set in motion at this very point. It is conceived in the form of a *possibility*, formulated by Onegin, who does not speak for or on behalf of himself: "If I wrote poetry like you." But given all that happens subsequently, it is no accident that these words come from him. Putting himself hypothetically in the ideal position of "poet," Onegin states his own preference. However, he does so hypothetically, from an ideal position—as if from the position of someone else,[41] and therefore it remains only a possibility: he *would choose* the elder.

This "raveling" [*zaviaska*], this possibility, is echoed at the end of the novel by Tatyana in her acknowledgment that the "unraveling" [*razviazka*] is an unrealized possibility: "So close, so possible/ Was happiness!" [VIII, 47]. *Possibility* in Pushkin's novel—we will see this again and again—is also a particular kind of reality parallel to that reality which actually occurs. If Onegin and Tatyana are "destined" for each other,[42] then in the words "I'd choose the elder" this fate is divined. But in the continuation, "If I wrote poetry like you,"[43] the opposite fate is divined, a fate which drives them apart. Simultaneously Onegin divines and does not recognize his "promised one," and this lack of recognition (compare Tatyana's letter: "I recognized you at first beholding") is really caused by the fact that he is *not a poet*.

However, the ideal position of poet, whence Onegin only ideally divines Tatyana, is not Lensky's position either. That is why Onegin, in the situation he supposes, occupies it *instead of* Lensky. He "would choose the elder" if he were a poet, but a poet of a different sort than Lensky. He would be sensitive to the "poetry of life" [Proffer, p. 128].[44] Onegin himself speaks of this later in his letter to Tatyana: "Though conscious of your tenderness,/ *I did not dare believe in it*" [the italics are Bocharov's].

In this speech of Onegin's, Lensky's poetic images are crudely deflated. Olga's image, executed in Lensky's "stylistic zone,"[45] is presented in Chapter II: "Pure-minded like the Muse's client,/ Dear as the kiss of youthful love," [II, 23]. In place of this Dulcinea, Onegin shows Lorenso an Aldonsa:

> "Your Olga's face is round and ruddy,
> Like that insipid [*glupyi*] moon aloft
> On that insipid dome suspended."

> (III, 5)

Thus, Onegin does not simply debate his friend's choice but opposes to his friend's consciousness and aesthetic his own consciousness and aesthetic, his own picture of the world. (Compare in the preceding stanza: "The country's so insipid here!") That Pushkin struggled to find the precise way to formulate Onegin's "image of the world" is evident from the fact that there are many variants of this passage. Initially the negative characteristics were not formulated so crudely: "Pink cheeks and gaze of innocence—/ I've had my fill of them long since"; "Believe me, innocence is piffle—/ I've had his Pamela's coy sniffle/ Ad nauseam in Richardson" [*PSS*, 6, 575]. In the course of working on the text, Pushkin made Onegin an "artist" and transformed his comments into a "picture of the world," while intensifying the subjective "deformation" of it. In the final text a picture of all of nature is executed by the same meager means with which Olga's portrait is drawn; everything is reduced to a single epithet, "insipid." When Pushkin introduced this epithet, he also changed a line in the preceding stanza, which read, "The country is so boring here!" [draft variant; *PSS*, 6, 306]. Thus in the final text Onegin's characterization of the world as a whole acquired stylistic unity.

Onegin's "artistic method" is a kind of aesthetic primitivism. It simplifies and trivializes to an extreme that which is exalted and ethereal to the "poet." The "romantic" image of life seems exaggerated because it is augmented by dreams. In Onegin's portrayal this imaginary reality is dispelled as an illusion, tendentiously debunked and depreciated. All of nature is "insipid." Onegin's aesthetic is the reverse of Lensky's aesthetic; hence, the traditional comparison to the moon is turned inside out. Moreover, in this characterization of the world a note of defiance is sounded. *Any and all* illusions—what Pushkin termed "the poetic predilections of the soul"—are challenged. And it is through Onegin that Pushkin's "lessons in pure atheism" are refracted in the novel.

"Your Olga's face is round and ruddy" is a translation into the language of folk primitivism of that ideal female image, which in Lensky's language is "Phyllis." In the novel the author "objectively" shows us very little of the "real" Olga; she is simple and predictable. On the other hand, Lensky and Onegin present two radically different, graphic portrayals of Olga, which are much more significant. For these portrayals, or "icons,"[46] reveal how both heroes view the world. Their pictures of the world, their *different* languages and stylistic systems, which express in different ways *one indivisible* world, simultaneously constitute in their diversity and unity the world of Pushkin's novel. For the world as a whole encompasses very different "images" and "pictures," images and pictures of reality which are also real and objective. In Pushkin's novel objectivity, reality is broadened "subjectively," broadened *stylistically* to an extraordinary degree. In many cases the image of reality arises out of juxtaposing two radically different stylistic variants which give expression to it in two radically different ways. The image of reality thus arises as "counterpoint." Two poles of expression evoke a particular content without supplanting it. Reality itself is situated "between" these radically different ways of expressing it.[47]

The intonations of Lensky and Onegin continually argue in the novel:

> "There'll be a frightful crowd and babble,
> A crush of every kind of rabble . . ."
> "Oh, nonsense, not like that at all!"
> "Who should be there?" "Just kin, that's all."

(IV, 49)

For the poet, "kin," that is, the Larins, is not the "external world," as it is for
Onegin. On the contrary, Lensky's "own" poetic world completely merges
with this immediate reality; what for him is everyday and personal is directly
elevated into an "ideal." "Kin" and dreams form the subjectively homoge-
neous (but to the detached observer heterogeneous and heterostylistic) "inner
world" of the poet, which he inhabits like a shell.

Conversely, Tatyana "seemed not born to them [that is, her "kin"] but
found—/ A stranger [*chuzhoi*] in the family round" [II, 25]. Tatyana also lives
in "her own" world, which is likewise a combination of things "her own" and
things "alien": "Insidious book in hand, she wanders/ Alone in forest hush and
ponders/ To seek and find in it *her own*/ Mute blaze, *her* dreams, *her* heart-
strings' tone;/ She sighs, and in herself discovers/ *Another's* glow, *another's*
smart," [III, 10; the italics are Bocharov's]. Onegin even destines her for the
"poet" on the basis of the ideal, proper stylistic affinity postulated by Lensky
himself (she is "like Svetlana"[48]). However, here as elsewhere in the novel, real
human relationships and inclinations do not coincide with stylistic coverings.
What is "one's own" and what is "alien" are allotted differently to the poet-
ically attuned Lensky and Tatyana. What for him is *one's own* ("kin"), for her is
alien. In the world of Pushkin's novel his world and her world are incom-
patible.

> To his ancestral hall returning,
> Vladimir Lensky sought the plot
> Of his old neighbor's last sojourning
> And sighed in tribute to his lot.
> And long he mourned for the departed:
> "Poor Yorick!" quoth he, heavy-hearted,
> "To think he nursed me in his day,
> And on his lap I used to play
> With his Ochákov decoration!"

(II, 37)

Here at the grave of Dmitri Larin, Lensky plays a scene from *Hamlet*.
Byron's poem "Lines Inscribed Upon a Cup Formed from a Skull" was the
model for this transformation of the Shakespearean situation (Hamlet musing
over the skull of poor Yorick) in Romantic poetry. Lensky, however, plays

naively, oblivious to the mixing of languages. Witness "Poor Yorick!" [quoted in English] and such mundane details as "Ochákov decoration."[49] For Lensky, "kin" exists as comfortably in the integument of the scene from *Hamlet* as in its natural attire. Lensky's world is *unconsciously heterostylistic*.

In the stanza which precedes Lensky's visit to the grave of Dmitri Larin, the author recounts the very same event to which Lensky responded as Hamlet:

> So they grew old like other mortals.
> At last a final mansion drew
> Asunder its sepulchral portals
> Before the husband, wreathed anew.
> Near dinnertime he died, contented,
> By friends and neighbors much lamented,

(II, 36)

The author's account is *consciously heterostylistic*. In these lines a single event, the death of Larin, is reported several times in different ways, in several stylistic variants. The simple and direct words—"grew old" [*stareli*], "died" [*umer*]—are paralleled by complex periphrastic metaphors: "drew asunder its sepulchral portals" [*otvorilis' dveri groba*], "wreathed anew" [*priial venets*].

The grand metaphors "elevate" the account of Larin's death. At the same time such details as "near dinnertime he died" tilt the account in a different direction, "downward." It is as if the direct words—"grew old," "died"—are located on the horizontal axis of this stylistic system of coordinates. Seemingly these words are equal to the event itself, while the stylistic variants in large measure constitute its interpretation. We cannot, however, assign one meaning to the event, for at one and the same time the tone is both ironic and serious. The solemn phraseology does not correspond to this simple, even "lowly," picture—hence the irony, and yet at the same time the phraseology does in fact elevate it and correspond to it as it would to the death of any man. "Wreathed anew/ Near dinnertime he died" are those very aspects of the simple event which are extracted from it by stylistic means, aspects which are relative and subjective (Larin's death refracted through two consciousnesses—one simple, the other archaic and lofty). At the same time, however, both aspects are objectively present in the event itself.

Here then is an example of the poetic "gnoseology" of Pushkin's novel. For in this fragment the words "wreathed anew" and "he died" relate to each other in the same way that the word relates to the event itself, to reality itself. The relationships between words re-create the structure of the relationship of the word to the world, the gnoseological structure of reality.

As we have said, the author's account of Larin's death is consciously heterostylistic, in contrast to Lensky's response to this event, which is unconsciously heterostylistic. The difference can be expressed as follows: the heterostylism in the *objective open context of the author* (in the context of actual reality, whose structure the text reproduces) versus the heterostylism in the *subjective closed context of Lensky* (which as such is encompassed in the author's objective context).

In a recent article Yury Lotman addressed this very problem, seeking to show how an image of reality is created in the structure of Pushkin's text. [50] Analyzing the stanza in which Larin's death is recounted, Lotman concludes: "The succession of semantic and stylistic breaks creates not a focused but a diffused multiple point of view, which thus becomes the center of a super-system perceived as an illusion of reality itself."

One must be careful, however, to distinguish whether such a stylistic juncture occurs in the author's open, "multiple" context or in the closed, "monological" context of one of the subjects. The same stanza demonstrates the difference. The account of Larin's death concludes with a "quotation," an epitaph:

> "A humble sinner, Dmitri Larin,
> God's servitor and brigadier,
> Found peace beneath this marble here."

(II, 36)

According to Lotman, the "repeated stylistic and semantic switches" are "synthesized" in this epitaph, "which simultaneously is both solemn . . . and comic." To be sure, both aspects of the event and their corresponding languages are "synthesized" in the "mixed" formula: "God's servitor and brigadier." Here "earthly and heavenly powers"—to quote Lotman—are naively equated. But precisely because of this the nature of the "synthesis" is qualitatively different. If a stylistic switch does take place in the author's speech when he recounts Larin's death, then in the line "God's servitor and brigadier" such a switch simply does not occur. In the stylistic reality of the author those elements which naively merge in the language of the patriarchal epitaph are differentiated. Lotman does not note this difference. He does not note the *boundary* which separates the authorial context, with its open heterostylism, from the closed context of the quotation, whose subject is the patriarchal consciousness speaking about the deceased in unconsciously mixed and therefore comical language.

Immediately after the patriarchal epitaph comes the epitaph of Lensky in the guise of Hamlet, which is an analogous mixture of elements ("Poor Yorick" and "Ochàkov decoration"). Unexpectedly, Lensky's poetic picture of the world turns out to be similar to the picture of the world formed by the naive patriarchal consciousness. Both closed "internal" worlds are presented in the text as they really appear in the "external" world of the author, in the world of the novel.

"This Grandison was fond of cards, / A fop, and sergeant of the Guards" [II, 30]. This is "Grandison" as he appears in the external world of the author, translated from "romantic" into "real" language. But here is the very same Grandison as he appears in a dialogue between characters, where no translation occurs:

> "Your Grandison, do you remember? . . ."
> "What Grandison? . . . Oh, *Grandison!*
> Yes, yes, of course . . . Where has he been?"
> "Why, here; he lives right by St. Simeon's."

> (VII, 41)

The contradiction in content and the technique used to create the effect seem to be the same in both cases. However, the effect itself is different. This suggests that artistic effect is not simply a matter of technique and that the device of the stylistic break in and of itself is not the only thing that matters. What matters most (and this also explains the different impression or effect) is the kind of significance the "device" acquires in both the subjective and the objective composition of the novel. In the first case the device is realized in the open context of the author, in the second case in a closed context—a conversation between two old ladies whose consciousnesses are in harmony. Their Grandison sounds "without translation" in their everyday language and exists in their everyday milieu; in fact, he lives right here in Moscow by St. Simeon's.

And, thus, the author's heterostylism is completely different from that of Lensky. The author consciously speaks in different languages and constructs from their relationships his own authorial text and his own objective world. In the context of the author this really constitutes the objective heterostylism of the world.

Here is how the "internal" world of Lensky, with its contradictions (which are not apparent to Lensky himself) and its stylistic discord, is displayed in the "external" world of the author:

> And find an ease as all-consoling
> As travelers drunk on inn-beds lolling,
> Or, gentler, butterflies that cling
> To honeyed blossoms in the spring.

> (IV, 51)

These two similes, illuminating the condition of all-consoling ease, are opposites and yet equivalents. "As travelers drunk" from the author's "external" point of view is the very same as "butterflies" from Lensky's "internal" point of view.[51] This is precisely how Lensky finds "an all-consoling ease" in a prosaic setting at the Larins'. A parallel can be drawn between Lensky's situation and the lines from Pushkin's 1822 epistle to Raevsky cited above: "Could I in that abyss of vice and slime/ Have really reveled, pure of heart?" "In that abyss of vice and slime" = "as travelers drunk on inn-beds lolling" = as "butterflies" = in blissful ignorance of the "eternal contradictions of being." However, we see how different the two situations are. The moment the lyrical "I" becomes conscious of this contradiction is quite unlike the way this contradiction is portrayed in the objective world of the novel, where it gives rise to a hetero-stylistic situation.

This then is another example of what we discussed above. An image of reality arises out of the coming together of two radically different stylistic variants which give expression to it in two radically different ways. It arises as "counterpoint." Here the counterpoint of "butterfly" and "traveler drunk on inn-bed lolling"[52] expresses the two aspects of Lensky's situation in the world. But right away, in turn, a counterpoint to this image of Lensky's world, which is portrayed from two different points of view, is formed by juxtaposing Onegin's image of the world:

> But wretched, whose foreboding vision,
> Whose wakeful mind is never blurred,
> To whom each movement, every word
> Spells shame and breeds a cold derision;

(IV, 51)

These lines, which portray Onegin's situation, also correspond to lines in Pushkin's epistle to Raevsky:

> But all has passed! The heart's blood is congealed,
> In all their nakedness before my eyes
> Stand world and life, friendship and love revealed,
> And my bleak wisdom I despise.

(PSS, 2, 265)

This *moment* in the development of the lyrical "I" almost coincides with the beginning of *Onegin*. In the novel in verse this moment is objectified and given alterity—transferred to the portrayal of the hero.

Just as initially in the final stanza of Chapter IV, an image of Lensky's world arises out of superimposing two opposing points of view = stylistic variants, so too subsequently does a broader and more complex image of the world arise out of superimposing Lensky and Onegin's opposing images of the world. It arises through counterpoint.

In this passage the author—or, more precisely, the "I" of the novel—seems to be close to Onegin and to form with him (as in many similar situations) a firm "we": "While we, his critics, . . ." [IV, 50]. But this union is relative and in large measure conditional; only up to a certain point does the "I" side with Onegin. We saw how Olga appears in Onegin's "translation" and with her the whole of nature. The author, however, does not "hate" life "in translation."

The kind of "translation" that Onegin practices is one of deflation, debunking. However, the concept of "translation" has much greater significance in the novel. "Translations" are the *creative* power of Pushkin's novel. The text, the world of the novel is *created, constructed* by means of "translations," switches from one stylistic language to another, and ultimately from any and all "subjective" languages into the "objective" language of life itself. Thus, the concept of "translation" is analogous to the structure of the world of the novel as a whole. In several passages of *Onegin* the word "translation" is particularly significant. Let us turn to the stanzas in Chapter III in which the author presents Tatyana's letter.

4

> I'll have to furnish a translation
> Of Tanya's letter in the end.
> She knew our language [Russian] only barely,
>
> . . . .
>
> She wrote in French, be it admitted . . .

(III, 26)

The author confesses, "What Tanya wrote is in my keeping" [III, 31]. But we have no idea just what this "original" is. In the text of the novel in place of it, we find:

> An incomplete and weak translation,
> A pallid copy of life's picture . . .

(III, 31)

And so, the classic verses of Pushkin, which all Russian children learn by heart, are passed off as the translation of a French text (to be sure, in prose) of a provincial miss. That is the author's empirical motivation, his mystification, which for some reason he finds necessary. Contemporary critics commented on this mystification: "But then we read Tatyana's letter rendered in charming verses."[53]

Pushkin's reasons for "translating" Tatyana's letter are rather complex. They form a special context all their own, which extends over six entire stanzas [III, 26–31]. Before presenting his own "translation," the author searches for another suitable way to translate Tatyana's letter, all the while expressing doubt and regret:

For Parny's pen, his gentle grace,
These days have lost their honored place.

(III, 29)

The name of Parny is the sign of a particular poetics which encompasses both the French poet himself and the Russian tradition of translations from his poetry.[54] This tradition was most notably represented in the poetry of Batyushkov and that of the young Pushkin.[55] "Prozerpina" ["Proserpina"], Pushkin's last translation from Parny, was written in 1824, the same year that Pushkin wrote these lines about Parny in Chapter III of *Onegin.* However, in this chapter Pushkin disassociates himself from the poetics of Parny, as he does in general throughout the novel. This disassociation is carried over into the following stanza, where the author addresses Baratynsky, "bard of feasts and languid sorrow":

> To see in your bewitching cadence
> New-rendered my impassioned maiden's
> Effusion of outlandish [foreign] words.
> Where are you? Come: my prior right
> I make it over to you gladly . . .

(III, 30)

Only because the "bard" is far away, " 'neath Finland's heaven," and does not hear his plea, does the author resolve to "translate" himself. Consequently, instead of "bewitching cadences," he presents an "incomplete and weak translation."

It is very characteristic of Pushkin to oppose "his own" and "another's" verse, as he does here in Chapter III of *Onegin,* to ascribe all the advantages to the "other's" and to characterize "his own" modestly. (In a certain sense this opposition is one of "poetry" versus "prose.") The model of "another's" poetry retains its own "poetic" language, all the while serving as a standard against which Pushkin defines his efforts in a modest and "prosaic" manner. The image of Baratynsky that is created here fully corresponds to the lyrical image found in Baratynsky's own early poetry. And the description of the way Baratynsky would have "new-rendered" "in bewitching cadence" the words of the impassioned maiden corresponds to a later description of just such a poetic process by Baratynsky himself. Young people, Baratynsky observed, find in the poetry of a young poet "almost their own feelings and their own thoughts clothed in brilliant colors" [*PSS,* 14, 6].

According to Vyazemsky, Pushkin confided "that for a long time he could not decide how to have Tatyana write, without being untrue to the feminine personality and violating verisimilitude of style. Out of fear that the letter would degenerate into an academic ode, he thought of writing it in prose. He even thought of writing it in French. But, finally, a happy inspiration came to him at just the right moment, and the feminine heart spoke simply and freely in Russian. It had no need for Tatishchev's *Dictionary* or Memorsky's *Grammar.*"[56]

Here an image of Tatyana's letter is sketched out. This is what it *could have been* "in the original," had "verisimilitude of style" been adhered to. Vyazemsky's testimony is most valuable not only because he transmitted Pushkin's own personal testimony, but also because he, Vyazemsky, could imagine this "original" ("real") letter of Tatyana, something impossible for a man not of his generation or background. It turns out that the verse equivalent of this "original" could have been an "academic ode," and the reference to Tatishchev's *Dictionary* and Memorsky's *Grammar* constitute a concrete historical stylistic indicator of this *possible* letter of Tatyana. In the text of the novel we do find examples of Tatyana's stylistic characteristics in the rare instances of her direct speech:

> She murmurs: "I shall be undone;
> Undone by him, I will be cheerful,"

> (VI, 3)

Or her farewell to favorite childhood haunts in VII, 28, whose model, as has been pointed out more than once, was the monologue of Joan in Zhukovsky's *Maid of Orleans*. This direct speech bears a stylistic imprint from which Tatyana's letter is free. For these are quotations, as it were, from the "verisimilar style" of Tatyana in the guise of "Svetlana," samples of her stylistically constrained language, which the author permits us to experience "in the original." In the text stylistic distance is created between these examples of Tatyana's direct speech and her letter in the author's "translation."[57]

But, in the case of the letter itself, distance is also created between the "translation" and the "original." Regarding Pushkin's mystification, Viktor Vinogradov observed: "Despite the preliminary apologies of the author, the language of Tatyana's letter is Russian, untranslated. It does not assume a French text behind it."[58] To be sure, Tatyana's letter does not assume an *actual* French text. Nevertheless, Pushkin does assume the fiction of this text, and it is a "fact" of the artistic reality which must be taken into consideration.[59] Given the premise of a foreign original, it is all the more significant that Pushkin's rendition of Tatyana's letter is free of "the French element in the Russian literary language" (which is more evident in Onegin's letter), free of "the periphrases and metaphors of milady's style characteristic of the Karamzinists."[60]

Pushkin's "translation" constitutes, as it were, an actual re-creation of precisely those most genuine qualities of Russian expression: "And the feminine heart spoke *simply* and *freely* in Russian." Here Pushkin's "happy inspira-

tion" is portrayed as bursting the empirical constraints that confined and
bound the consciousness and language of the real Tatyana. (The examples of
her direct speech in the text give us an idea of what these constraints are like.)
Her heart spoke, and not merely her constrained and limited language, stylis-
tically conditioned in a particular manner. Several times in the text of the novel
Tatyana's "heart" is called the "subject" of her letter. Pushkin's "translation"
then is not a translation of the French text of a young provincial miss in love,
not a translation of this "verisimilar" reality whose sign is the assumed letter
"in French," but a "translation" of profound reality, of Tatyana's "heart." To
distinguish this reality from empirical reality the fiction of the original in
French is used. Thereby, the empirical "textual intermediary" and its "foreign
words" are *separated* from "the innermost original," "the living picture" of
Tatyana's Russian soul.

Here it should be noted that all the variants which, according to
Vyazemsky, Pushkin considered in his search for an appropriate way to express
his intent found expression in one way or another in the text of the novel.
There is Tatyana's stylized direct speech, there is the "fact" of her letter in
French (to be sure, in prose), and finally there is her free "conversation of the
heart" in Pushkin's "translation" of that same letter. Instead of "new-render-
ing" Tatyana's "foreign words" in "bewitching cadences," which would have
concealed the distance separating poetry from reality, Pushkin emphasizes that
distance. He constructs the entire composition out of the relationship between
his own poetry (the "translation"), "factual" reality (Tatyana's letter, which is
"in his keeping"), and "true reality," the "innermost original."[61] And in
relationship to *this* original and to *this* reality, Pushkin's rendition of Tatyana's
letter is only

> An incomplete and weak translation,
> A pallid copy of life's picture . . .

> (III, 31)

Thus Pushkin's mystification can be said to embody the profound *composi-
tional idea* of his novel, which is conscious of being only a "translation" of the
real world.[62] Pushkin the "translator" does not compete with the "original" of
reality, and therein lies the true and profound meaning of the opposition
"bewitching cadence"–"incomplete, weak translation."

Further on in the text of the novel (in draft variants to VII, 24) we come
across a definition which is similar to the formula used to characterize Tatyana's
letter:

> Perhaps a rather weak translation
> Of others' vices, others' cares.

> (*PSS*, 6, 442)

This occurs in the scene in which Tatyana unmasks Onegin. The formula is similar, but its meaning is quite the opposite.

Let us recall the circumstances surrounding the unmasking [VII, 19–25]. Tatyana visits the home of her hero in his absence. The account of this visit sustains the style of their "romantic" relations: "Spellbound, Tatyana mused and lingered/ Within that modish hermit's cell" [VII, 20]. Tatyana is enveloped by the atmosphere of Onegin. In his absence she reads his books, wherein "On every page there are revealed/ Involuntary intimations/ Of where he nodded or demurred/ With query, cross, or scribbled word" [VII, 23]. This system of signs gives a more spontaneous ("involuntary") expression to Onegin's soul than did the living person Tatyana encountered. In this system "the sharp mark of a fingernail" [VII, 23] signals those models which this living person follows. For Tatyana, "the sharp mark of a fingernail" distinguishes these "originals" from their "rather weak translation." In the final text this definition was not included. (Was it perhaps because it coincided too closely with the formula in Chapter III?) Nonetheless it corresponds to the situation. For it is as if Tatyana finds the "romantic" guises left behind by Onegin, the "cloaks" in which he appeared to her, and thus for the first time (and in his absence!) can distinguish the real Onegin from these "costumes." Instead of "real substance" she discovers "nothingness," a "translation" from a foreign source—seemingly without an "innermost original."

The series of variants given in VII, l. 24, indicate that Pushkin was searching for a way to define this relationship between the reproduction, the repetition, and the "original." Here, for example, we find "imitation," "phantom," "interpretation," "whole lexicon of modish words." Thus, the enigma of Onegin in large measure is a stylistic problem. Finally:

A parody, perhaps . . . who knows?

(VII, 24, line 14)

It is as if the literal translation of "foreign" content ("alien whims") into Russian, which gives rise to stylistic discord ("A Muscovite in Harold's cloak"—VII, 24, l. 11), constitutes parody. In principle this is the very same phenomenon as Lensky playing Hamlet at the grave of Dmitri Larin. The hero and his "cloak," which heretofore in Tatyana's eyes constituted an inseparable and indivisible image of Onegin, now are separated from one another and compared as model and "copy." Tatyana seems to examine a transfer, a calque. Obviously the formula "weak translation," which appeared in the draft variants, signifies "weak" in relation to a completely different kind of original than was the case with Tatyana's letter.

Conversely, in the final chapter, Tatyana appears surrounded largely by *untranslated* foreign concepts:

. . . She seemed a faithful likeness
Du comme il faut (Shishkov, be kind!
This won't translate, so never mind).

(VIII, 14)

Not one in her could much as find
A single blemish of the kind
That London's fashionable classes
In their fastidious slang decry
As *vulgar.*[63] (And I vainly try . . .

I'm very fond of this locution,
But vainly try to render it;
And yet, with us, its distribution
Is small, and it is scarcely fit
For any use but rhyming meanly . . .)

(VIII, 15–16)

For Pushkin it is very important to express this quality of the new Tatyana "in the original," to convey it in its own terms. (In the Russian context these appear to be the proper names for the realities they render.) By superimposing the two foreign terms from different languages, which illuminate Tatyana from different perspectives (positively and by contrast), Pushkin suggests that this quality in the new Tatyana is not imitation, not translation, but a "faithful likeness." In the same stanza [VIII, 14] an equivalent definition is given: "Without affected mannerism."[64]

At the same time, however, these foreign realities—for the foreign words given here in the original seem to constitute their own realities—convey in the Russian context not only the distance between the new Petersburg Tatyana and the former Tatyana, but in this new Tatyana the distance between the "lady" [VIII, 16], "High Priestess of the polished floor" [VIII, 28], and the unchanged "simple maiden" [VIII, 41] concealed within her. Foreign originals constitute Tatyana's "role"—a role she does not simply play but seriously lives: "How she had grown into her role!" [VIII, 28]. Tatyana herself, however, knows that this is "pretentious masquerading" [VIII, 46].

In a certain sense there is a parallel between Tatyana in the final Petersburg chapter of the novel and Onegin in the first Petersburg chapter—that Onegin who is compared to "playful Venus" joining a "masquerade" [I, 25]. That chapter too is full of foreign terms given in Latin script. However, the relationship of the role to the hero is different in Chapter I. It is expressed by the formula, "Like *dandy* clad in London dress" [I, 4], which Pushkin immediately translates in a note: "Dandy, *frant*" [note 2]. Apropos of this, Grigory Vinokur's comments are illuminating: "A dandy . . . if he is a hero, is a stylized hero, not simply a hero, but forever 'like' a hero. Strictly speaking, Onegin is not even a dandy, but only *like* a dandy: 'Like *dandy* clad in London dress.' "[65]

Earlier in this essay we talked about the opposite stylistic pole in Chapter I, where "The peddler struts, the merchant dresses" [I, 35]. It is interesting that this particular stanza concludes with a Russianized German word:

> The baker, punctual German, bustles
> White-capped behind his service hatch
> And more than once has worked the latch [*vasisdas*].

(I, 35)

The draft version read: *Was—ist—das* [*PSS*, 6, 242]. Just imagine this word in that [i.e., the Latin] orthography in the final text. It would then fall into the same category as all the other foreign terms in Chapter I, which are given in Latin script and which constitute the reality of the "young good-for-nothing" Onegin. The baker, although he is a German, shares a common environment with the merchant, the peddler, and the cabman. Therefore, the word *vasisdas* is translated for the Russian ear, given in the Russian transcription of popular speech, presented as a specific term of ordinary Russian reality.

The reverse of this is found too. For example, in II, 33, where Russian *N* is "ejected/ A la française" and "Praskovya smartened to Paulina." Calques such as these play no small role in the stylistic reality of *Onegin*. In a very real sense they constitute "the encyclopedia of Russian life." In conjunction with this we should not forget Pushkin's "macaronic" epigraph to Chapter II: "O rus! . . ." —"O Russia! [*Rus'*]."[66]

In an article on Chateaubriand's translation of *Paradise Lost,* which Pushkin wrote shortly before his death, the poet commented: "There is no doubt that in trying to render Milton *word for word,* Chateaubriand could not adhere to fidelity of thought and expression. A literal translation can never be faithful" [*PSS*, 12, 144]. Translating word for word gives rise to *parody,* as Pushkin demonstrates in IV, 47: "The hour that people class/ As 'wolf-and-dog time'[67] (for some reason/ That I for one could never see)." But how much in the content of the novel that is extremely serious and profound is linked with this playful passage! The very phrase "Muscovite in Harold's cloak" [VII, 24], which is so important to the novel, is such a calque. At the opposite pole stands Tatyana's letter, which, precisely because it is an "incomplete and weak translation," manifests "fidelity of thought and expression."

And so, in the vocabulary of significant words in Pushkin's novel, "translation" is one of the most important. This word characterizes the "multilingualism" of the novel—specifically, the linguistic relations between foreign and Russian verbal realities. In a broader sense, however, "translation" signifies the interrelations between stylistic "languages" and their relationship to the "simple," "direct" ("nonstylistic") word, and ultimately the relationship of verbal expression in general to reality as content. The true and final original, as it were, is life itself.

Let us consider an example from Chapter I:

> A malady to whose causation
> We have, alas, as yet no clues,
> Known as [like] the *spleen* to Albion's nation,
> In the vernacular: the *blues*—
> With this disease he was infected;

(I, 38)

We see, however, that this precise definition is not immediately arrived at. There are lengthy approaches; an approximation is given. It is as if words keep circling around the object. First, instead of the anticipated characterization of the "malady," there is oblique movement off to the side. Then we draw closer: the malady is *likened* to an analogous phenomenon, but one that is foreign[68] and belongs to a different language and hence is not exactly the same thing. Finally, there is the translation into Russian, and with it the distance between the word and reality is bridged. Nevertheless the distance is not completely bridged; the word does not merge with reality. For Russian *"blues"* [*khandra*], like English *"spleen,"* is given in italics. In this way the *word* is emphasized as well as its specific terminological nature, which still does not adequately cover the "malady" itself. English spleen correlates with Russian blues (as a likeness to the original) in the same way that the latter correlates with its own reality, which is present behind the word. And just as the essential Russian quality of these blues cannot be expressed in a language of foreign likeness, so too the "malady" in and of itself, reality in and of itself, cannot be completely translated into a word.

But these "blues," which in I, 38, appear in italics as a *marked* word, shortly thereafter [in I, 54] appear without italics, like reality itself: "The blues hovered near him like a sentry." And this kind of thing happens over and over again in the text of the novel. In a particular passage, a word—most often of all a word that is current, "modish"[69]—will be marked, singled out, and thereby separated from its own reality, presented as a *word* which is not at one with reality (as if it were given in quotation marks or italics). Thereby in "the encyclopedia of Russian life" this word will also seem to be an object, a reality alongside that object, that reality which it signifies. In other passages of the novel it will merge with its own reality. The distance between a word and reality will be demonstrated and then eliminated.

In Chapter VI, 23, we read: "Upon the modish word *ideal,*/ Did dreamless sleep on Lensky steal." But this modish word, which is displayed to us here as a material thing, lives as meaning in the novel. As it moves from one stylistic context to another, it ceases to be an alien, empty, and comical word and becomes a word rich in content, replete with that which is the author's *own.* Let us compare: "One droopy sort of fool contended/ She was ideal to earth descended," [VII, 49],[70] but the author himself says: "The dear Ideal of Tatyana" [VIII, 51] and in the preceding stanza: "You, too, strange travel-mate unsteady,/ Farewell, and you, my true Ideal" [VIII, 50]. Moreover, in the concluding stanzas the word is transformed, capitalized. This process of moving a word from one context to another and filling it with new content is clearly demonstrated in "Onegin's Journey," where we are told: "I felt I had to pay addresses/ . . . To that proud maiden, my ideal" [J, 17] and then in the next stanza: "Now my ideal is the *khoziaika* ["housewife"]." This is a very interesting passage from the standpoint of the question of "translations" in the novel. Strictly speaking, the only word that moves here from one context (the former, the "poetic" one) to another (the new, "prosaic" one) is "ideal." It seems to move without translation, but in return the content which fills it out is plainly translated into another language—"proud maiden" transformed into "housewife."

Marked, "modish" words are not the only words to undergo transformations in the text. Side by side we will find a word italicized, set off as a word, and the same word without italics, brought to life as living reality.

Here is an instance where a simple word (actually a phrase) is italicized, and this time the plot is affected. In VI, 27, Onegin recommends his servant as his second: "Although he is outshone by many,/ He is a fine as lad as any" [*malyi chestnyi*]. Onegin's recommendation is designed to transform "the servant, a Frenchman named Guillot" [VI, 25], into a completely different kind of person, one worthy to be his second. Therefore, in making his recommendation he translates the Russian pronounciation and orthography of the servant's French name back into the language of the original: "He's here: my friend, Monsieur Guillot" [VI, 27].[71] Within just a few lines this new character, this verbal phantom, leads an independent existence: "While some way off, Zaretsky and/ His colleague, the *fine lad* [*chestnyi malyi*], have started/ A grave discussion. . . ." Repeated in italics, Onegin's characterization seems to acquire new power, to be objectified, externalized, turned into a verbal role. Thus it is linked in the world of the novel to other similar formations: for example, to the verbal masks of Onegin himself.

Truly, Pushkin is like a "lexicon," to invoke Gogol's remarkably apt word.[72] Here we should repeat what we said earlier: namely, that in Pushkin's text the poetic world of the novel and its stylistic laboratory are one. Stylistic problems, contradictions, distinctions, intermingle and unite with the very lives of the novel's heroes. Speaking about the way styles and languages of the era ("images of language") mutually illuminate one another in *Eugene Onegin*, Mikhail Bakhtin emphasizes that this interillumination is not accomplished at the level of linguistic abstraction: "Images of language are inseparable from images of various world views and from the living beings who are their agents—people who think, talk, and act in a setting that is social and historically concrete."[73] Thus, Pushkin's "encyclopedia," or his "lexicon," is a *world* in which different "languages" and "words" do not appear in isolation or in a state of separation, as is the case in a lexicon or an encyclopedia,[74] but in living combinations and unexpected contexts created in the conscious and speaking reality of the novel, which is expressed by the indivisible, uninterrupted, and heterostylistic authorial speech.

In Chapter VII, when Tatyana unmasks the hero, "words" ("Whole lexicon of modish words?"—VII, 24, l. 13) is contrasted to "word" as genuine reality, as truth: "But can it be the *word*'s been found?" [VII, 25, l. 2]. Note that here "word" itself, as a word, is italicized. But just what is this problematic *word*? It is of course not some "individual," even "simple" word or group of words (a single stylistic cluster). We are talking about the matter of solving the riddle of Onegin, which represents a fundamental problem in the novel. However, "parody"—Tatyana's word, her solution [VII, 24, l. 14], which also seems to be implied in VII, 25, by *"word"*—is not the final pronouncement on Onegin; it is not the answer to the riddle. For what is at issue here is the revelation of reality. The "word" which meets that objective is the entire text of the novel in verse as a whole, as a structure. A stylistic stratification of the text that is properly organized can bring us closer to experiencing this *word* in Pushkin's novel.

5

Let us examine the stylistic system of *Eugene Onegin* in action, by following the development of a particular theme in the text:

> He mourned the wilt of life's young green
> When he had almost turned eighteen.

(II, 10)

This couplet, which is typical of the stanzaic codas in *Onegin,* concludes the characterization of Lensky's "song" by translating it and the image of the "bard" himself into "real language" in the final line. Here the mechanism of the ironic switch from the "ideal" world to the "real" world is obvious. The sober second line cancels out and destroys the image of Lensky's poetry in the first line. The second line relates to the first as reality to illusion, as Lensky's real image (compare: "Vladimir Lensky, in the flower/ Of youthful looks and lyric power"—II, 6) to his elegiac double.

This tendency in the text—this deflation, whereby the text (= world) of the novel is divided into the "real" and the "ideal"—can be called the "analyzing" force of Pushkin's novel. Every reader of *Onegin* feels the constant pull of this force in the text of the novel. Where it is strongest, this tendency signifies the "dispelling" of various verbal and life-engendered illusions or fantasies ("elegiac poses"—VI, 44), which constitute no small part of the reality of the novel and play no small role in the lives of its heroes. The stylistic translations from one language to another "dispel" these illusions one by one. Pushkin's irony strips reality to its "simple foundation." The following quotation illustrates this tendency. Lensky's phraseology is deflated, simplified, and the author himself is the "translator":

> He thinks: "I will be her redeemer,
> Will not permit the shameless schemer
>
> . . . .
>
> And all this meant was, in the end:
> I shall be shooting at my friend.

(VI, 17)

In this case Lensky's style is subjected to translation *in toto:* "And all this meant." It is simply canceled out.[75]

This tendency in the text of the novel corresponds to the program in the 1822 note "On Prose": "Why not simply say 'horse' "—where "simply" means "in truth." But, as we stated above, the matter is not nearly so simple in Pushkin's novel in verse. In the 1822 note this tendency totally defines the stylistic system constructed. Every expression is reduced to "simple" words. All other modes of expression (the "nonsimple") are "simply" considered untrue, meaningless, written off as having no reality. Therefore they are debunked, cancelled out through "simple" translation.

In *Onegin,* however, things are much more complex, and this tendency does not fully characterize the text. Rather it combines with another tendency which is its exact opposite: the joining, the synthesis of all "languages" and modes of expression into a single poetic entity—the "ontology" of Pushkin's novel. From this opposing point of view all illusions, all stylizations, all "words" possess reality and constitute the "encyclopedia of Russian life," its "lexicon"—the conscious and speaking world of the novel in verse.

In the novel the unriddling of its "strange" and enigmatic hero Onegin is also reduced to a "simple" solution. Such, at least in part, is Tatyana's conclusion: "But can it be the *word*'s been found?" (this word being "parody"). In "Onegin's Album," which in the manuscript of Chapter VII Tatyana also read, another "simple" solution is proposed by another intelligent lady: "Did you not know, as long you should,/ That you are simply—very good?" [*PSS,* 6, 615]. In the final text "Onegin's Album" was not included, but the association of this formula ("simply") with Onegin is significant. In the last chapter the formula occurs again in another variant. Now it becomes the viewpoint of philistine "realism," the voice of the crowd: "Or will he be like everybody,/ Like you and me, just [simply] a good egg?" [VIII, 8]. However, the "reality" of Onegin (according to Dostoevsky, he is a man of "fantasy"[76]) simply cannot be reduced to such "simplicity." The same holds true for the entire reality of *Eugene Onegin,* which constantly *is reduced* to "simple truth" ("prose") but at the same time *is not reduced* to it.

Returning to the portrayal of Lensky in the final two lines of II, 10, we can feel that here too deflation does not completely resolve the matter. If, in one sense, the elegiac image in the first line (poetic illusion) is completely reduced to simple reality in the second line, then in another sense the "actual," "real" Lensky is not reduced to his mundane image. Instead he combines young ruddiness and "the flower of youthful looks" with the elegiac "wilt of life" in his dreams and "songs." In these two lines the authentic, real Lensky, with his real consciousness, is presented as a single whole, where "subjective" and "objective" merge:

> He mourned the wilt of life's young green
> When he had almost turned eighteen.[77]

To be sure, the couplet does divide internally into the "ideal" and the "real," expression and content. But at the same time this "analytical" tendency (the "gnoseology" of Pushkin's novel) unites with the reverse tendency, that of synthesis: the synthesis of both one and the other image of Lensky, the "poetic" and the "prosaic." On this "ontological" plane Lensky's poetic *expression* of his life also constitutes the *content* of his life, his very life. Here it should be noted that there is a significant difference in the way our two examples are constructed. In both cases [II, 10 and VI, 17] Lensky's phraseology is deflated, translated into simple language. In the second case the author himself openly acts as the "translator" and thereby simply cancels out Lensky's speech, his manner of expression. Lensky's speech as the speech of "another" is clearly distinguished from the author's interpretation. In the concluding couplet of II, 10, however, the switch takes place within authorial speech. Thus, "subjective" and "objective" are not distinguished as they are in VI, 17, but are *juxtaposed* as if they constituted a single entity. If in one sense the "ideal" image of the first line is canceled out in the second, then in another sense the two images *coexist* in the unity of this couplet.

In these lines the correlation between the ideal and the real is not fixed; the ideal viewed otherwise is also real. That is why images of Lensky's poetic consciousness and style appear in different "positions" in different passages of the author's text. Their real meaning continually changes. They are portrayed "almost as a material thing"[78] and subjected pitilessly to "translation": "Thus he wrote *murkily* and *limply*" [VI, 23]. But immediately after this verdict, Lensky's poetry comes alive in authorial speech—in the scene of the duel, where the author seriously and openly recounts Lensky's death in the language of Lensky's consciousness: "The bell tolls out his term, unheard"—VI, 30 (compare with Lensky's elegy: "The bell doth toll for every man"—VI, 21). Unexpectedly Lensky's "ideal" poetry is *realized:* it "comes to life." This poetry as such, with all its conventional images, is transformed into the direct speech of the author himself. The author recounts the death of the young bard and mourns him in the bard's own language, in the language of "another," with its typical periphrases, all on the same stylistic level: "Our youthful friend/ Has gone to his untimely end./ Becalmed the storm; by searing cancer/ Spring's lovely blossom withered lies;/ The altar fire grows dim and dies!" [VI, 31].

In the following stanza "counterpoint" is created as two distinct and *equal* voices sound:

> Quite still and strangely placid seeming,
> He lay in deathly torpor swooned,
> His breast pierced through and through, and steaming,
> The lifeblood trickled from his wound.

(VI, 32)

The first two lines approximate Lensky's stylistic zone; in the second couplet this sight is translated into the sober language of facts. Here, however, the two categories do not correlate, the way they do in so many other passages of the novel, as illusion and reality. In this portrayal of the bard's actual early death, his "song" unexpectedly takes on the same reality in authorial speech as does the sober account of the facts. The author speaks seriously and openly in two voices—one "alien" and the other "his own"—and thus he constructs an all-embracing image of Lensky's death, giving equal weight to Lensky's "subjec-tivism" and his own "objectivism" and making them symmetrical.

The two variants of Lensky's possible fate crown this symmetry: "Perchance the world would have saluted/ In him a savior or a sage" [VI, 37] and "Or we might guess with equal reason/ A fate of far more common cast" [VI, 39]. These two prospects, however, indicate that the unified "subjective–objective" image has disintegrated for they are *variants, possibilities* instead of *life*. Here the two aspects forming the "duality-in-oneness" of the lines "He mourned the wilt of life's young green/ When he had almost turned eighteen" are singled out in their "primary state."

Earlier, apropos of Onegin's words "If I wrote poetry like you,/ I'd choose the elder" [III, 5], we talked about the fact that *possibilities* possess a particular kind of reality in Pushkin's novel. In Onegin's words, for example, a fate is divined which remains a possibility, ideal relations are divined which do not coincide with the actual fate of Onegin and Tatyana. But on another plane of the novel these ideal relations are real—real in the profoundest sense of the word. As we read the text, we observe how the action of the novel advances amid many possibilities, potential variants, which the author continually sketches out as the plot unfolds.[79] These possibilities either do not come to pass or, conversely, come to pass unexpectedly. Tatyana pronounces the words, "So close, so possible/ Was happiness . . ." [VIII, 47], at a time when another possibility has become reality, a possibility which she at one time rejected: "I would have been a loving mother/ And a devoted, faithful wife"[80] [letter to

Onegin, Chapter III]. Compare this to her words in Chapter VIII: "But I was pledged another's wife,/ And will be faithful all my life" [VIII, 47].

The composition of the novel unfolds through a consideration of the *variants* of a given situation as it arises. Take Chapter III, for example. Tatyana sees all novelistic heroes "blended/ Into a single essence warm,/ Embodied in Onegin's form" [III, 9]. But immediately, two types of novels, the old moralistic novel [III, 11] and the new Romantic novel [III, 12], are considered separately. And the two fictional hypostases of Onegin that Tatyana conjures up in her imagination—"dear hero" [III, 10] and "modish tyrant" [III, 15]—correspond to these two types of novels. The same two images are developed in Tatyana's letter—again as variants, supposed possibilities: "My angel then, my preservation,/ Or the fell demon of temptation,/ Which are you?" And again in the episode of unmasking: "Issue of Heaven or of Hell,/ Proud demon, angel—who can tell?" [VII, 24]. The unriddling of Onegin usually proceeds the same way by laying out opposing variants of a solution. A fundamental question—indicated by such formulas as "really" [*vpravdu*], "truly" [*na samom dele*], "indeed" [*i vpriam*]—will be raised, and then variants of the answer will be considered (in the form of "whether . . . or . . .").

Take the following stanza, for example:

> And while he made a silent bow,
> A glance went with it which, somehow
> Was strangely tender. Was it *really* [*vpravdu*]
> The touch of pity at his heart,
> *Or* did he act the amorous part
> From kindness, *or* by habit merely?
> But tenderness it did express,
> And Tanya warmed to its caress.
>
> (V, 34) [the italics are Bocharov's]

This stanza is highly characteristic of the way the text of *Onegin* is constructed. (Incidentally, when Dostoevsky insisted in his "Pushkin Speech" that Tatyana "solved the riddle," he ignored the *conjectural* and *interrogative* forms this riddle solving takes in VII, 24–25. In actual fact Pushkin uses this problematic question and the different variants of the answer, which also remain in question, to shed light on his hero and to characterize him. For the most part Onegin is *in question* in the novel.)

The matter of the two types of novels found in literature is resolved in III, 13: "This surely, friends, defies all reason!" The author opts for a third path, "humble prose." However, in the world of Pushkin's novel the Sentimental and Romantic variants of the European novel become models for different interpretations of Onegin as "hero." Further on in Chapter III (in connection with Tatyana's letter) once again variants are juxtaposed. Two opposing types of female behavior, with which Tatyana's behavior is compared, are presented—each in a separate stanza: "With beauties have I been acquainted/ As pure as winter and as kind" [III, 22]; then: "And others shine there, proudly wielding/ Adherents to their service bent" [III, 23]. In the following stanza the situation is resolved: "How is Tatyana's failing greater?" "Beauties" and "weird lionesses" [the "others" of III, 23] have no bearing, as it were, on Tatyana's special case. Thus the narration moves forward. At certain points when a situation is commencing, a fan of possibilities is spread and variants are sketched out, amid which the action proceeds. This resembles the way in which the drowsy state of the hero is described in the novel's last chapter: "Imagination deals and shuffles/ Its rapid motley solitaires" [VIII, 37]. Usually in the novel situations are constructed by presenting *two* variants, falling "to the left and to the right" of a plot and a compositional axis.

Returning to the two variants of Lensky's possible fate, we see that they are perfectly balanced. The stanzas [VI, 37 and 39; stanza 38 was omitted] are constructed in such a way that we cannot say that one of them is "more possible," "more real" than the other. It is significant that when Belinsky and Herzen made such a choice they picked different variants. Subsequently, following in Belinsky's footsteps, critics came to prefer the second, everyday path, claiming that it was "realistic."[81] This meant, however, that "reality" in Pushkin's novel was identified with the deflated image that is presented in the following picture of the "poet's" fate: "There he would learn life's essence truly,/ By forty would contract the gout,/ Would eat and drink, be dull, grow stout" [VI, 39]. The formula "life's essence truly" [*zhizn' na samom dele*] would seem to support this choice. However, this is hardly Pushkin's direct answer to the question. Rather it is simply one variant of the answer to this question which is raised more than once in the novel—indicated by such formulas as "indeed," "truly," and "really." ("Life's essence truly" in VI, 39, correlates with the "philistine" pole—the ambivalent speech about man's life, where the voice of the author and the voice of the crowd mingle: "Blest he who, green in adolescence" [VIII, 10] and "But sad to feel, when youth has left us" [VIII, 11]. This is a typical example of the "diffused" point of view in the text of *Eugene Onegin*.) To return to Lensky, we repeat: VI, 37 and 39, constitute *possibilities, variants* of Lensky's unrealized life; they represent the disintegration of his unified, "dual-in-one" image. Therefore we cannot say that one of these paths is "more likely," "real." The construction of these stanzas does not give grounds for this.

The two variants are presented by the author on equal terms, and the contradiction between them is neutralized in VI, 40, where we are brought back to the facts and everything is left a possibility:

> But futile, reader, to uncover
> *What once his future might have held—*

Dead lies our dim young bard and lover,
By friendly hand and weapon felled.

(VI, 40) [the italics are Bocharov's]

In these lines the "complex movement is resolved, synthesized."[82]

However, in the following stanzas (the concluding stanzas of Chapter VI) the complex movement continues, as Pushkin switches from the sphere of the heroes to the sphere of the author of the novel (from the "reality of the heroes" to the "reality of the 'I' "[83]), and in this context develops the very same theme which was linked with the portrayal of Lensky's life and death:

Oh, dreams, my dreams, where is your sweetness?
Oh, youth's (the rhyme fair beckons) fleetness!
Can it be really true at last,
Its lovely bloom is past, is past,
In truth, in sober earnest ended?
All elegiac pose aside,
The springtime of my days has hied
(As hitherto I just pretended)?

(VI, 44)

The lyric of the "I" emerges directly from the lyric concerned with Lensky's fate. In the author's own life "in truth, in sober earnest" [*i vpriam, i v samom dele*] also comes to pass that which up to now was only an elegiac pose. The elegiac line—"Oh, dreams, my dreams, where is your sweetness"" (a quotation from Pushkin's own Lyceum lyric "Probuzhdenie" ["The Awakening"])—is translated and negated in the following line, where the mechanism is laid bare—i.e., the rhyme is demonstrated.[84] As we know, this is the prosaic course Pushkin's poetry takes: verse is displayed as verse, presented from a "prosaic" point of view. It is very easy to attribute the significance of this movement to "laying bare the device," to exposing the "laboratory," as the Formalists would tend to do. But in these very lines Pushkin renders such an explanation meaningless. The poet does not examine the rhyme "youth" from a laboratory but from experience, from his own mature life. Together with the rhyme, he examines "in truth" his own youth. Paradoxically, at the same time that poetic illusion is dispelled, poetry is identified with the poet's real life.

The traditional rhyme is subjected to analysis from the standpoint of a question which is fundamental to the novel and which is raised repeatedly: "In truth, in sober earnest?" From this vantage the elegiac pose disintegrates into rhymes and is transformed into a "material thing." However, at the same time this conventional, "unreal" content is *realized "all elegiac pose aside."* Stylistically, the stanza is constructed on this discovery: "Can it be really true at last,/ Its lovely bloom is past, is past?" That is precisely it: *in truth its bloom is past,*

which translated into simple language means "Shall I be really thirty soon?"
[VI, 44, l. 14]. And here as well, paradoxically, the simple language negates,
cancels out the conventional "poetic" language and at the same time, as it
were, affirms it, unites with it to form a single poetic entity within the *unity of
authorial speech*. Yet all the while the two languages are clearly distinguished
and juxtaposed as "poetry" and "reality."

The theme, whose development in the text of the novel we have followed,
concludes with the concluding lines of *Eugene Onegin:*

> Blest he who left in its full glory
> The feast of Life, who could decline
> To drain the brimming cup of wine,
> And, loath to finish Life's long story,
> Abruptly made his parting bow,
> As I to my Onegin now.

(VIII, 51)

Thus, the novel which was inspired in part by Pushkin's opposition to the
periphrastic style (recall the 1822 note "On Prose") concludes, not ironically,
but seriously—with a classical periphrasis, with the metaphor of life as a feast.
Moreover, the traditional "crowning power of poeticisms"[85] acts here in full
measure. It would seem that in the novel the image of the "poetic cup" is
canceled out. After all, in "Onegin's Journey" the author confesses: "The wine
in my poetic cup/ Has since been watered down a lot" (J, 17). We see, however,
that in the concluding lines of the novel it is revived—its poetic persuasiveness
restored, its meaning expanded (it becomes the "cup" of the "feast of Life").
The traditional situation, which has been "played through" many times in
Pushkin's poetry and which seemed to be "played out," recurs once more.

Let us recall Pushkin's 1817 lyric, "Krivtsovu" ["To Krivtsov"]:

> Let another keep on drinking
> From the cup of life grown stale;
> We will spend our youth unthinking,
> And with it lose life as well;

(*PSS*, 2, 50)

In the last stanza of the novel, composed in 1830, we find a variation on just
this motif. However, let us see what kind of variation it is and how it differs
from the 1817 lyric.

First of all, we should note the difference in poetic time. The early lyric
speaks in the *future* tense about that which in the concluding lines of the novel is
said to have already *taken place*. In the world of the author, "some are no more"
[VIII, 51].[86] In the world of the novel itself Lensky, likewise, has lost his youth
and with it life as well, precisely when he was the age of Pushkin in the 1817

lyric—"When he had almost turned eighteen." Finally, the author's parting with his novel and with his hero in the final "cathartic stanza"[87] is likened to a man parting with life.

In the 1817 lyric, with its light trochaic verses, a situation is expressed which antecedes the experiences of life. The subject of these verses not only does not know the experiences but does not want to know them. The very notion of these experiences is conveyed in the repulsive image of a cup grown stale, from which *another* keeps on drinking. "Blest" in the concluding lines of *Onegin* is pronounced from the viewpoint of a man who has already lived through these experiences, from the viewpoint of *"another"*—one could say of that other who "keeps on drinking" from the cup grown stale, which he himself has watered down. The poet has changed with time, and it could be said that his "blest" relates to the subject of the 1817 lyric and to his unburdened perception of life prior to the experience of life itself.

The traditional epicurean motif is thus presented from a new point of view, complicated by the experience of life. Gone is the former "lightness." Now the author speaks not about some conventional poetic death, which in his early lyric was depicted in advance (in a conventional future time) as a "light" event, but about the fact that in truth "some are no more." He recalls those in whose fate the traditional situation has been *realized*. And the traditional "light" phraseology becomes "lofty."[88] Consequently Pushkin reverently elevates the word "life" in these final lines of the novel ("the feast of Life," "Life's long story").

Thus, in the poetic "ontology" of the novel in verse, traditional phraseology, canceled out in the text of that same novel, is also shown to be valid.

Originally the line "brimming cup of wine" read "phials of sparkling wine" [*PSS*, 6, 636]. In the text of the novel the word "phial" occurs in Chapter V:

> The glass that slimly, trimly tapers,
> So like your slender waist, Zizi,
> Heart's crystal, you that used to be
> Game for my first poetic capers,
> Allurement's phial that I adored,
> Drunk with the wine of love you poured!
>
> (V, 32)

The Zizi addressed here is Evpraxia Vulf of Trigorskoye, and it is as if these lines are presented in Yazykov's stylistic zone, illuminated simultaneously by Pushkin's irony. Pushkin often met Yazykov at Trigorskoye in 1826, when he was writing Chapter V of *Onegin*. In the context of that chapter, wine, poetry, and love are linked. Possibly Pushkin changed "phials" to "cup" in the final stanza of the novel in order to distinguish this context from the seemingly "Yazykovian" context. In Pushkin's concluding stanza the wine of Life is a much more complex image with much more complex stylistic meaning, resulting from a synthesis of "poetic" and "prosaic" points of view. On the one hand, the poeticality of the image is elevated in comparison with the "light" semantics of "intoxication," but at the same time the "prosaic" point of view of the author of the novel "waters down" this poeticality.

In the final lines of *Onegin*, however, the transformed traditional image is augmented by a second comparison:

> And, loath to finish Life's long story,
> Abruptly made his parting bow,
> As I to my Onegin now.

(VIII, 51)

The image of Life as a poetic work, as a novel embracing the whole of existence, was widespread in the Romantic period. Here such an image is equated, on the one hand, with the traditional poetic image of life as a feast, but, on the other, with this very novel, with the text which is ending now. In the staircase-like construction of the concluding stanza of *Eugene Onegin* all planes of being come together; life and death merge with the novel and with its conclusion, with the dispelling of artistic illusion. Demonstrating at the end of the novel this end, displaying the limits of his own work, the author emerges from his novel not into a "laboratory" but into the sphere of the novel of Life, into the ontological sphere.

The image of the novel of Life crowns the theme of the "novel" in relation to life, a theme which in the text of Pushkin's novel is developed into a complexly structured whole. This theme of the "novel" within Pushkin's novel functions on four different levels. First there is the matter of Sentimental novels: "But novels, which she early favored,/ Replaced for her all other treats;/ With rapturous delight she savored/ Rousseau's and Richardson's conceits" [II, 29]. Such novels, which from the viewpoint of Pushkin's novel can be called a "deception" or a "fantasy," differ significantly from Onegin's reading, which opens a completely different world to Tatyana in Chapter VII: "Two or three novels" (that's all) where "contemporary man/ Is *rather faithfully* depicted" [VII, 22; the italics are Bocharov's]. This type of European novel *(Adolphe)* correlates more closely with Pushkin's but is not identical to it. Then there is "our novel": *Eugene Onegin* as it appears in its own text. Finally, there is the author's parting with this "our" ("my") novel in the concluding "cathartic" stanza, which is likened to a man parting with the novel of Life.

The capitalization of the words "Life" and "Life's" creates a lofty notion of the novel of Life and suggests that it in some way surpasses the novel *Eugene Onegin*, which is concluding now. *Eugene Onegin* relates to the novel of Life in the same way as one man's life relates to "life without beginning or end"—to use the words of another poet from another era.

The question whether *Onegin* is "complete" or "incomplete," which has evoked so many arguments, is fully resolved—and resolved poetically—by this comparison of "my novel" with the novel of Life in the final lines. The former is ending right now and its ending is openly displayed; Onegin's portrait, however "abruptly," is "finished."[89] The latter is truly "life without beginning or end." It is introduced into Pushkin's novel as an image embracing all its being, against the background of which the novel appears to be only an excerpt, a fragment from "Life's novel"; therefore, it ends "abruptly." But at the same time, the novel *Eugene Onegin,* which is ending now, *as a whole* correlates with the *whole* of the novel of Life, and the "abrupt" character of the "ending" reproduces the incompleteness and infinitude of this great whole.[90]

The Transformation of the Tradition Generated by *Onegin* in the Subsequent History of the Russian Novel

YURY LOTMAN
(1975)

Usually when we read the text of a novel,[1] we experience it simultaneously in the following ways: (1) Reading the novel, we become absorbed in its internally organized and locked-in world, and we identify that world with reality. From this perspective we do not distinguish the personages and events in the text from those in empirical reality. (2) At the same time as we become absorbed in the world of the novel, we continue to be situated outside that world, for we remain participants in actual reality. From this position we evaluate the text; we compare it with the life in which we are participants—biographically, historically, ideologically—as real people, as thinkers. From this perspective we no longer see the novel as a part of reality but as its explanation. (With respect to life the novel is situated on some metalevel.) We no longer see the text as a fragment of life but as its model.

Something quite different happens when we read Pushkin's novel in verse. (1) Because of the abundance of metastructural elements in the text of *Onegin*, we are never allowed to forget in the process of reading that what we are dealing with is a *literary* text. Although we become absorbed in the inner world of the novel, we do not experience the illusion of reality, because the author not only informs us about the course events are taking but constantly shows us the scenery from backstage. He involves us in a discussion of ways in which the narrative could be constructed differently. (2) However, if we move beyond the confines of this position and view the text in light of the opposition "literature–reality," we discover to our amazement that *Eugene Onegin* breaks out of the purely literary category into the world of reality. (3) But simultaneously we run up against a process which works in the opposite direction. Although the entire internal structure of *Onegin* is designed to evoke from the reader the feeling of "non-novel," the subtitle of the work, "novel in verse," the initial situation of the heroes, the narrative focus on the story of their lives, the love

Translated and published with the permission of the Copyright Agency of the USSR.

element as the basis of the conflict—all these things prompt the reader to include the text in the category of novelistic works he already knows and to interpret the work as a novel. Here the reader's perception runs counter to the author's design. Because of the way the reader perceives the text, he endows it again with the qualities of a model, situated on a higher level than empirical reality.

The transformation of the *Onegin* tradition in the subsequent history of the Russian novel provides a clear illustration of these complex shifts in the functioning of a text. As has been pointed out repeatedly, the entire nineteenth-century Russian novel stems from *Onegin* and in one way or another reinterprets its content. However, we are specifically interested in two aspects of this process. On the one hand, with respect to the subsequent tradition *Onegin* acts as a distinctive kind of standard. What Pushkin thought of as being in direct opposition to the norms of the poetics of the novel became itself the norm of novelistic poetics. It was *Onegin* that determined many features which subsequently became associated with the specific character of the *Russian* novel. On the other hand, in the subsequent tradition the text of *Onegin* invariably underwent significant and very characteristic transformations. Different authors extracted from the complex whole of Pushkin's novel individual semantic sections, developing, yet at the same time schematizing, the novel's structure. To interpret *Onegin* was to project it onto a somewhat more defined and more limited semantic space. With respect to the subsequent tradition *Onegin* appeared to be not so much a literary fact as a fact of reality.

The similarity between Onegin and Lermontov's hero Pechorin is all too obvious. But it is not only in this regard that Lermontov's novel intersects with Pushkin's. There are numerous echoes of *Eugene Onegin* in *A Hero of Our Time* which attest to the fact that they are interrelated. Compare: "Her glance seemed to me wondrously tender"[2] and "Tenderness it [Onegin's glance] did express" [*Eugene Onegin*, V, 34].

Entire scenes from *A Hero of Our Time* can only be understood as responses to *Onegin*. Take, for example, the episode at the ball in "Princess Mary," when the young officer Grushnitski becomes jealous of Pechorin:

> "I did not expect this of you," he [Grushnitski] said, coming up to me [Pechorin] and taking me by the arm.
> "What, exactly?"
> "You are dancing the mazurka with her, aren't you?" he asked in a solemn voice. "She confessed to me. . . ."
> "Well, what of it? Is it a secret?"
> "Naturally . . . I should have expected this from a frivolous girl, from a flirt . . . But I'll have my revenge!" [Nabokov, pp. 134–135].

Compare this to *Onegin,* where Lensky, in response to Onegin's attentions to his fiancée, thinks: "Olga, scarce unswaddled,/ Become a flirt . . ." [V, 45]. And, as in *Onegin,* the clash leads to a duel.

Finally, Belinsky's famous statement that Pechorin is "the Onegin of our time" and that "the difference between Onegin and Pechorin is much less than the distance between the Onega and Pechora rivers"[3] fixed this parallel in the minds of readers for generations. One could give many reasons why the antithesis Onegin-Lensky is reflected in the pair Pechorin-Grushnitski (significantly, as early as 1837 Lermontov was inclined to identify Lensky with Pushkin) or why the narrative principles of *Onegin* are transformed in the system of *A Hero of Our Time,* revealing a clear line of succession. However, this does not really interest us; nor are we interested in the objective differences between the characters of Onegin and Pechorin, which have been examined repeatedly by critics all the way from Belinsky and Apollon Grigoriev to Soviet authorities on Lermontov. What is intriguing is to try to reconstruct on the basis of the portrayal of Pechorin how Lermontov interpreted the Onegin type, how he saw Onegin.

The principle of comprehending self through a prism of literary clichés, which is characteristic of *Onegin,* is applied productively in *A Hero of Our Time.* Grushnitski's goal is "to become the hero of a novel" [Nabokov, p. 85]. Princess Mary strives "not to depart from the role she has assumed" [Nabokov, p. 118]. Dr. Werner informs Pechorin: "In her [Princess Mary's] imagination, you became the hero of a novel in the latest fashion" [Nabokov, p. 95]. In *Onegin* such literary comprehension of self is a sign of naiveté, a sign that the hero's view of life is childish and false. As the heroes mature inwardly, they are freed of their literary eyeglasses. In Chapter VIII they no longer appear in the guise of literary figures from well-known novels and poems but emerge as *people,* which is much more serious, profound, and tragic.

In *A Hero of Our Time* a different arrangement is utilized. In Lermontov's novel there are two types of heroes: (1) those who have nothing to do with literary self-coding—that is, characters like Bela, Maksim Maksimich, or the smugglers, all of whom are simple people; (2) their opposite—that is, characters who are coded in a literary tradition, whether they are noble or base. The only difference being that Grushnitski is a character from the prose fiction of Bestuzhev-Marlinsky brought to life, while Pechorin is coded as an Onegin type.

The literary coding of a character in a Romantic text is fundamentally different from that in a realistic text. In a Romantic text if the mark "Cain," "Napoleon," or "Brutus" were transferred to the hero, then the space surrounding him underwent a corresponding transformation (the "Russian Brutus," for example, implied the existence of a "Russian Caesar"[4]). Consequently, the basic indices of the plot situation were repeated.

In a realistic text the traditionally coded figure is placed in a space which is fundamentally alien to him and seemingly extraliterary (for example, "the genius chained to the clerk's desk"). As a result, plot situations are displaced. The hero's perception of self proves to be in conflict with those contexts that surround him, that are given as analogues of reality. A clear example of this kind of transformation is found in *Don Quixote*. Titles like "A Knight of Our Time"[5] or *A Hero of Our Time* involve the reader in the conflict.

Pechorin is coded in the image of Onegin, but precisely because of this he is not Onegin but an interpretation of Onegin. For Pechorin, to be Onegin is to play a role. Onegin is not a "superfluous man." This definition, as well as Herzen's "intelligent superfluity," appeared later and was then projected onto Onegin. In Chapter VIII of Pushkin's novel in verse, Onegin does not conceive of himself as a literary character. Herzen revealed the political implications of the "superfluous man," Dobrolyubov the social implications.[6] We would like to point out that the historical psychology of this type is inseparable from the perception of self as "hero of a novel" and the perception of one's own life as the realization of some plot. When a man sees himself in this light, he inevitably is confronted by the question of his "fifth act," whether apotheosis or ruin will conclude the play of life, life's human novel. The theme of death, of the end, of "the fifth act," of the denouement of one's own novel, became a major theme in the psychological self-definition of man in the Romantic period. Just as a literary character "lives" for the sake of the final scene or the final cry, so man in the Romantic period lived "for the sake of the outcome." "We will die, brothers; ah, how gloriously we will die!" exclaimed Alexander Odoevsky, coming out on Senate Square, December 14, 1825.[7]

"The end! How tuneful is this word. . . ."[8] The theme of the end, of "triumph or defeat," runs through all of Lermontov's works. It is also extremely important to Pechorin, who continually sees himself as a participant in the denouement of plots: "I am the indispensable persona in the fifth act" [Nabokov, p. 133]. "I am like a man who yawns at a ball and does not drive home to sleep, only because his carriage is not yet there. But now the carriage is ready . . . good-by!" [Nabokov, p. 158].

The psychology of the "superfluous man" is the psychology of a man whose part in life is to seek death but who nevertheless does not die. The novel's plot finds the "superfluous man" after the conclusion of the fifth act of his life's drama, deprived of a scenario for further action. For the generation of Lermontov's "Duma" ["Meditation"][9] the concept of the fifth act was still imbued with historically real content—the Decembrist uprising. Subsequently, it turned into a conventional symbol for reading the plot's code. Nor surprisingly, activity after activity turned into lingering inactivity. With utmost clarity Lermontov revealed the link between the death which does not occur and the aimlessness of further existence when he had Pechorin in the middle of "Princess Mary" bid farewell to life, settle all accounts with it, and yet not die. "And I now feel that I still have many years to live," Pechorin confesses [Nabokov, p. 160]. Subsequently Leo Tolstoy showed how this literary situation in turn became a plan for real action. The cycle kept repeating: The Romantic hero as a plan of action was realized in the actual deeds of the Russian nobleman [the Decembrist] and became a "superfluous man." In turn, the "superfluous man" became a literary fact and then subsequently a plan of action for a particular segment of the Russian nobility.

Like Pechorin, Tolstoy's hero Andrey Bolkonsky in *War and Peace* experiences a moment of "triumph or defeat" in the middle of the narrative[10] but then lives on after the end of his own role. And here it is important to note the difference between the life journey of this kind of literary hero and that of the "reborn hero." On the surface they are similar, but the journey of the latter, who from the standpoint of origin has distinctly mythological features, is constructed quite differently. Dying in some initial, lower incarnation in the middle or even at the beginning of the narrative, the hero is reborn, like a new man for a new life (". . . and you will be a man reborn"[11]). The reborn hero is typical of Tolstoy's plots[12] and is fundamentally different from the character type "Romantic hero–superfluous man." The latter, dying in the middle of the action, drags on his existence as a living dead man. He goes on but is not reborn, or he makes hopeless attempts to be restored to life but cannot change his inner nature. For example: Pechorin in his love for the Caucasian princess Bela, Prince Andrey in his love for Natasha.

The theme of the "living dead man" became especially important not so much in texts of the Russian Romantic period as in works which transferred the Romantic hero into everyday situations and examined his conduct under real-life conditions—ranging from Turgenev's "Yes, for he truly was a dead man"[13] to Alexander Blok's narrative poem *Retribution.*

The transformed *Onegin* situation is present not only in Turgenev's novels *Rudin, A Nest of Gentlefolk,* and *On the Eve* but also in *Fathers and Sons.* The almost parodistic resemblance of a whole series of episodes makes this apparent. Consider, for example, the conversation between Pavel Kirsanov and the young nihilist Bazarov [Bazarov speaks first]:

> "We won't have any seconds, but there is the possibility of a witness."
> "Who, precisely, if I may inquire?"
> "Why, Peter."
> "What Peter?"
> "Your brother's valet. He's a man who stands on the peak of contemporary culture, and he will play his role with all the *comme il faut* required in cases such as this" [Chapter 24; Guerney, p. 209].

The reference to Onegin's bringing his valet as a second to the scene of the duel is obvious [*Eugene Onegin,* VI, 25–27]. The choice of a hired servant as a second or witness could not be contested formally, from the standpoint of the rules of dueling. In *Onegin,* however, it represented a conscious insult to the other second, Zaretsky, since it implied that the seconds were equal before a court of honor (in certain situations the possibility of a duel between seconds was envisaged). In *Fathers and Sons* it represents a mocking insult not only to Pavel Kirsanov but to the duel as such, since the witness must act as an arbitor in questions of honor.

Thus in the tradition created by *Onegin* the features of *Onegin* were not repeated but transformed.

The bifurcation in interpretations of the plot provides clear evidence that the *Onegin* tradition was invariably accompanied by a transformation of the characters, a transformation which simplified the structural nature of the text and led it to be incorporated into other literary traditions, including here even the tradition created by Pushkin's novel itself. Naturally, the author and his contemporaries could not correlate *Onegin* with this tradition, just as subsequent generations could not separate *Onegin* from it. In one tradition the "Onegin situation" became a conflict between the "Onegin" hero and a heroine who was linked with the character of Tatyana. The principal novels of Turgenev [*Rudin, A Nest of Gentlefolk,* and *On the Eve*] and Goncharov [*Oblomov*] were constructed in this way, as was Nekrasov's narrative poem *Sasha.* Moreover, the Turgenev version of the *Onegin*-type novel became so firmly entrenched in the Russian tradition that it even began to determine the way Pushkin's text was perceived.

However, the "Onegin situation" was simultaneously interpreted as a clash between the two male characters (the Onegin–Lensky conflict). Lermontov in "Princess Mary," the longest tale in *A Hero of Our Time,* acted as the founder of this tradition. (Actually in his earlier novel *The Princess Ligovskaya,* which remained unfinished, a conflict was sketched out between the romantic Krasinsky and the skeptic Pechorin.) In this regard it is significant that in his novel *A Common Story* Goncharov "took" from *Onegin* precisely this kind of plot structure before shifting to the "Pushkin–Turgenev" type of interpretation in *Oblomov,* while Turgenev in *Fathers and Sons* abandoned his favorite way of organizing novelistic material for the sake of the "masculine conflict."

To be sure, the ways the *Onegin* tradition was appropriated, even within the relatively narrow confines of plot, were very diverse and are not limited to those enumerated above. One could, for example, point to what appears to be an obvious connection between the initial plan for *Anna Karenina* ("a novel about an unfaithful wife") and the lively debate about Tatyana's "retrogressive" behavior in nineteenth-century Russian criticism.[14] It is as if Tolstoy set up an experiment showing what would have happened, had Pushkin's heroine conducted herself as a "progressive woman," one above prejudice.

However, while it generated a complex and diverse novelistic tradition, *Eugene Onegin* really stands outside this tradition.

To be sure, the subsequent tradition did not simply read into Pushkin's text the strictly novelistic structure. *Onegin* does possess a structural layer, organized according to strictly novelistic conventions, that "works" productively. It is manifested in the oft-noted symmetry of the compositional construct, which simultaneously can be viewed as an "unorganized" fragment without a beginning or an end and as a strictly proportioned edifice in which parallel plot moves are repeated in mirror-like fashion.[15] It is also manifested in the "novelistic" plot moves which are spontaneously present in the text. However, this novelistic structure does not completely encompass the whole body of the work. The same thing is true of the author's reflections on the principles of art and the flaunted "literariness." These too constitute definite layers, but they do not embrace the whole work either.

In the general structure of Pushkin's novel in verse the characters occupy a unique place, which attests to the duality of their construction. As Lev Vygotsky pointed out some time ago, taking his cue from Yury Tynyanov, if we isolate the "characters" from the living fabric of the novel and assume that they are constant and static entities ("man in the 1820s" or "the ideal Russian girl"), entities that have an independent existence above and beyond their place in the general structure of Pushkin's text, we reduce the artistic and ideological significance of the work. To quote Vygotsky: "Then the heroes are interpreted naively. Not only are they conceived to have everyday significance, but, more importantly, they are conceived to be static, finished entities that do not change during the whole course of the novel. In actual fact, however, the novel itself demonstrates that Pushkin treats the heroes dynamically."[16] Vygotsky clearly had Tynyanov's position in mind here, and he even quoted Tynyanov.

Tynyanov believed that the artistic unity of the hero is fundamentally different from our conception of the unity of man's extraliterary personality in everyday life. Opposing the view that man is static, all of a piece, devoid of any inner contradictions (and the naive transference of this view into the world of literary works), Tynyanov argued that from the contradictory pieces of narrative which are dynamically correlated, the artistic consciousness, through an act of creative violence, reconstitutes the secondary unity of the fictional character. According to Tynyanov: "It is sufficient that there is a sign of unity, that there is a category which justifies the boldest instances of violation and compels us to regard them as *equivalents of unity*. But it is quite obvious that such unity is very different from the unity of the hero as it is naively conceived. Instead of being marked by static wholeness, the hero is marked by dynamic integration and wholeness. . . . All we need is the sign of the hero, the name of the hero. We do not painstakingly scrutinize the hero in every case."[17]

Although Tynyanov's thesis has proved to be fruitful, it is somewhat one-sided and should be amended.

On the one hand, the notion that a literary character is the product of the dynamic integration of contradictory qualities, which are marked by a conventional sign of structural unity, is by no means true of all types of fictional generalization. In the Western European literary tradition this notion is usually associated with the names Shakespeare and Cervantes; in the Russian tradition it stems from *Eugene Onegin* (in this regard the examples that Vygotsky gives from Dostoevsky are stronger proof that the Pushkinian tradition is present in these novels than that this kind of construction is normative for the novel in general). There exists in world literature another no less significant tradition of narrative genres in which there is a tendency to eliminate from the hero's character any contradictory qualities. The novelistic tradition which Pushkin may well have had in mind was defined in large measure by this latter tendency. It is characteristic of Richardson, Maturin, Nodier, and Rousseau (as the author of *La Nouvelle Héloïse*). Against this background works like *Rameau's Nephew, Manon Lescaut,* or Rousseau's *Confessions* appeared atypical and played no part in shaping the tradition.

On the other hand, we cannot say categorically that man's extraliterary personality in everyday life is completely static. It is when we give a *verbal account,* in the form of a nonliterary narrative, of our impressions of a certain individual that such static wholeness is produced. Direct observation is always disconnected, fragmentary, and contradictory. The gluing together and unification of these impressions into a single character is the result of secondary psychological operations, which are not free from the influence of literature.

Thus, it is foolhardy to maintain that the literary and nonliterary modeling of the human personality are distinguished by fixed, opposing indicators that never change and that can be described apart from their correlation with each other. The notion that they constitute a dynamic interrelated system seems to correspond better to the spirit of Tynyanov's argument. This system is unchanging insofar as its indicators remain distinct, yet its function consists of periodic acts of aggression across the boundary that separates the indicators in the structure of culture.

In Pushkin's time people attributed greater organization and order to literary narratives than is characteristic of the stream of life:

> And I perceived that world entire
> That is the realm of poetry,
> And sued for thy consent, o lyre,
> To dedicate my life to thee.[18]

Pushkin destroyed the even development and continuity of his hero's history, as well as unity of character, and transferred to the literary text a sense of immediacy, a sense of the impressions one has from contact with a living person. Only after the *Onegin* tradition had entered the literary consciousness of the Russian reader as a kind of aesthetic norm was this series of momentary glimpses of the hero on the part of the author transformed into an explanation of the hero's character. Direct observation was elevated in status and began to be perceived as the model. Simultaneously, properties of simplicity, wholeness, and harmoniousness (i.e., noncontradictoriness) were ascribed to life. Earlier, there was a tendency to view life as a series of disconnected observations and to regard the artist as the one who could see the underlying unity and harmony; now the reverse occurred. To the ordinary observer man seemed simple and noncontradictory and life appeared unified, while the artist saw that "which unheeding eyes see not"[19]—tragic ruptures and profound contrasts.

Eugene Onegin signifies the moment when these two tendencies were in equilibrium. This meant not only that qualities of life were ascribed to literature but that characteristics of literature were ascribed to life. And in this sense the ending of Pushkin's novel is extremely significant. After making so many efforts to ensure that the conclusion of *Onegin* is not reminiscent of the traditional descriptions "at the end of the final quire,"[20] Pushkin suddenly equates Life (with a capital *L!*) to a novel and concludes the history of his hero with the image of reading cut short:

> Blest he who left in its full glory
> The feast of Life, who could decline
> To drain the brimming cup of wine,
> And, loath to finish Life's long story,
> Abruptly made his parting bow,
> As I to my Onegin now.

(VIII, 51)

The poet, who throughout the work played the contradictory role of author and creator (whose creation, however, turns out not to be a literary work but something exactly its opposite—a fragment of living Life), suddenly appears before us as a reader,[21] that is, as a man linked with the text. But here the text turns out to be Life. This view of Life as a text links Pushkin's novel not only with diverse phenomena in subsequent Russian literature but also with a profound tradition whose origins are very ancient.

When we speak of Pushkin, we are fond of calling him progenitor, thereby emphasizing his link with the following period and his break with the preceding one. Pushkin himself was more inclined to emphasize the continuity of cultural development. The striking originality of the construction of *Eugene Onegin* simply underscores the fact that it is deeply linked to the culture of both the preceding and the following periods.

An analysis of the inner world of Pushkin's novel in verse convinces us that concealed within *Onegin* is the "embryo" of the subsequent history of the Russian novel. Therefore, each new step in the development of Russian literature brings to light new ideological and artistic elements which are objectively present in the novel but are only revealed by a later artistic vision. Because of this we cannot hope to find a "final" solution to the problem of *Onegin*. We can only advance, drawing closer to the goal. To reach it, so long as the novel remains a living cultural phenomenon, clearly is impossible.

The seed of the future history of the Russian novel is concealed within *Eugene Onegin*. At the same time the work is also the fruit of the literary development that preceded it. It was this aspect of the work that corresponded to Pushkin's conscious orientation.

To conclude: In the case of *Onegin* the opposition between intrinsic textual analysis and historical analysis proves illusory. When we analyze the historical relationship of *Eugene Onegin* to the preceding and following traditions, we find ourselves inevitably analyzing the text as such, and when we do a textual analysis we inevitably find ourselves investigating extratextual historical ties.

Only where these two perspectives intersect can we find the gates to the artistic world of *Eugene Onegin*.

Notes

INTRODUCTION

1. Letter to Pyotr Vyazemsky, November 4, 1823; Shaw, p. 141.

2. Letter to Ivan Kireevsky, 1832. Quoted in A. S. Dolinin, ed., *Russkie pisateli XIX veka o Pushkine* (Leningrad, 1938), pp. 64–65.

3. A good source for the intellectual history of this era is Andrzej Walicki, *The Slavophile Controversy: History of a Conservative Utopia in Nineteenth-Century Russian Thought,* trans. Hilda Andrews-Rusiecka (Oxford: Clarendon Press, 1975).

4. For a discussion of Belinsky, see Victor Terras, *Belinskij and Russian Literary Criticism: The Heritage of Organic Aesthetics* (Madison: University of Wisconsin Press, 1974); and René Wellek, *A History of Modern Criticism, 1750–1950,* 4 vols. (New Haven: Yale University Press, 1955–1965), vol. 3, pp. 243–264.

5. Belinsky made this observation in the first of eleven articles on Pushkin he published between 1843 and 1846.

6. Actually Belinsky wrote two articles on *Eugene Onegin.* The second one, which is not included in this volume, dealt with Tatyana and for its time was a sensitive treatment of feminist issues.

7. Other critics in other European countries underwent a similar evolution: Carlyle in England, Taine in France, De Sanctis in Italy.

8. For a discussion of Pisarev, see Evgenii Lampert, *Sons Against Fathers: Studies in Russian Radicalism and Revolution* (Oxford: Clarendon Press, 1965), pp. 272–337; and Wellek, vol. 4, pp. 254–265.

9. The conservative critics as a group are discussed in Wayne Dowler, *Dostoevsky, Grigor'ev, and Native Soil Conservatism* (Toronto: University of Toronto Press, 1982); Walicki, pp. 531–558; and Wellek, vol. 4, pp. 266–277.

10. The links between the conservative critics and Belinsky are discussed in Terras, pp. 214–226.

11. There are striking similarities between Dostoevsky's interpretation of *Eugene Onegin* and Tchaikovsky's operatic rendition of Pushkin's work, which was composed at about the same time and which quickly became one of the most popular operas in the Russian repertoire.

12. For a discussion of the Russian Formalist movement see Victor Erlich, *Russian Formalism. History—Doctrine,* 3d ed. (New Haven: Yale University Press, 1981); and Peter Steiner, *Russian Formalism: A Metapoetics* (Ithaca: Cornell University Press, 1984).

13. In this sense they paralleled the New Critics in England and America, although there were differences in ethos and emphasis. For a comparison of Formalism and New Criticism, see Ewa M. Thompson, *Russian Formalism and Anglo-American New Criticism: A Comparative Study* (The Hague: Mouton, 1971).

14. "Art as a device" was the battle cry of early Formalism. It was coined by Viktor Shklovsky, whose 1917 article by that title is regarded as the Formalist manifesto.

15. A good example is Boris Eikhenbaum's famous essay "How Gogol's 'Overcoat' is Made," in *Gogol from the Twentieth Century,* ed., trans., and introduced by Robert A. Maguire (Princeton: Princeton University Press, 1974), pp. 269–291.

16. Shklovsky's essay, which was published in 1923, is translated in *Twentieth-Century Russian Literary Criticism,* ed. Victor Erlich (New Haven: Yale University Press, 1975), pp. 63–80.

17. The concept of *ostranenie* [defamiliarization] was Shklovsky's most original contribution to Formalist theory.

18. The Formalists were particularly drawn to parody since it "laid bare" the conventionality of art.

19. For a discussion of the relationship between Russian Formalism and Czech Structuralism, see Peter Steiner, "The Roots of Structuralist Esthetics," in *The Prague School: Selected Writings, 1929–1946,* ed. Peter Steiner (Austin: University of Texas Press, 1982), pp. 174–219.

20. The official Soviet approach to *Eugene Onegin* found its fullest formulation in Grigorii Gukovskii, *Pushkin i problemy realisticheskogo stilia* (Moscow, 1957).

21. Iu. M. Lotman, *Struktura khudozhestvennogo teksta* (Moscow, 1970); English translation, *The Structure of the Artistic Text,* trans. Ronald Vroon (Ann Arbor: Michigan Slavic Contributions, 1977). *Analiz poeticheskogo teksta* (Leningrad, 1972); English translation, *Analysis of the Poetic Text,* ed. and trans. D. Barton Johnson (Ann Arbor: Ardis, 1976). *Semiotika kino i problemy kinoestetiki* (Tallin, 1973); English translation, *The Semiotics of Cinema,* trans. Mark E. Suino (Ann Arbor: Michigan Slavic Publications, 1976).

22. Bakhtin formulated this idea in *Problems of Dostoevsky's Poetics,* first published in 1929.

23. A good selection of Lotman's recent papers on Russian cultural history is found in *The Semiotics of Russian Cultural History,* ed. Alexander Nakhimovsky and Alice Stone Nakhimovsky (Ithaca: Cornell University Press, 1985). Boris Gasparov's introduction to that volume is also very useful.

24. M. M. Bakhtin, *Problemy poetiki Dostoevskogo,* 2d rev. ed. (Moscow, 1963); English translation, *Problems of Dostoevsky's Poetics,* ed. and trans. Caryl Emerson (Minneapolis: University of Minnesota Press, 1984).

25. M. M. Bakhtin, *Tvorchestvo Fransua Rable* (Moscow, 1965); English translation, *Rabelais and His World,* trans. Helen Iswolsky (Bloomington: Indiana University Press, 1984).

26. For a discussion of Bakhtin and a bibliography of his works see Katerina Clark and Michael Holquist, *Mikhail Bakhtin* (Cambridge: Harvard University Press, 1984).

27. The translation is taken from *The Dialogic Imagination: Four Essays by M. M. Bakhtin,* ed. Michael Holquist, trans. Caryl Emerson and Michael Holquist (Austin: University of Texas Press, 1981).

28. See Edward Wasiolek, *Tolstoy's Major Fiction* (Chicago: The University of Chicago Press, 1978), pp. 210, 243.

29. Another essay from the same book, dealing with Pushkin's short story "The Queen of Spades," appeared in translation in *New Literary History* 9 (1978):315–332.

30. The analogy stems from Bakhtin's notion of polyphony.

31. Bocharov's notion of heterostylism [*raznostil'nost'*] is related to Bakhtin's notion of heteroglossia [*raznorechivost'*], the living mix of varied and opposing voices, which Bakhtin sees as fundamental to the novel.

BELINSKY: *EUGENE ONEGIN:* AN ENCYCLOPEDIA OF RUSSIAN LIFE

1. This article, originally published in the journal *Otechestvennye zapiski* [*Notes of the Fatherland*] in 1844, is the eighth in a series of eleven articles on Pushkin that Belinsky wrote between 1843 and 1846. The text used here is from V. G. Belinskii, *Polnoe sobranie sochinenii,* vol. 7 (Moscow, 1955), pp. 431–472.—Tr.

2. Ivan Krylov (1769–1844) was Russia's greatest fabulist.—Tr.

3. Vladislav Ozerov (1769–1816) was a Russian dramatist whose French-inspired tragedies were very popular in the first decade of the nineteenth century.—Tr.

4. *The Bridegroom,* Pushkin's only ballad, was written in 1825 and published in 1827.—Tr.

5. Initially Pushkin published *Eugene Onegin* chapter by chapter. The first complete edition did not appear until 1833.—Tr.

6. From the Prologue to *Ruslan and Lyudmila,* translated in Walter Arndt, *Ruslan and Liudmila* (Ann Arbor: Ardis, 1974), p. 5.—Tr.

7. *Zipun* is a type of peasant coat.—Tr.

8. *Nemets,* the word for German in the Russian language (originally applied to all northern Europeans), comes from *nemoi* [dumb] and thus had a pejorative meaning. —Tr.

9. A *sarafan* is a kind of loose dress worn by Russian peasant women.—Tr.

10. Quoted from Gogol's 1834 article, "Neskol'ko slov o Pushkine" ["A Few Words on Pushkin"], in N. V. Gogol', *Polnoe sobranie sochinenii,* vol. 8 (Moscow/Leningrad, 1952), pp. 50–55.—Tr.

11. Ivan Dmitriev (1760–1837) was a late eighteenth-century poet who wrote light verse.—Tr.

12. Denis Fonvizin (1745–1792) was the greatest Russian dramatist of the eighteenth century.—Tr.

13. Ivan Khemnitser (1745–1784) was the first Russian fabulist to write original fables in a colloquial style.—Tr.

14. Belinsky alludes here to journalist Nikolay Nadezhdin (1804–1856), who complained in his review of *Eugene Onegin,* Chapter VIII, that Pushkin's work lacked unity and wholeness; that Pushkin had no goal, no plan; that *Eugene Onegin* was not a novel but simply a "poetic album of lively impressions." *Teleskop* [*Telescope*] 9 (1832):107–108.—Tr.

15. The Charter of 1785 recapitulated and expanded the privileges of the Russian nobility.—Tr.

16. Ippolit Bogdanovich (1743–1803) was an eighteenth-century poet, best known for his verse tale *Dushenka.*—Tr.

17. Nikolay Novikov (1744–1818), journalist and book publisher, was one of the most important figures of the Russian enlightenment.—Tr.

18. A reference to Karamzin's most famous story, "Poor Liza" (1792), the sentimental tale of a young peasant girl who was seduced and abandoned and who then drowned herself out of remorse.—Tr.

19. Belinsky refers here to Vasily Zhukovsky.—Tr.

20. A quotation from Krylov's fable "Zerkalo i obez'iana" ["The Mirror and the Monkey"], about a monkey who refuses to recognize his own ugly mug in the mirror. —Tr.

21. Belinsky assumes that "Onegin's Journey" is an integral part of the plot.—Tr.

22. Martin Zadeka is the alleged author of a dream-book that Tatyana treasures and to which she turns in an effort to interpret her frightening dream [V, 22–24].—Tr.

23. The gifted individual who fails to act because of a stultifying environment subsequently came to be known as the *lishnii chelovek* [superfluous man]. By linking Pechorin with Onegin, Belinsky also introduces the notion of a recurring social type. —Tr.

24. Both Pushkin and Lermontov were killed in duels, Pushkin at 37, Lermontov at 26.—Tr.

PISAREV: PUSHKIN AND BELINSKY: *EUGENE ONEGIN*

1. This article was originally published in the journal *Russkoe slovo* [*The Russian Word*] in 1865. The text used here is from D. I. Pisarev, *Sochineniia v chetyrekh tomakh,*

vol. 3 (Moscow, 1956), pp. 306–364. Pisarev begins by quoting from Belinsky's essay in the present collection.—Tr.

2. Belinsky made this observation in his fifth article on Pushkin, citing the very lines about Onegin's beaver collar. Belinskii, *PSS*, 7, 336.—Tr.

3. Charles-Louis Didelot (1767–1837) was a French balletmaster and choreographer associated with the Russian ballet in the early nineteenth century.—Tr.

4. Pavel Kirsanov is the elegant aristocrat in Turgenev's novel *Fathers and Sons*.—Tr.

5. Beltov is the hero of Alexander Herzen's novel *Who Is to Blame?* (1847).—Tr.

6. Mitrofan Prostakov is the imbecile hero of Denis Fonvizin's play *The Minor* (1782), which satirizes the vulgarity and ignorance of the Russian provincial gentry. From *The Minor,* Act III, Scene 7.—Tr.

7. Chatsky is the hero of Griboedov's comedy *Woe from Wit* (1833), Rudin the hero of Turgenev's novel *Rudin* (1856).—Tr.

8. Bazarov is the hero of Turgenev's novel *Fathers and Sons* (1862). Lopukhov and Rakhmetov are central characters in Nikolay Chernyshevsky's radical novel *What Is to Be Done?* (1862).—Tr.

DOSTOEVSKY: PUSHKIN

1. This speech was delivered in Moscow on June 8, 1880, at the dedication of the Pushkin monument. It was subsequently published in Dostoevsky's journal, *Diary of a Writer.* The text used here is from F. M. Dostoevskii, *Polnoe sobranie sochinenii v tridtsati tomakh,* vol. 26 (Leningrad, 1984), pp. 136–149. Dostoevsky begins by quoting from Gogol's article "A Few Words on Pushkin" (1834).—Tr.

2. The Table of Ranks promulgated by Peter the Great in 1722.—Tr.

3. When Zemphira tires of Aleko and takes a young gypsy lover, Aleko murders them both.—Tr.

4. From Nikolay Nekrasov's 1845 lyric, "Otradno videt', chto nakhodit" ["It's Pleasant Finding There Are Moments"].—Tr.

5. Turgenev's heroine sacrifices happiness to duty.—Tr.

6. Belinsky calls the young Tatyana a "moral embryo" in his ninth Pushkin article. Belinskii, *PSS*, 7, 499.—Tr.

7. Father Pimen in Pushkin's historical drama *Boris Godunov* (1825).—Tr.

8. From Pushkin's 1826 lyric "Stansy" ["Stanzas"]; translated in Arndt, *PuCP,* p. 77.—Tr.

9. Dostoevsky refers here to Pushkin's little tragedy, *The Stone Guest* (1830), a recasting of the Don Juan legend.—Tr.

10. Dostoevsky paraphrases the final stanza of Fyodor Tyutchev's 1855 lyric, "Eti bednye selen'ia" ["These Poor Villages"], which expresses the belief that the poverty, suffering, and Christ-like meekness of the Russian peasant mark him as chosen by God.—Tr.

TYNYANOV: ON THE COMPOSITION OF *EUGENE ONEGIN*

1. This article, written in 1921–1922, was first published in 1975. The text used here is from Iu. N. Tynianov, *Poetika, istoriia literatury, kino* (Moscow, 1977), pp. 52–77.—Tr.

2. Andrey Bely (1880–1934) was an important symbolist poet and ornamental prose writer, best known for his novel *Petersburg* (1913).—Tr.

3. The genre *petites poèmes en prose* [lyrics in prose], practiced by such writers as Baudelaire and Turgenev, is based precisely on the fact that verse cannot merge with prose. The reader's initial response to the verse form in works of this kind only emphasizes the fact that they belong to prose.

4. We seem to have the same reaction to the inversion of adjectives in Karamzin's

prose. The original reason for these inversions was sound perceptibility, but in time they began to be perceived solely from the standpoint of syntax and semantics.

5. *Zaumnyi iazyk* [transrational language] was advocated by such early twentieth-century avant-garde Russian poets as Alexey Kruchonykh and Velimir Khlebnikov, who sought to write verse composed solely of arbitrary combinations of sounds.—Tr.

6. P. A. Viazemskii, *Polnoe sobranie sochinenii,* vol. 7 (St. Petersburg, 1882), p. 149.

7. K. N. Batiushkov, *Sochineniia,* vol. 2 (St. Petersburg, 1885), pp. 331–332.

8. Thus, for Pushkin and for all those in the second, younger tradition, prose was primary (not in and of itself but as a principle). We are of the opinion that Pushkin's *prose* developed naturally from the prose plans he made for his verse. (Boris Eikhenbaum takes a different point of view.) [In his 1922 article, "Put' Pushkina k proze," Eikhenbaum argued that Pushkin consciously developed his prose in opposition to his verse.—Tr.]

9. I. V. Kireevskii, *Polnoe sobranie sochinenii,* vol. 1 (Moscow, 1861), p. 15. [In the 1820s Kireevsky was a member of a literary and philosophical circle called the Lovers of Wisdom.—Tr.]

10. I discuss this more fully in *Problema stikhotvornogo iazyka* [*The Problem of Verse Language,* trans. and ed. Michael Sosa and Brent Harvey (Ann Arbor: Ardis, 1981)]. In the present article examples from *Eugene Onegin* serve as partial *proof* of my thesis.

11. This also happens because the *prosaism* is perceived as a *prosaism*—that is, it is immediately associated with two categories: the prosaic and the poetic.

12. Just how far such enrichment can go without turning prose into poetry or poetry into prose (so long as the constructive principle is observed) is demonstrated by the extremes: *vers libre,* on the one hand, and *petites poèmes en prose* on the other. These I have already mentioned. Often the division of the text into lines is the only indicator of the verse nature of the speech, of its constructive principle, as the specifically verse (motor and dynamic) functions are reduced to a minimum.

13. Letter to his brother, Lev Sergeevich Pushkin, January–February 1824. [Translated in Shaw, pp. 150–151. All the French quotations are from *Phèdre.*—Tr.]

14. These prefaces and notes afforded Pushkin yet another forceful way to emphasize or lay bare the very dynamics of the novel, to create a *novel about a novel.* In addition, they gave Pushkin reason to include *prose* introductions and digressions, which thus set off the verse. Only in rare instances did Pushkin provide prefaces and notes for his other works, and, when he did so, they were very brief.

15. Katenin viewed the problem from the standpoint of the *plan.*

16. The fact that the omission of chapters (or their transposition) is frequently used as a device of compositional play in the works of Sterne, Byron, Brentano, and Hoffmann only serves to strengthen my argument.

17. This becomes even clearer if we take into consideration the fact that, when Pushkin published the first complete edition of *Eugene Onegin* in 1833, he *excluded* the poem which had served as an introduction to Chapter I ["Conversation between Bookseller and Poet"], several notes, and even seven stanzas he had published earlier (IV, 1–4; V, 37–38; and VI, 47, which was transferred to note 40), yet he *retained* "The Fragments from Onegin's Journey."

18. Pushkin had an entire stanza ready, but he preferred to end *Onegin* with a fragment, with only the first line.

19. "Refutations of Criticisms," translated in Proffer, pp. 105, 107, 108. In all the above quotations the italics are Tynyanov's.—Tr.

20. Just as he did in the work's subtitle: *novel in verse.*

21. Rendered as "oh" and "why" by Arndt.—Tr.

22. In the Russian text all three lines begin "A ia tak."—Tr.

23. There are hints of this in *Eugene Onegin.* Onegin is introduced as "a dear friend of

mine" [I, 2], and Pushkin made a drawing of himself with Onegin. [The drawing, intended to accompany stanza I, 48, is reproduced in Shaw, facing page 187.—Tr.] Also in "Onegin's Journey" it is said: "Onegin in my footsteps wandered/. . . And recollected me . . ." [J, 19].

24. Arndt reverses the syntax. In the Russian text *upala* [sank] is the first word in III, 39.—Tr.

25. In the Russian text "E" comes last in the line and rhymes with the final word in the preceding line, *stekle* [window].—Tr.

LOTMAN: THE STRUCTURE OF *EUGENE ONEGIN*

1. This article was originally published in *Uchenye zapiski Tartuskogo gosudarstvennogo universiteta* 184 (Tartu, 1966):5–32.—Tr.

2. G. A. Gukovskii, *Pushkin i problemy realisticheskogo stilia* (Moscow, 1957), p. 168.

3. This term was adopted by Belinsky to designate socially committed literature of the 1840s.—Tr.

4. Iu. M. Lotman, "K evoliutsii postroeniia kharakterov v romane 'Evgenii Onegin,'" in *Pushkin: Issledovaniia i materialy,* vol. 3 (Moscow/Leningrad, 1960), pp. 131–173.

5. It is assumed that the informed reader recognizes the link between the present article and several ideas set forth in the following works: Iu. N. Tynianov, *Problema stikhotvornogo iazyka* (Leningrad, 1924); M. M. Bakhtin, *Problemy poetiki Dostoevskogo,* 2d ed. (Moscow, 1963); V. B. Shklovskii, "'Evgenii Onegin' (Pushkin i Stern)," in *Ocherki po poetike Pushkina* (Berlin: Epokha, 1923), pp. 199–220; G. O. Vinokur, "Slovo i stikh v 'Evgenii Onegine,'" in A. M. Egolin, ed., *Pushkin: sbornik statei* (Moscow, 1941), pp. 155–213.

6. Quoted from Pushkin's letter to Anton Delvig, November 26, 1828 [Shaw, p. 361].—Tr.

7. In the dedication to *Eugene Onegin,* Pushkin characterized his novel in verse as a collection of "motley chapters."—Tr.

8. In Russian the phrase is *beg pakhuchii* [odorous flight].—Tr.

9. M. Iu. Lermontov, *Sochineniia v shesti tomakh,* vol. 2 (Moscow/Leningrad, 1954), p. 147. [The quotation is from Lermontov's poem, "Zhurnalist, chitatel' i pisatel'" ("Journalist, Reader, and Writer"; 1840).—Tr]

10. V. N. Orlov and S. I. Khmel'nitskii, eds., *Dnevnik V. K. Kiukhel'bekera* (Leningrad, 1929), p. 40.

11. See my article "O probleme znachenii vo vtorichnykh modeliruiushchikh sistemakh," *Trudy po znakovym sistemam* 2 (Tartu, 1965): 22–37.

12. In his review of Chapter I in *Moskovskii telegraf* [*The Moscow Telegraph*] 5 (1825): 46.—Tr.

13. "Master," "sir," the form used to address one's betters.—Tr.

14. G. O. Vinokur, "Slovo i stikh v 'Evgenii Onegine,'" p. 186.

15. Ibid., p. 187.

16. B. M. Eikhenbaum, *Melodika russkogo stikha* (Petrograd, 1922).—Tr.

17. In his 1960 article Lotman argued that Pushkin's ideas about what determines an individual's character evolved through four stages while he was working on *Onegin.* —Tr.

18. However, the boundary of the synchronic section does not always coincide with the boundary of the chapter. In Chapter I of the novel, for example, two systems are presented in succession: in the first Onegin is a superficially educated dandy and in the second a man who "has lived and thought" [I, 46], a companion to the author, someone who thinks as he does.

19. Vinokur, pp. 167–168.

20. The Union of Welfare, formed in 1818, was a secret union of cultured young noblemen opposed to tyranny and slavery.—Tr.

21. In his article in the present collection.—Tr.

BAKHTIN: DISCOURSE IN *EUGENE ONEGIN*

1. This translation by Caryl Emerson and Michael Holquist is reprinted from *The Dialogic Imagination: Four Essays by M. M. Bakhtin,* ed. Michael Holquist (Austin: University of Texas Press, 1981), pp. 42–50. However, I have substituted a different system of transliteration. "Discourse in *Eugene Onegin*" is actually an extract from a larger essay, "From the Prehistory of Novelistic Discourse" (1940), which is translated in its entirety in *The Dialogic Imagination.* The extract was published as a separate article in *Voprosy literatury* [*Problems of Literature*] 8 (1965):84–90 under the title "Slovo v romane."—Tr.

2. A reference to *Onegin,* VII, 24, ll. 11–14: "A Muscovite in Harold's cloak,/ An alien whim's interpretation,/ Compound of every faddish pose . . .?/ A parody, perhaps . . . who knows?"—Tr.

BOCHAROV: THE STYLISTIC WORLD OF THE NOVEL

1. This essay appeared in S. G. Bocharov, *Poetika Pushkina* (Moscow, 1974), pp. 26–104. The Dostoevsky quotation is taken from "Bookishness and Literacy: Article One" (1861), which in many ways anticipates the "Pushkin Speech." The Bakhtin quotation comes from "Discourse in *Eugene Onegin.*"—Tr.

2. "Razgovor knigoprodavtsa s Poetom" (1824) [Arndt, *PuCP,* pp. 55–60].—Tr.

3. This quotation from a letter by Pushkin to Pyotr Vyazemsky, dated November 4, 1823 [Shaw, p. 141], is the first mention of *Eugene Onegin* in Pushkin's correspondence.—Tr.

4. The word performs the same "switching" function in the 1822 note "On Prose" [Proffer, pp. 18–20], which can be regarded as a kind of theoretical premise for the stylistic constructs in *Eugene Onegin,* particularly those in Chapter I. [Here and elsewhere in this essay when Bocharov uses the term "speech" *(rech'),* he is referring to a manner of speaking and not to individual speeches by particular characters or the narrator.—Tr.]

5. "On Prose." In this note the crucial stylistic problems of literature are reduced to an opposition between a figurative manner of expression—that is, periphrasis (associated with the Karamzinian tradition)—and the simple word.

6. Iu. N. Tynianov, *Arkhaisty i novatory* (Leningrad, 1929), p. 234.

7. A Petersburg society Pushkin joined in 1819.—Tr.

8. Dmitry Pisarev, retelling Chapter I of *Onegin* from his own point of view [in his essay "Pushkin and Belinsky: *Eugene Onegin*"], took note of the truffle, "which Pushkin *for some reason* called 'youth's delight.'"

9. L. Iu. Ginzburg, *O lirike* (Leningrad, 1964), p. 232.

10. *Syn otechestva* [*Son of the Fatherland*] 8 (1825): 380–381 [Proffer, p. 295]. The article was signed "-v."

11. *Moskovskii telegraf* 15 (1825): 10–11 (special supplement).

12. A reference to the passage in "Onegin's Journey" in which the author confesses that he now prefers the simple Russian life.—Tr.

13. A quotation from Pushkin's 1828 note "On Poetic Style" [Proffer, p. 71].—Tr.

14. "Elegiia iz Tibulla" in K. N. Batiushkov, *Polnoe sobranie stikhotvorenii* (Moscow/ Leningrad, 1964), p. 167.

15. *Deva* is the poetic form.—Tr.

16. I. M. Semenko, *Poety pushkinskoi pory* (Moscow, 1970), p. 51.

17. *Atenei* 4 (1828): 84.

18. Pushkin uses the colloquial form, which at that time was considered disrespectful.—Tr.

19. *Atenei* 4 (1828): 88.

20. Baratynsky wrote Pushkin in February 1828: "I really like the vast plan of your *Onegin*, but the majority of the public does not understand it. . . . The lofty poetic simplicity of your work strikes them as poverty of invention. They do not notice that old and new Russia, life in all its manifestations is passing before their very eyes" [*PSS*, 14, 6].

21. *Byvalo—teper'* ["it used to be—these days"] is one of the formulas, or "links," which is constantly repeated in the text of the novel in verse.

22. Like the English "clear," the Russian *iasnyi* denotes brightness and serenity as well as unambiguousness and pellucidness.—Tr.

23. Often "spring" [*vesna*] is rhymed with "clear" [*iasna*], as in Pushkin's 1822 lyric "Adeli" ["To Adele"]—*PSS*, 2, 275.

24. The Lyceum was a special imperial school for young noblemen. Pushchin and Pushkin were classmates there.—Tr.

25. "Moe bespechnoe neznan'e"—*PSS*, 2, 293.

26. "Ty prav moi drug—naprasno ia prezrel" ["You're Right My Friend—I Should Not Have Disdained"]—*PSS*, 2, 266.

27. B. V. Tomashevskii, *Pushkin*, vol. 1 (Moscow/Leningrad, 1956), p. 551.

28. In the 1818 version the lines quoted were followed by seventeen more verses. But when Pushkin edited the lyric for the 1826 edition, he discarded them, and, thus, his "comprehension" of Zhukovsky's world became the final word in the lyric.

29. "Liubliu vash sumrak neizvestnyi"—*PSS*, 2, 255.

30. This is the opening line of the second part of the lyric.—Tr.

31. The Salgir is the stream that waters Bakhchisaray.—Tr.

32. Quoted in A. N. Veselovskii, *V. A. Zhukovskii: Poeziia chuvstva i "serdechnogo voobrazheniia"* (St. Petersburg, 1904), p. 179.

33. V. A. Zhukovskii, *Polnoe sobranie sochinenii v dvenadtsati tomakh*, vol. 12 (St. Petersburg, 1902), p. 96.

34. L. Iu. Ginzburg, *O psikhologicheskoi proze* (Leningrad, 1971), p. 27. Grigory Vinokur investigated this phenomenon of biographical stylization in his book *Biography and Culture*. On the basis of many examples (Andrey Turgenev and the young Zhukovsky, "Werterism" in Goethe's own biography), Vinokur concluded that "what was fictitious was not the facts themselves but the expressive atmosphere imparted to them. What was created was not personal life but its style." G. O. Vinokur, *Biografiia i kul'tura* (Moscow, 1927), p. 53.

35. G. A. Gukovskii, *Pushkin i russkie romantiki* (Moscow, 1965), p. 163. [Denis Davydov (1784–1839), a soldier and a hussar poet, used his military celebrity to promote his literary works and vice versa.—Tr.]

36. Pushkin refers here to the hero of *The Prisoner of the Caucasus.*—Tr.

37. From Baratynsky's 1828 letter to Pushkin, *PSS*, 14, 6.—Tr.

38. In twentieth-century Russian poetry Anna Akhmatova's lyrics are heir to this Pushkinian situation in which love and poetry part ways.

39. In the Russian text, *priamym poetom* [like a true poet].—Tr.

40. V. I. Tumanskii, *Stikhotvoreniia i pis'ma* (St. Petersburg, 1912), p. 117. [Vasily Tumanskii (1800–1860) was a minor poet, who clerked with Pushkin in the Odessa chancery, 1823–1824.—Tr.]

41. The opposition that Bocharov uses here and subsequently of "one's own" [*svoi*] versus "another's" [*chuzhoi*], implying "otherness" (frequently translated as "alien"), is also fundamental to Bakhtin's thinking.—Tr.

42. G. A. Gukovskii, *Pushkin i problemy realisticheskogo stilia* (Moscow, 1957), p. 197.

43. In Arndt's translation the lines are reversed.—Tr.

44. A quotation from Pushkin's article "Baratynsky" (1830).—Tr.

45. The term is Mikhail Bakhtin's. [See "Discourse in *Eugene Onegin*."—Tr.]

46. "Each prays to his own icon"—"drily answered" Vladimir in one of the variants [*PSS*, 6, 307]. Possibly, the variant was discarded because it did not correspond to Lensky's character, for Lensky simply does not distinguish between the real image of his Olga and her "icon," to which he "prays" in his imagination.

47. Compare in *The Gypsies,* which was begun and completed about the same time as Chapter III of *Onegin,* the argument between Aleko and Zemphira about city life, which is similar to the collision of Lensky's and Onegin's "artistic systems." Aleko: "There man in throngs, hemmed in by fences,/ Tastes not the morning cool. . . ." Zemphira: "But there they have such spacious mansions,/ With rugs of many-colored plaid,/ And festive games and lively dancing,/ And girls there go so richly clad!" [*PuCP,* pp. 272–273]. Here the two conventional emblems of the city form two subjective poles, two voices and two intonations, two completely discordant and incompatible images of what is undoubtedly *one indivisible world.*

48. Lensky compares Tatyana to Svetlana, the heroine of Zhukovsky's ballad, in the opening lines of III, 5.—Tr.

49. The decoration awarded to all officers who took part in the storming of the Black Sea fortress of Ochakov during the Turkish campaign of 1788.—Tr.

50. In "The Structure of *Eugene Onegin*," which is translated in the present collection.—Tr.

51. The image system in this quatrain correlates with other passages in the novel. For example, Olga through Lensky's eyes: "Like the shy lily of the meadow,/ Unknown in her secluded lea/ To butterfly and bumblebee" [II, 21]; the motifs of sleep and a hostel [inn] bed in the portrayal of Lensky's death and bliss beyond the grave: "Or does he drift down Lethe's healing/ Dream currents, blissfully unfeeling" [VII, 11]; and ". . . on melting snow-sheet dozing/ A lad, quite still, as if reposing/ Asleep upon a hostel bed" [VIII, 37].

52. The draft manuscript read: "As travelers poor on inn-beds lolling,/ As gay, lighthearted butterflies. . ." [*PSS*, 6, 377]. Here the two similes do not yet constitute an opposition but merely follow one another. The "counterpoint" is not yet formed. It is created when the epithet in the first line is "deflated" and the disjunctive "or" is introduced in the second line.

53. *Moskovskii telegraf* 19 (1827): 223.

54. In the numerous variants Parny's name is more directly linked with the problem of translation: "Are they translating in our day, Is there translated in our day// A letter worthy of Parny, A letter styled as by Parny" [*PSS*, 6, 311]. In variants of the fair manuscript it is precisely the tradition of translations from Parny's poetry that is emphasized: "The tracks of magicking Parny, The traces of divine Parny// We have forgotten in our day, Have they been lost then in our day"; "I miss the footsteps of Parny,/ They've been forgotten in our day" [*PSS*, 6, 584–585].

55. See V. N. Toporov, " 'Istochnik' Batiushkova v sviazi s 'Le torrent' Parni: 1. K probleme perevoda; 2. Analiz struktury," *Trudy po znakovym sistemam* 4 (Tartu, 1969): 309.

56. P. A. Viazemskii, *PSS,* vol. 2 (St. Petersburg, 1879), p. 23 (originally published in *Moskovskii telegraf* in 1827).

57. What has been said about Tatyana's direct speech has no bearing on her last speech to Onegin [VIII, 42–47], which is as free an expression as her letter.

58. V. V. Vinogradov, *Iazyk Pushkina* (Moscow/Leningrad, 1935), p. 222.

59. Its "verisimilitude" is motivated by the fact that "To speak milady's love, but

few/ Have thought our native language fitted,/ Our haughty Russian hardly knows/ How to adjust to postal prose" [III, 26].

60. Vinogradov, pp. 223–230.

61. Compare this complex motivation with the motivation for Onegin's letter: "Here is his letter word for word" [VIII, 32].

62. Compare Pushkin's use of this word in conjunction with Tatyana's letter to the understanding of "translation" in the art of Russian icon painting. Here the very representation is called a "translation," while the "originals" are the system of rules governing the representation. But these originals (guides) are only an intermediate stage, a guarantee, as it were, that the translation of the "innermost original" is faithful, that it represents transcendent reality.

63. In the Russian text *du comme il faut* is given in French and *vulgar* is given in English; both are italicized.—Tr.

64. Compare Pushkin's letter to his wife (October 30, 1833): "You know how I dislike everything that smacks of the Moscow young lady, all that is not *comme il faut*, all that is *vulgar*" [Shaw, p. 617].

65. G. O. Vinokur, *Biografiia i kul'tura*, p. 51.

66. In the Russian text, the first "rus," meaning "countryside" in Latin, is given in Latin script; the second *Rus'*, an old form for "Russia," is given in Cyrillic.—Tr.

67. A literal translation of the French expression *entre chien et loup*, meaning dusk. —Tr.

68. The Russian text uses "spleen," given in Cyrillic.—Tr.

69. As Leonid Grossman points out, "It is no accident that one of the most characteristic epithets in *Onegin* is 'modish' [*modnyi*]. In the context of Pushkin's work it often takes on the nuance of the later European term *moderne*, in the sense of extreme and excessive contemporaneity." L. P. Grossman, *Bor'ba za stil'* (Moscow, 1927), p. 117.

70. In the draft variant "ideal" was given in italics [*PSS*, 6, 458]. In the printed text the italics were deleted and thus transformed into what Bakhtin calls "intonational quotation marks." This then is another way of setting off an alien word in the authorial speech of the novel. It is not obvious, but it is extremely effective, *stylistically* speaking.

71. In this stanza "Monsieur Guillot" is given in Latin script, but not in VI, 25, where the name is pronounced in Russian fashion as *Gil'o*.—Tr.

72. "In him," observed Gogol, "as in a lexicon, was encompassed all the richness, strength, and versatility of our language." N. V. Gogol', *PSS*, vol. 8, p. 50 [quoted from Gogol's article "A Few Words on Pushkin"].

73. Bakhtin, "Discourse in *Eugene Onegin*."

74. In the dream-book of Martin Zadeka, Tatyana attempts to find an explanation for her dream: "She finds in alphabetic order/ The entries; Bear, Bench, Blizzard, Briar,/ Bridge, Dagger, Darkness, Feasting, Fire,/ And so on. But for once the Master/ Has no reply to what she asks" [V, 24]. The import of the horrible dream is not revealed through "alphabetic order." It is as if the "alphabetic" principle of the lexicon is shown here against the background of Pushkin's "living" lexicon—the speaking world.

75. For Lotman's analysis of this stanza, see his article "The Structure of *Eugene Onegin*."

76. "He loves a fantasy and is himself a fantasy," observed Dostoevsky in his "Pushkin Speech."

77. This is the coda as it appeared in the final text. In manuscript variants these concluding lines described what Lensky "sang," and there was no stylistic switch, no shift into another reality and into another language. Thus the initial ending to II, 10, did not possess that concluding and synthesizing significance which is so important for the characterization of Lensky. That emerged in the final text, thanks to the stylistically bi-compositional construction that the coda acquired.

78. Mikhail Bakhtin, "Discourse in *Eugene Onegin.*"

79. For example, here is an ironic variant, but it corresponds to the possibility of the "lofty" poet concealed in Lensky's elegy: "As freedom's lover, glory's gallant,/ His mind on stormy fancies fed,/ Vladimir would have tried his talent/ On odes—which Olga never read." [IV, 34.] The subjunctive mood used here is continually operative in the text of the novel in verse.

80. The significance of these words, as well as Onegin's words ("If I wrote poetry like you,/ I'd choose the elder"—III, 5), was pointed out by Lev Vygotsky in his very interesting, though brief interpretation of *Eugene Onegin.* Vygotsky observed that these words "hint at another course the novel could take . . . and thereby bring it to life," that these words "seem unexpectedly to lay bare the true course of the novel." L. S. Vygotskii, *Psikhologiia iskusstva,* 2d ed. (Moscow, 1968), pp. 285–286.

81. See, for example, G. A. Gukovskii, *Pushkin i problemy realisticheskogo stilia,* pp. 235–239.

82. L. Iu. Ginzburg, "K postanovke problemy realizma v pushkinskoi literature," *Vremennik Pushkinskoi komissii,* vol. 2 (Moscow/Leningrad, 1936), p. 397.

83. For a discussion of the difference between these "realities," see my article, "Forma plana," *Voprosy literatury* 12 (1967): 115–136.

84. In the Russian text *sladost'* [sweetness] rhymes with *mladost'* [youth].—Tr.

85. V. D. Levin, ed., *Poeticheskaia frazeologiia Pushkina* (Moscow, 1969), p. 136.

86. Presumably Pushkin alludes here to Decembrist friends, who were executed or exiled as a result of the unsuccessful revolt.—Tr.

87. L. S. Vygotskii, *Psikhologiia iskusstva,* p. 287.

88. In traditional poetic phraseology there were two aspects to the image of the cup of life, linked with different traditions: the "lofty," harking back to church literature, and the "light," linked with the epicurean view of life as a feast or banquet and harking back to the Western, secular tradition. See V. D. Levin, ed., *Poeticheskaia frazeologiia Pushkina,* pp. 152, 331.

89. Therefore, all the talk about Onegin's "subsequent fate" makes no sense.

90. In poetic drafts (1835) of his answer to the proposal that he continue *Onegin,* Pushkin renders the opinion of friends that the novel is incomplete as the point of view of someone else: "You are quite justified in saying/ That it seems strange, in fact betraying/ Bad form, to break the novel off. . ." [*PSS,* 3, 1, 397]. (Compare the draft of Pushkin's letter to Pletnyov from September 1835: "You advise me to continue *Onegin,* assuring me that I haven't finished it. . ." [Shaw, p. 723].) But obviously the structure of the ending of *Onegin* does interest Pushkin, and he strives to express its complete, yet incomplete character by passing on the opinion of friends.

LOTMAN: THE TRANSFORMATION OF THE TRADITION GENERATED BY *ONEGIN* IN THE SUBSEQUENT HISTORY OF THE RUSSIAN NOVEL

1. This article is the final chapter of Iurii M. Lotman, *Roman v stikhakh Pushkina 'Evgenii Onegin'* (Tartu, 1975), pp. 92–108.—Tr.

2. A quotation from the tale "Taman" in M. L. Lermontov, *A Hero of Our Time,* trans. Vladimir Nabokov in collaboration with Dmitri Nabokov (New York: Doubleday, 1958), p. 75. Hereafter Nabokov's translation is cited in the text.—Tr.

3. V. G. Belinskii, *PSS,* vol. 4 (Moscow, 1954), p. 265.

4. Compare in Pushkin: "Here's Caesar; where is Brutus?"—*PSS,* 2, 311 [a quotation from Pushkin's poem "Nedvizhnii strazh dremal na tsarstvennom poroge" ("The Guard Immobile Dozed upon the Doorstep of His Lord"; 1824)].

5. One of Nikolay Karamzin's stories.—Tr.

6. Alexander Herzen, *Du développement des idées révolutionnaires en Russie* (1851), in A. I. Gertsen, *Sobranie sochinenii v tridtsati tomakh,* vol. 7 (Moscow, 1956), pp. 73–76; Nikolay Dobrolyubov, "Chto takoe oblomovshchina?" (1859), in N. A. Dobroliubov, *Sobranie sochinenii,* vol. 4 (Moscow/Leningrad, 1962), pp. 307–343; English translation: "What Is Oblomovitis?" in *Belinsky, Chernyshevsky, and Dobrolyubov: Selected Criticism,* ed. Ralph E. Matlaw (Bloomington: Indiana University Press, 1976), pp. 133–175.—Tr.

7. The Decembrist Alexander Odoevsky (1802–1839) was sentenced to twelve years of hard labor in Siberia for taking part in the ill-fated insurrection.—Tr.

8. M. Iu. Lermontov, *Sochineniia v shesti tomakh,* vol. 2 (Moscow/Leningrad, 1954), p. 59 [a quotation from Lermontov's lyric, "Chto tolku zhit'! . ." ("What Sense to Living! . ."; 1832)].

9. In "Duma" (1838), one of Lermontov's most important civic poems, the poet ponders the fate of his generation which had lost its outlet for heroism because of the repressive regime of Nicholas I.—Tr.

10. At the Battle of Austerlitz; Book 3, Chapter 13.—Tr.

11. A quotation from Pushkin's dramatic poem *Andzhelo* [*PSS,* 5, 112].—Tr.

12. For example, Dmitri Nekhlyudov in Tolstoy's novel *Resurrection.*—Tr.

13. Said of the middle-aged aristocrat Pavel Kirsanov in Ivan Turgenev, *Fathers and Sons* [Chapter 24], trans. Bernard G. Guerney (New York: Random House, 1961), p. 228. Hereafter Guerney's translation is cited in the text.—Tr.

14. The debate was initiated by Belinsky, who, in his ninth article on Pushkin, criticized Tatyana for pledging fidelity to a husband she did not love.—Tr.

15. The idea of plot symmetry is developed most extensively by Dmitry Blagoy. See Dmitrii Blagoi, *Masterstvo Pushkina* (Moscow, 1955), pp. 178–198.

16. L. S. Vygotskii, *Psikhologiia iskusstva,* 2d ed. (Moscow, 1968), p. 283.

17. Iu. N. Tynianov, *Problema stikhotvornogo iazyka,* 2d ed. (Moscow, 1965), p. 27.

18. E. A. Baratynskii, *Polnoe sobranie stikhotvorenii,* vol. 1 (Leningrad, 1936), p. 188. [Quoted from Baratynsky's 1831 lyric, "V dni bezgranichnykh uvlechenii" ("In Days of Boundless Fascination").—Tr.]

19. Quoted from Nikolay Gogol, *Dead Souls* [Chapter 7], trans. Bernard G. Guerney (New York: Holt, Rinehart and Winston, 1948), p. 151.—Tr.

20. Quoted from *Eugene Onegin,* III, 11, where Pushkin pokes fun of the all too predictable ending of Sentimental novels.—Tr.

21. Compare: "With loathing I peruse the record of my years" [quoted from Pushkin's 1828 lyric "Vospominanie" ("Remembrance"); *PuCP,* p. 83].

Glossary of Proper Names and Works

Authors and works frequently cited in the text.
(Works are listed under the name of the author.)

Baratynsky, Evgeny (1800–1844). Major nineteenth-century Russian poet; Pushkin's friend and poetic rival.

Batyushkov, Konstantin (1787–1855). Important early nineteenth-century Russian poet. His poetry strongly influenced the young Pushkin.

Bestuzhev, Alexander (1797–1837). Romantic poet and prose writer; pen name Marlinsky.

Derzhavin, Gavrila (1743–1816). The greatest Russian poet of the eighteenth century, best known for his odes.

Griboedov, Alexander (1795–1829). Author of the first great Russian comedy, *Woe from Wit* (1833), which satirizes the stupid and selfish world of Moscow society, epitomized by Famusov and Repetilov, and pits against it the caustic and spirited young hero Chatsky.

Karamzin, Nikolay (1766–1826). Important Sentimental poet and prose writer. He reformed the Russian literary language by introducing a periphrastic "middle" style, based on the language of polite society and modeled on French.

Küchelbecker, Wilhelm (1797–1864). Nineteenth-century Russian poet, defender of the "high" genres, who was exiled to Siberia for participating in the abortive Decembrist insurrection.

Lermontov, Mikhail (1814–1841). Russia's greatest Romantic poet; author of the first major prose novel in Russian literature, *A Hero of Our Time* (1840). It centers on the enigmatic personality of Pechorin, whose character is gradually revealed in a series of five tales told from different points of view.

Lomonosov, Mikhail (1711–1765). Founder of modern Russian literature. He codified the Russian literary language, establishing a system of three literary styles: "high," "middle," and "low."

Pletnyov, Pyotr (1792–1865). Minor poet and literary scholar; Pushkin's friend and literary agent.

Polevoy, Nikolay (1796–1846). Critic and journalist. He reviewed *Eugene Onegin,* as it appeared, in his journal, *The Moscow Telegraph.*

Pushkin, Alexander (1799–1837).

—*Count Nulin* (1825). Playful tale in verse about the frustrations of a Frenchified Russian dandy stranded for a night in the country.

—*Eugene Onegin.* Begun in 1823 and completed in 1831. Initially published chapter by chapter (Chapter I appeared in 1825, Chapter VIII with "Fragments from Onegin's Journey" in 1832). When the first complete edition appeared in 1833, 44 notes were appended to it. Quotations of the notes are taken from Nabokov's translation, since Arndt does not include all of the notes in his rendition.
"Onegin's Journey" was initially intended to be an integral part of *Eugene Onegin* (it was to have been Chapter VIII and the present Chapter VIII would have been Chapter IX), but only fragments of it were actually published. When the first complete edition of *Onegin* appeared, these fragments were placed after the notes. This order is observed in Russian editions and by Nabokov in his translation.

—*The Fountain of Bakhchisaray* (1823). Pushkin's most popular narrative poem and his most romantic. Inspired by the poet's visit to the ruined Palace of the Crimean Khans in 1820, it was presumably linked with a secret and unrequited love Pushkin experienced at that time.

—*The Gypsies* (1824). A dramatic poem about a disillusioned Russian Aleko who joins a gypsy camp and falls in love with Zemphira, a gypsy girl, in hopes of becoming a natural man.

—*The Prisoner of the Caucasus* (1821). The first of Pushkin's southern, Romantic poems. The hero is a disenchanted Russian, captured by Circassians, who finds himself no longer capable of love.

—*Ruslan and Lyudmila* (1820). A mock-heroic fairy tale in verse, the first large poem Pushkin published. It brought him immediate success.

Venevitinov, Dmitry (1805–1827). Promising philosophical poet who died at the age of 22.

Vyazemsky, Pyotr (1792–1878). Poet, critic, and one of Pushkin's closest friends.

Yazykov, Nikolay (1803–1846). Important poet of the 1820s. His anacreonic verse had an intoxicating quality.

Zhukovsky, Vasily (1783–1852). Russia's leading pre-Romantic poet; Pushkin's early mentor and lifelong friend. A remarkable translator and adaptor, Zhukovsky introduced English and German poetry to Russia.

Bibliography

Criticism on Eugene Onegin *in English*

Bayley, John. *"Evgeny Onegin."* In Bayley, *Pushkin: A Comparative Commentary.* Cambridge: Cambridge University Press, 1971, pp. 236–305.

Clayton, Douglas. *"Ice and Flame": Aleksandr Pushkin's "Eugene Onegin."* Toronto: University of Toronto Press, 1985.

Fanger, Donald. "Influence and Tradition in the Russian Novel." In John Garrard, ed., *The Russian Novel from Pushkin to Pasternak.* New Haven: Yale University Press, 1983, pp. 29–50.

Fennell, John. *"Evgeny Onegin."* In Fennell, *Nineteenth-Century Russian Literature: Studies of Ten Russian Writers.* Berkeley: University of California Press, 1973, pp. 36–55.

Freeborn, Richard. *"Eugene Onegin."* In Freeborn, *The Rise of the Russian Novel from "Eugene Onegin" to "War and Peace."* Cambridge: Cambridge University Press, 1973, pp. 13–68.

Gibian, George. "Love by the Book: Pushkin, Stendhal, Flaubert." *Comparative Literature* 8 (1956): 97–109.

Gregg, Richard. "Rhetoric in Tat'jana's Last Speech: The Camouflage That Reveals." *Slavic and East European Journal* 25 (1981): 1–12.

———. "Tat'yana's Two Dreams: The Unwanted Spouse and the Demonic Lover." *Slavonic and East European Review* 48 (1970): 492–505.

Gustafson, Richard. "The Metaphor of the Seasons in *Evgenij Onegin." Slavic and East European Journal* 6 (1962): 6–20.

Hoisington, Sona. *"Eugene Onegin:* An Inverted Byronic Poem." *Comparative Literature* 27 (1975): 136–152.

———. *"Eugene Onegin:* Product of or Challenge to *Adolphe?" Comparative Literature Studies* 14 (1977): 205–213.

———. "The Hierarchy of Narratees in Pushkin's *Eugene Onegin." Canadian-American Slavic Studies* 10 (1976): 242–249. Reprinted in A. S. Pushkin, *Eugene Onegin.* Trans. Walter Arndt. 2d ed., rev. New York: E. P. Dutton, 1981, pp. lxiii–lxxv.

Jakobson, Roman. "Marginal Notes on *Eugene Onegin."* In Jakobson, *Pushkin and His Sculptural Myth.* Trans. and ed. John Burbank. The Hague: Mouton, 1975, pp. 51–57. Reprinted in A. S. Pushkin, *Eugene Onegin.* Trans. Walter Arndt. 2d ed., rev. New York: E. P. Dutton, 1981, pp. xxxviii–xlvi.

McLean, Hugh. "The Tone(s) of *Evgenij Onegin." California Slavic Studies* 6 (1971): 3–15.

Matlaw, Ralph. "The Dream in *Evgeny Onegin* with a Note on *Gore ot uma." Slavonic and East European Review* 37 (1959): 487–503.

Meijer, Jan M. "The Digressions in *Evgeni Onegin."* In A. G. F van Holk, ed., *Dutch Contributions to the Sixth International Congress of Slavicists.* The Hague: Mouton, 1968, pp. 122–152.

Mirsky, D. S. *"Evgeni Onegin,* 1823–1831." In Mirsky, *Pushkin.* New York: E. P. Dutton, 1963, pp. 137–152.

Mitchell, Stanley. "The Digressions of *Yevgeny Onegin:* Apropos of Some Essays by Ettore Lo Gatto," *Slavonic and East European Review* 44 (1966):51–65.

Nabokov, Vladimir. *Eugene Onegin: A Novel in Verse by Aleksandr Pushkin.* Trans., with a commentary, by Vladimir Nabokov. Rev. ed. 4 vols. Princeton: Princeton University Press, 1975.

Picchio, Riccardo. "Dante and J. Malfilâtre as Literary Sources of Tatjana's Erotic Dream (Notes on the Third Chapter of Pushkin's *Evgenij Onegin*)." In A. Kodjak and K. Taranovsky, eds. *Alexander Pushkin: A Symposium on the 175th Anniversary of His Birth*. New York: New York University Press, 1976, pp. 167–177.

Shaw, J. Thomas. "The Author–Narrator's Stance in *Onegin*." *Russian Language Journal* 120 (1981):25–42. Reprinted in A. S. Pushkin, *Eugene Onegin*. Trans. Walter Arndt. 2d ed., rev. New York: E. P. Dutton, 1981, pp. xlvii–lxii.

Todd, William Mills III. "*Eugene Onegin:* 'Life's Novel.'" In Todd, *Fiction and Society in the Age of Pushkin*. Cambridge: Harvard University Press, 1986, pp. 106–136.

Vickery, Walter. "Byron's *Don Juan* and Pushkin's *Evgenij Onegin:* The Question of Parallelism." *Indiana Slavic Studies* 4 (1968):181–191.

Weil, Irwin. "Onegin's Echo." *Russian Literature Triquarterly* 10 (1974):260–273.

Wilson, Edmund. "In Honor of Pushkin: *Evgeni Onegin*." In Wilson, *The Triple Thinkers*. London: J. Lehmann, 1952, pp. 37–51.

Woodward, James B. "The Principle of Contradictions in *Yevgeny Onegin*." *Slavonic and East European Review* 60 (1982):25–43.

Index

Akhmatova, Anna, 186n.38
Aleko, Onegin and, x, 56–59, 62
Alexander I, 25
"André Chénier" (Pushkin), 136
Anna Karenina (Tolstoy), 174
Apposition, 125
Authorial discourse, xii, 86, 110, 112, 118–120
"The Awakening" (Pushkin), 164

Bachelard, Gaston, 12
Bakhtin, Mikhail, xi, xiv, 10–12. *See also specific works*
The Bandit Brothers (Pushkin), 18
Baratynsky, Evgeny, 2, 13, 76, 133, 136, 140, 150, 186n.20, 191
"The Bard" (Pushkin), 139
Batyushkov, K. N., 18, 72–73, 129, 136, 150
Belinsky, Vissarion, 44, 47, 120; credulity of, 52; criticism of, 43–55; errors of, 54; on *Eugene Onegin,* 112, 163; importance of, ix, 4; on Lensky's fate, 163; on Pechorin, 171; Romanticism and, 4, 95; social values of, ix, 45; Westernizers and, 3
Beltov, and Onegin, 52
Bely, Andrey, 71
Beppo (Byron), 22
Bestuzhev, Alexander, 101, 125
Biography and Culture (Vinokur), 186n.34
Blok, Alexander, 173
Bocharov, Sergey, xi, 11–13
Bogdanovich, Ippolit, 25
Bolkonsky, Andrey, 173
Boredom, 35, 45–48, 59, 83
The Bridegroom (Pushkin), 18
"Buria" (Pushkin), 130
Byron, Lord George, 60, 104; *Beppo,* 22; *Childe Harold,* 21, 60, 92, 117; *The Corsair,* 75; "Lines Inscribed Upon a Cup Formed from a Skull," 144; Pushkin and, 2, 21–22, 56, 117

Calques, 155
Catherine the Great, 24
Censorship, 2
Cervantes, Miguel de, 64, 175
Chapter divisions, 110
Character, of individuals: determination of, 92, 184n.17; environment and, 91; essence of, 111; national character, 126; periphrastic treatment of, 124
Characters: construction of, 110; contradictory qualities, 175; dynamic systems of, 176; internal reference to, 130; isolation of, 175; literary coding of, 171, 174; paradigms of, 112. *See also* Hero(es); Heroine(s); *specific characters; works*
Charter of 1785, 24
Chatter. *See* Colloquial speech
Chekhov, Anton, xiv
Childe Harold (Byron), 21
Christ, 66
Clarity, emphasis on, 134, 136
Classicism, 93
Class values, 47
Clayton, J. Douglas, ix, xiii
Clichés, 103, 171
Closure, of world view, 146
Colloquial speech, 10, 84–85, 103–105
Comedy, 90, 101, 103. *See also* Irony
A Common Story (Goncharov), 174
Composition, Tynyanov on, 8, 71–90
Confessions (Rousseau), 176
Conservative criticism, x, 5
Constructivism, 7
Contradictions, 93, 175–176. *See also* Opposition
"Conversation between Bookseller and Poet" (Pushkin), 122
The Corsair (Byron), 75
Counterpoint, 13, 148, 161
Count Nulin (Pushkin), 21, 54

Davydov, Denis, 138
Dead Souls (Gogol), 21
The Dead Tsarevna and the Seven Heroes (Pushkin), 19
Death, theme of, 172–177 *passim*
Decembrists, 172, 189n.86, 190n.7
Deconstruction, xii
Delvig, Anton, 101
"The Demon" (Pushkin), 135
Derzhavin, Gavril R., 17–18, 22, 25, 72
Descriptive excess, in *Onegin,* 45–46
Dictionary (Tatishchev), 151
Didelot, Charles L., 45–46
Dimitry of the Don (Ozerov), 18
Dmitriev, Ivan I., 21–25 *passim*
Dobrolyubov, N. A., 172
Don Juan (Pushkin): Byron and, 21; Dostoevsky on, 65; *Eugene Onegin* and, 80; omitted stanzas of, 77
Don Quixote, 117, 172
Dostoevsky, Fyodor, 5, 175; authorial comments, 86; on *Eugene Onegin,* 159; *pochvenniki* and, 5

195

Infinity, principle of, 113
Interjections, 88, 90
Interpretation, 153. *See also* Translation
Intonation, xii, xiv, 10, 104; colloquial, 84–85, 103–105; of incompleteness, 108; stanza divisions and, 109
Intuition, vs. reason, 5
Irony, 100–101, 111, 158

Jakobson, Roman, 7, 10
Jeanne (Sand), 19
Juvenal, 101

Karamzin, Nikolay, 25, 71–72, 95, 172
Katenin, Pavel, 77–78
Katzenjammer, mood of, 47
Khlebnikov, Velimir, 183n.5
Kireevsky, Ivan, 73
A Knight of Our Time (Karamzin), 172
Kozhinov, Vadim, 11
"Krivtsovu" (Pushkin), 165
Kruchonykh, Alexey, 183n.5
Krylov, Ivan, 18–19, 22, 25
Kuchelbecker, Wilhelm, 100–101, 140

Languages, in *Eugene Onegin,* 118–120 *passim;* images of, 121, 157. *See also* Intonation
Larin, Dmitri, 138, 144–145; death of, 103, 144, 146; family of, 33–34, 130; Lensky and, 103, 145, 147. *See also* Tatyana
Lensky, Vladimir, 51, 135, 138, 164; duel with Onegin, 41, 49–50, 158–160; fate of, 161, 163; heterostylism and, 146; internal world of, 147; language of, 117–120; Larin and, 103, 145, 147; monologue of, 96; Olga and, 33, 41, 100, 111, 141–142, 187n.46; Onegin and, 29, 33, 49, 98, 143–144, 148, 161; persona of, 40–42; poet-author and, 137; poetry of, 115–116, 133–134, 137; portrayal of, 159–160, 189n.77; Romantic style and, 12, 40, 42; situation of, 148; subjectivism of, 101, 161; youth of, 139, 160
Lermontov, Mikhail, 23, 95, 104, 171–172; "Duma," 190n.9; *A Hero of Our Time,* 4, 20–21, 26, 39, 170–172; "Meditation," 172; *The Princess Ligovskaya,* 174
Lexicons, order in, 188n.74
"Lines Inscribed Upon a Cup Formed from a Skull" (Byron), 144
Little House in Kolomna (Pushkin), 54
Lomonosov, Mikhail, 71–72
Lotman, Yury, 146; Bakhtin and, xi; Formalism and, x; Structuralism and, 9, 10; on "superfluous man," 11
Love: marital, 60; poetics and, 140, 186n.38; Pushkin on, 137–139. *See also* Romanticism
Lyudmila (Zhukovsky), 18

Maiden, defined, 130–132
Maid of Orleans (Zhukovsky), 151
Marital love, 60
Marxist criticism, 9
"Meditation" (Lermontov), 172
Merleau-Ponty, Maurice, 12
Mikhavlovskoe estate, 137
Miller, J. Hillis, 12
Milton, John, 155
Minus device, 104
Models, literary, 93
Modish Wife (Dmitriev), 21

Nadezhdin, Nikolay, 181n.14
Narodnost, 19, 20
Narrator. *See* Authorial discourse
National character, debate on, 126
Naturalism, 57, 91
Negativism, of Onegin, 45–47
Nekrasov, Nikolai, 174
A Nest of Gentlefolk (Turgenev), 59, 173–174
Nicholas I, 4, 64, 190n.9
Nietzsche, Friedrich, 71
Nobility, in Russia, 24–26
La Nouvelle Héloïse (Rousseau), 176
Novel: Bakhtin on, 11; colloquialism in, 10, 84–85, 103–105; construction of, 94–96; deformation by verse, 90; of experience, 169; "fifth act" in, 172; image of novel in, 76, 167; metalevel of, 169; narration in, 86, 110, 112, 118–120, 165; other genres and, 121; poetic genres in, 80, 115; speech in, 11–12, 115–121; stylistic structure of, 121–168; types of, 162. *See also specific authors, styles, works*
Novikov, Nikolay I., 25

Objectivity, structure and, 104
Oblomov (Goncharov), 174
Ode, theory of, 72
"Odessa" (Tumansky), 128, 140–141
Odoevsky, Alexander, 172
Olga, 81, 99, 137; image of, 143, 149; Lensky and, 33, 41, 100, 111, 141–142, 187n.46
"Onegin's Journey" (Pushkin), 125–132 *passim,* 140, 157, 165, 181n.21, 185n.12, 191
Onegin, Eugene, 124, 126, 130, 140–141, 155; Aleko and, 56–59, 62; author and, 111–112, 118; books of, 153; boredom of, 45–48, 52, 59, 83; Byron and, 81, 117; callousness of, 29; daily life of, 44, 47; duel with Lensky, 41, 49–50; as egotist, 27, 32; fate of, 32; as hero, 98; image of the world, 143, 148; language of, 118; Lensky and, 29, 33, 49, 143–144, 161, 171; as noble, 26; normality of, 31; objectivism of, 161; peasants and, 33; Pechorin and, 39, 171–172; periphrastic descriptions of, 124; in Petersburg, 154; poetic nature of,